Rationality

The Problems of Philosophy
Their Past and Present

General editor: Ted Honderich
Grote Professor of the Philosophy of
Mind and Logic
University College London

Rationality

Harold I. Brown

London and New York

First published in 1988

First published in paperback in 1990
by Routledge, 11 New Fetter Lane, London EC4P 4EE

Simultaneously published in the USA and Canada
by Routledge, a division of Routledge, Chapman and Hall, Inc.
29 West 35th Street, New York, NY 10001

Printed in Great Britain by T. J. Press (Padstow) Ltd, Padstow, Cornwall

British Library Cataloguing in Publication Data
Brown, Harold I.
    Rationality. – The problems of philosophy).
    1. Rationality
    I. Title   II. Series
    153.43

Library of Congress Cataloging in Publication Data
Brown, Harold I.
Rationality/Harold I. Brown.
    p.   cm.—(Problems of philosophy)
Bibliography: p.
Includes index.
1. Science—Philosophy.   2. Rationalism.   I. Title.   II. Series:
Problems of philosophy (Routledge)
Q175.B7963   1988
121-dc19   87-31662
ISBN 0-415-05517-2

Contents

Contents

Preface

My aim in this book will be to describe and criticize a widely
accepted model of rationality, and to propose an alternative.
According to the classical model that I shall discuss, a rational
decision or belief must be based on an evaluation of relevant
evidence by the application of appropriate rules. I will develop
this model in chapter I, and I will argue that although this is not
the only view of rationality that we may have encountered, it
is a view that has in fact played a pervasive role in Western
epistemology.

Chapters II and III will be devoted to a critique of this model
of rationality. In chapter II I will argue that the model requires a
foundational epistemology, and I will discuss the major problems
with foundationalism, and the significance of these problems for
the classical model of rationality. From a foundational perspective, rational justification ultimately requires both premises and
rules that can be justified without appealing to other premises
and rules. We will see that the familiar attempts to satisfy these
requirements fail, and attempts to produce a rational justification
of any claim threaten infinite regresses of premises and rules. The
need to break such justificatory regresses will be a major concern
in our attempt to develop an alternative model of rationality.

Chapter III will be concerned with the relation between rationality and science. Science provides our best example of a rational
endeavor, and it has long been held that scientific practice
conforms to the classical model of rationality. Recent work in the
history and philosophy of science has cast considerable doubt on
this second claim, and this, in turn, has led to surprising new
questions about the rationality of science, while adding fuel to
doubts about the viability of any notion of rationality. In this

chapter I will argue that crucial scientific decisions are not rational when viewed in terms of the classical model, but that this should be read as a mark against the classical model of rationality, rather than as an argument against the rationality of science. The rationality of science will provide an important constraint on our attempts to construct a new model of rationality. This does not mean that the rationality of science is an *a priori* truth, but only that, at the present stage in the development of knowledge, we have no clearer example of a rational endeavor. Thus we might as well pay close attention to scientific practice in attempting to develop a model of rationality.

One theme which will emerge in our discussion of science is that standards for scientific choice must be relativized to particular stages in the development of science, and this will lead to a discussion of some of the arguments for a thoroughgoing social relativism in cognitive matters. If that view is correct, it is impossible to construct a transculturally legitimate model of rationality, and I will be attempting to construct such a model. Moreover, according to this form of relativism science is only a feature of a particular culture, so my use of science as a basis for developing a model of rationality would assure that the resulting model would have no significance beyond that culture. In response I will argue that this brand of relativism is a result of attempting to maintain the classical model of rationality without the required foundations, and that the arguments for a complete social relativism lose their force once we abandon that model.

The last two chapters will be devoted to the constructive portion of our discussion. In chapter IV I will examine the idea of *judgement*, an idea that will play a central role in our new model of rationality; in chapter V I will develop and defend that new model. On this model, the key situations that call for rationality are those in which we lack a sufficient set of rules to settle a question, and I will argue that rational beliefs arise out of informed judgements that have been submitted to the community of competent individuals for evaluation and criticism. This will lead to discussions of the relation between rationality and truth, and between rationality and objectivity, and to an examination of the nature of rational disagreement. I will explain my use of the term 'model' in section 5.1, and those who are curious should feel free to read ahead. The precise meaning of this term will not be important before the final chapter, and until then it will suffice to think of a model as a way of understanding what it is that makes some belief or decision rational.

Acknowledgements

I want to thank Donna Baird, Peter Barker, Maurice Finocchiaro, Andrew Lugg, Thomas Nickles, Morton Schagrin and Harvey Siegel for comments on earlier drafts of my manuscript. This is a considerably better book than it would have been without their interest and efforts, but I have not always taken their advice, and I am fully responsible for the remaining errors. The Graduate School at Northern Illinois University duplicated the manuscript, and the Philosophy Department did the mailing.

Part One

CHAPTER I

A Classical Model of Rationality

I want to begin by describing a model of rationality that has been pervasive in Western thought, even though it has not always been explicitly formulated. We can approach this task by considering a problem posed by Douglas Hofstadter in one of his *Scientific American* columns (1983), and Hofstadter's solution to this problem.

Hofstadter asked 20 people to consider themselves members of a group who are going to receive financial rewards that depend on whether they, and other members of the group, decide to 'cooperate' or 'defect'. The awards will be based on two rules:

1. An individual who cooperates receives $3 for each other member of the group who cooperates, and nothing for each member who defects.
2. An individual who defects receives $5 for each other member who cooperates, and $1 for each other member who defects.

Each player's goal is to maximize her own financial gain; each individual must decide whether to cooperate (*C*) or defect (*D*) without communicating with any other player; and the decision to cooperate or defect must be made in a completely rational manner.

Consider the results of some of the different combinations of decisions. A player gets the maximum possible gain, $95, if she defects and everyone else cooperates – but all of the players know this, and a defector's reward is reduced by $4 for each additional defector; if everyone defects, the payoff is only $19. When everyone cooperates each player receives $57, but the payoff for a person who cooperates is reduced by $3 for each defector. When

3

nine people cooperate and eleven defect a defector's income is $55, which is less than she would receive if everyone cooperated. The worst position (economically) is to be the only cooperator: this gets you no income while each defector receives $23. For each possible combination of decisions the defectors receive more income than the cooperators, but everyone knows this, and as a rational being you must take this into account as you attempt to find the strategy that will maximize your income. Here is Hofstadter's analysis.

Hofstadter compares the task of reasoning one's way through this situation to that of doing an arithmetic problem such as dividing 507 by 131. He notes that anyone, anywhere, who does the arithmetic problem rationally must come up with the same answer, and he maintains that this is equally the case for his cooperation/defection problem. Once this is recognized, Hofstadter argues, it follows that the only rational choice is to cooperate:

> if reasoning dictates an answer, then everyone should
> independently come to that answer. . . . Seeing this fact is
> itself the critical step in the reasoning toward the correct
> answer. . . . Once you realize this fact it dawns on you that
> *either* all rational players will choose *D* or all rational players
> will choose *C*. That is the crux.
>
> Any number of ideal rational thinkers faced with the same
> situation and suffering through similar throes of reasoning
> agony will necessarily come up with the same answer
> eventually, as long as reasoning alone is the ultimate
> justification for their conclusion. Otherwise reasoning would
> be subjective, not objective as arithmetic is. A conclusion
> reached by reasoning would be a matter of preference, not
> one of necessity. Now *some* people may believe this of
> reasoning, but rational thinkers understand that a valid
> argument must be *universally* compelling, otherwise it is
> simply not a valid argument.
>
> If you grant this, then you are 90 percent of the way. All
> you need ask now is: 'Since we are all going to submit the
> same letter, which one would be more logical? That is, which
> world is better for the *individual* rational thinker: one with
> all cooperators or one with all defectors?' The answer is

4

immediate: 'I get $57 if we all cooperate, $19 if we all defect. Clearly I prefer $57, hence cooperating is preferred by this particular rational thinker. Since I am typical, cooperating must be preferred by *all* rational thinkers. And so I'll cooperate.' (1983, p. 22)

I want to develop the conception of rationality involved in this passage, but before doing so, there is a preliminary matter that should be dealt with. The term 'rational' is regularly applied to a large variety of items. One recent list includes, 'beliefs, prefer-ences, choices or decisions, actions, behavioural patterns, persons, even collectivities and institutions' (Elster, 1983, p. 1); we must narrow down this list if we are to proceed in a coherent manner. To begin with, I will not be concerned here with collectives or institutions, and I will not be concerned with the rationality of persons in the sense in which we might assess whether someone is, on balance, a rational individual. Nor will I be concerned with the rationality of overall behavior patterns, although I will consider the rationality of specific behaviors, and I will apply the term 'rational' to the remaining items on Elster's list. In other words, I will be concerned with what makes a specific belief, decision, act, etc. rational, and I will also talk of situations that call for rational behavior, a rational decision, and so forth. Note that in many cases we use the terms 'belief', 'decision', etc. to ask the same question in different ways; e.g., we can ask whether a decision to cooperate is rational, or whether the belief that it is better to cooperate is rational, or whether it is rational to act on a decision to cooperate, and more. I now want to discuss three major ideas involved in the view of rationality that Hofstadter's discussion illustrates: rational results must be universal, necessary, and determined by rules.

1.1 Universality

Hofstadter maintains that all rational thinkers must arrive at the same solution to his problem – they all begin with the same information, and in such cases correct reasoning can only lead to one conclusion. In general, if two individuals arrive at different results in a particular situation it must be either because they do not both have the same information, or because at least one of them is not proceeding in a wholly rational manner. As Hofstadter suggests, mathematics and logic provide a paradigm of rationality. Given a specific problem in long division, there is no room for judgement or opinion as to the correct solution; there is simply a correct answer, and anyone, anywhere, who follows the appropriate procedures correctly will arrive at this answer. Someone may make a mistake in doing such a problem, but that is beside the point. The key idea is that there exists both a definite solution and a definite procedure for arriving at that solution, and all who follow that procedure must arrive at the same result. Similarly, in the case of logic, an argument is either valid or invalid, and there are unequivocal procedures for assessing validity.

While mathematics and logic provide clear examples of problems with a single universal answer, situations involving taste provide clear examples on the opposite side. If I like cream in my coffee while you prefer your coffee black, this is a difference in taste; there is no single answer to the question, 'Should coffee be drunk black or with cream?' We acknowledge this difference in a number of ways: we do not offer arguments or evidence on behalf of our tastes, and the common maxim 'One does not dispute about tastes' expresses our recognition that there is no point to such disputes. We do not consider people who prefer black coffee to be guilty of a cognitive failing in the way in which we take people who believe that *modus ponens* is invalid or that the product of 25 and 7 is something other than 175 to be guilty of a cognitive failing. But we do not consider tastes to be irrational. Properly speaking, questions of rationality do not arise when we are dealing with tastes, and I will describe such cases as 'nonrational', reserving the term 'irrational' for situations in which the demands of rationality are violated. It is irrational to refuse to accept the results of a correctly done problem in arithmetic, or to refuse to apply the standard arithmetical techniques to such problems, but to rely instead on intuition or on random selection of an answer; it is neither rational nor irrational to prefer black coffee.

The above examples provide fairly clear cases in which issues of rationality do and do not arise; many cases are not nearly so clear, and there is often considerable debate as to whether rational results are obtainable in a particular field. I want to look at some examples of this sort of debate, not to attempt to settle any of the issues involved, but only to illustrate how the thesis that rational results must be universal often serves as a guiding principle. Ethics provides one common arena in which this debate takes place, and it will be useful to distinguish two different kinds of disagreements that occur in this context. First, there are disagreements on the correct principles for making ethical judgements; second, there are disagreements over whether any such principles exist at all. I will begin with some examples of the first sort of dispute in order to indicate how philosophers who agree that ethics has a universal foundation can disagree over which principles provide that foundation.

It is always appropriate to begin with Plato. According to Plato, there is a set of nonphysical entities, the forms, which correspond to the properties that an item can have, and any item that has a particular property participates in the appropriate form.[1] In particular, anything which may properly be described as 'good' participates in the form of 'The Good', and this holds equally whether we are concerned with an individual, a state, an act, or what have you. An item is good just in case it has the relevant property, not good if it lacks this property. We assess the goodness of an item by determining whether it has this property, and the ability to do this well requires that we first develop a clear grasp of The Good – not an easy task. If I do not have an adequate grasp of The Good, then I will often be unable to determine if some item is good, but this is a failing on my part analogous to being unable to determine if a physical object is square or yellow. Moreover, The Good is an atemporal, unalterable entity. Thus the criteria or standards for goodness cannot change with time or from place to place, and ethics is built on a universal foundation that is grounded in a permanent feature of the universe.

Kant provides us with a different attempt to achieve a universal ethic. For Kant an ethic must provide us with a set of moral laws, and Kant argues that just as the characteristic feature of a scientific law is its universality, so a moral law must also be universal. This, in turn, yields a test for the moral acceptability of a proposed action: '*Act only on that maxim through which you can at the same time will that it should become a universal law*' (1956, p. 88). For example, Kant argues that the practice of making promises that we do not intend to keep is morally unacceptable because it cannot

7

be universalized. If people universally adopted the practice of making such promises when they found it convenient, no one would believe any promise, and promising would become impossible: 'I then see straight away that this maxim can never rank as a universal law of nature and be self-consistent, but must necessarily contradict itself' (1956, p. 90). Note that Kant is concerned with the ethical evaluation of specific forms of behavior, while Plato attempts to cast his net much wider. At the same time, Kant takes 'duty' as the fundamental ethical notion and maintains that we determine our duty by the application of criteria (Kant offers other criteria besides universality, but believes that these criteria can never give conflicting results), while Plato takes The Good as the primary ethical notion and holds that we assess goodness by determining whether an item has this property. These are quite different moral theories, but both philosophers are seeking a universal foundation for ethics.

Utilitarianism will provide our final example. There is a version of utilitarianism that is, on one level, much more flexible than the moral theories of Plato or Kant, for this view allows for the possibility that any act, even making a promise that I do not intend to keep, might be morally permissible in one set of circumstances, but not in another.[2] Whether an act is morally permissible depends on its consequences, and in particular on whether those consequences tend to promote the general happiness. Since the consequences themselves, as well as their tendency to promote happiness, can vary with the attendant circumstances, an act can be good on one occasion, and bad on another. But this does not remove the demand for a universal ethic. Utilitarians require that all acts are to be judged by a single criterion – their tendency to promote the greatest happiness of the greatest number. This criterion allows us to take circumstances into account in a way that is analogous to the way we take circumstances into account in logic: different situations provide different premises, but the principles of correct reasoning from these premises do not vary. Just as we apply the same laws of logic in all circumstances, utilitarians maintain that we apply the same principles to assess morality in all circumstances, and in both cases it is not possible for two rational individuals who begin with the same information to arrive at contrary conclusions.

All three of these approaches seek not only a universal basis for ethics, but a rational basis as well. For Plato, we come to grasp The Good through the practice of dialectic, which is, in his view, the paradigm of a rational activity, and it is only after we have grasped this form that we become capable of behaving in a fully rational manner. Kant considered universality to be the foundation of rational thought, and he sought a system of ethics that would be applicable not only to all human beings, but to all rational beings just in so far as they are rational. Similarly, utilitarians wish to reduce ethics to the determination of the consequences of acts and to an assessment of the import of those consequences against a standard, but they take this to be the model of a rational evaluation. Recall here Jeremy Bentham's attempt to construct a 'hedonic calculus' which would completely assimilate decision-making in ethics to decision-making in arithmetic. For all of these philosophers there is no way in which individuals who proceed in accordance with the prescribed procedures could arrive at different moral assessments in a given case, and they would all insist that this is required if ethical questions are to be subject to rational resolution.

Now these are all examples of the first sort of disagreement that I noted, disagreement about how we are to establish a universal, rational, objective basis for ethics. But there are also those who reject this project, i.e., who not only oppose specific attempts to find this foundation, but attack the idea that a universal ethic is possible at all. Those who take this position generally agree that rationality requires universality, and in rejecting a universal basis for ethics they are also rejecting the view that ethics can be rational. Let me note two such examples. The first, 'ethical emotivism', is an offshoot of logical positivism. Briefly, logical positivists attempted to distinguish claims which have cognitive content from those which do not. The former set consists of all claims whose truth or falsity can be assessed either on purely logical grounds or on the basis of empirical evidence. Depending on the appropriate logical considerations, or on the available evidence, it may be rational or irrational to believe such a claim, but questions of rationality do not arise for claims which do not fall into one of these classes. Since ethical claims are neither logically true nor capable of empirical test, positivists typically held that such claims are no more than expressions of emotion. To say that a particular act is good, or to tell someone that she ought to behave in a particular manner, is to express approval of that act or that behavior. Ethical judgements thus fall among the tastes about which we do not dispute, and there is no universal, or rational, basis for ethics. It is this last point that concerns me: the notions of rationality and universality go hand in hand; here the positivists were in complete agreement with the moral philosophers we have already considered.

The second example comes from anthropology. Many anthropologists have been impressed by the diversity of ethical systems in different societies, and this diversity has led to the relativist view that ethical systems are features of specific cultures, and that there are no transcultural grounds for the comparative evaluation of different ethical systems. When we attempt such comparisons, the argument goes, we typically end up judging other people's cultures against our own, but we have no greater right to judge their culture than they have to judge ours, and there is no 'method of ethical reasoning that can be expected in principle to show, when there is a conflict of values or ethical principles, that one and only one solution is correct in some important and relevant sense of "correct" . . .' (Brandt, 1967, p. 76). In other words, there is no rational basis for making such comparisons. Note particularly that advocates of this form of relativism do not reject the view that rationality requires universality; rather, they assume it.

Let us now consider the tie between universality and rationality in a different context. Science has long been considered a paradigm example of a rational endeavor, but a number of philosophers have recently raised doubts – or been interpreted as raising doubts – about the rationality of scientific procedures. There are many sides to this discussion, and we will consider several of these in later chapters, but for the moment I want to note one argument that is supposed to show that we lack a rational basis for evaluating scientific theories. This argument derives from a study of the history of science, and in particular from the existence of 'scientific revolutions' in which the accepted body of science in a field is radically transformed. In this century, for example, physics has undergone two major revolutions with the introduction of relativity theory and quantum mechanics. These revolutions transformed our understanding of the physical world, and also raised serious questions about what had previously been taken to be universal standards for judging scientific results. To take one instance, quantum theory rejects the thesis that every event has a cause, yet before quantum theory came on the scene, the causal principle was widely considered to be not just another scientific thesis that could be reconsidered as science developed, but rather a much deeper principle that was constitutive of science. That is, it was claimed that what science is is in part determined by its adherence to the causal principle. Thus the attempt to find causes was viewed as a necessary feature of science, and the failure to find a cause for some event always reflected on the scientist, not on the causal principle. Scientists might disagree about specific causes for specific events, but they could not disagree about whether an event has a cause.

With the advent of quantum theory this has changed, and this change raises fundamental problems about the basis for accepting one scientific theory rather than another. If scientists need not adhere to the causal principle, need they adhere to any principle at all? Quantum theory introduces its own ways of deciding what proposals are acceptable, but might not these also be subject to future reconsideration? And if so, why must we accept these principles now? If a principle is truly universal, then we understand what we are doing when we invoke it as a reason for a decision, but if it is not universal, and if there may not even be any universal principles that we can appeal to in making scientific decisions, then what rational grounds can we have for making one decision rather than another? Indeed, why shouldn't we consider people who accept quite different principles, e.g., principles of magic, to be as rational in assessing conclusions on the basis of their principles as is the scientist who accepts results that conform to those principles of evaluation that are currently accepted by scientists?[3] Paul Feyerabend explicitly draws this conclusion (e.g., 1975, pp. 298–9). At the end of an extended attack on the thesis that science is guided by a universal method, Feyerabend writes:

> if science has found a method that turns ideologically contaminated ideas into true and useful theories, then it is indeed not mere ideology, but an objective measure of all ideologies. . . . But the fairy tale is false, as we have seen. There is no special method that guarantees success or makes it probable. . . . Basically there is hardly any difference

between the process that leads to the announcement of a new scientific law and the process preceding passage of a new law in society. . . . (1975, p. 302.)

I am not concerned at the moment to evaluate these claims, but only to emphasize, again, that the demand for universality is so deeply embedded in our current understanding of rationality that to question the universality of a discipline's foundations is equivalent to questioning the rationality of that discipline.

Now reflection on the above examples suggests that there is an ambiguity in the notion of 'universality': some claims or principles are universal in the sense of being applicable in every possible domain, while some are only universal with respect to a limited domain. Formal logic provides the clearest example of the former, since the validity of an argument is independent of any particular subject matter, and a valid argument is valid everywhere. Similarly, Plato's form of The Good was to provide the basis for evaluation in all domains, even science (cf. *Phaedo*, 96a–99c). Utilitarianism is more restricted: it offers a universal criterion for every ethical assessment, but this criterion applies only to ethical questions. In philosophy of science there is a long tradition that has sought a logic of theory evaluation that would allow us to determine how well a particular body of evidence supports an hypothesis. This logic would be applicable to all scientific domains, but it might only be relevant to assessing scientific hypotheses. To be sure, some philosophers have attempted to limit rationality to those domains in which the logic of science applied, but others, such as Kant, have sought different criteria for evaluation, e.g., in science and ethics. And we must be a bit careful about mathematics: although we can add apples and battleships and sums of money, we cannot add temperatures, and we do not 'add up' the capacitance of the elements in an electrical circuit by the same rules we use to add up their resistance.

I will return to these topics in chapters II and III, but for the moment let me note that proponents of our classical model of rationality have typically taken the full universality that we find in logic as an ideal, and only reluctantly moved to principles that are domain-specific. Moreover, there are good reasons for this preference. On this model, a belief or decision is rational if it conforms to a set of criteria, and if the same criteria are applicable in every context, then rational individuals need not debate over which criteria should be applied. If alternative criteria are admitted, we may find ourselves having to choose between them, and we will need some way to make *this* choice on a rational basis. Even if we attempt to restrict different criteria to different domains, we may find that domains which seemed clearly distinct at one stage are found to overlap at another stage, and our domain-specific criteria can come into competition. It may well be that we only achieve full blown universality in the case of formal logic, and the recognition of this possibility is surely part of the reason for the common tendency to identify 'rational' with 'logical'. For the remainder of the present chapter I will take the full blown universality that is exemplified by formal logic as the ideal, and any principle which is put forward as a basis for rational decision-making will have to be measured against this ideal.

Let me emphasize one respect in which the possession of time-less, universal principles for evaluating claims is highly desirable: when we have such principles we know what we are doing, and in their absence we might encounter situations in which we have no coherent basis for making an important decision. Suppose, for example, that a new scientific theory included a new set of criteria for evaluating scientific theories, and that these criteria conflicted with those that were previously accepted. Moreover, suppose that our new theory was preferable on the new criteria, while the older theory was preferable on the older criteria. How would we decide between these two theories? Similarly, suppose a new political theory not only proposed a new social order, but also a new set of criteria for evaluating political institutions, and that the new order was clearly superior to the older order given the new criteria, but not on the basis of the older criteria. These are troubling cases, and for the moment I only want to note that they would not arise if we had a truly universal set of criteria for evaluating proposals, and that the lack of such criteria has played a significant role in generating doubts about the possibility of a rational resolution of such questions. At the same time, we should not fear that universal principles would block innovation. In the case of science, we might have principles for evaluating hypotheses against the evidence, and all rational individuals who possess the same evidence would have to arrive at the same evaluation of any scientific proposal. Yet this leaves open the possibility that this

13

evaluation would change as new evidence became available, and even the possibility that a radically new proposal would do better on the available evidence than an older theory. Similarly, it might be possible to invent new political institutions that would do a better job of promoting universal goals. Again the parallel with formal logic is appropriate. Given the constraints of validity we can still construct valid arguments that move from new premises that no one has previously considered to new conclusions, but these constraints do prevent us from attempting to evade a charge of invalidity by introducing a new logic tailored to the conclusions at which we wish to arrive.

There is one small point that should be noted before we leave this topic. Suppose that, at the beginning of this discussion, we had taken the solution of a quadratic equation as our example, instead of a division problem. All of the above points would obtain except that we would end up with two solutions, but this does not contradict the demand for universality. It is a property of quadratic equations that they have a two member solution set, but there is one and only one correct solution set for a given equation, and all individuals who solve a given quadratic equation in a rational way will arrive at the same solution set. Anyone who arrives at a different solution set must have either made a mistake, which can be found and corrected, or failed to arrive at a solution in a rational manner.

1.2 *Necessity*

Consider, now, a second requirement for rationality. It is not enough that all rational thinkers arrive at the same conclusion since this might occur as a result of a massive coincidence, rather than through reasoning. A rationally acceptable conclusion must follow with necessity from the information given.[4] Again mathematics and logic provide the central model: the answer to a problem in arithmetic follows with necessity from the information supplied, while the conclusion of a valid deductive argument follows necessarily from the premises, and any deductive argument is necessarily valid or necessarily invalid.

In one sense the requirement of necessity is more fundamental than the requirement of universality: the existence of a necessary tie between the available information and a rationally acceptable result allows us to understand *why* all rational individuals who start at the same point must arrive at the same conclusion. The requirement of necessity permits us to distinguish those cases in which everyone arrives at the same result because they have reasoned their way to that result in an appropriate manner from those in which universality is achieved as a result of, say, ignorance or indoctrination. And this points to another crucial aspect of this requirement: not only must there be a necessary tie between premises and conclusion for that conclusion to be rationally acceptable, it is also required that we accept the conclusion because we recognize the existence of that necessary connection. Suppose, by way of contrast, that I guess the solution of a problem in arithmetic, and that it happens that I arrive at the correct result. The relevant necessary connection does in fact obtain, but *my* acceptance of that solution is still not rational.

One important example of the connection between necessity and rationality in the history of philosophy is provided by the sharp distinction that is often drawn between accepting a result on a rational basis and accepting it on the basis of experience. The grounds for this distinction typically lie in the claim that conclusions accepted on the basis of experience do not have the necessity that characterizes reasoned results. For example, Locke believed that the perceived properties of a natural substance are necessarily determined by its essence, i.e., by its atomic constitution, and he held that if we knew the essence of a substance we would be able to deduce its properties. But Locke doubted our ability to discover these essences, and argued that we lack a rational grasp of which qualities go together in a particular substance, and are reduced to relying on experience. Thus Locke tells us that 'the want of *Ideas* of their real *Essences* sends us from our own thoughts to the things themselves, as they exist. *Experience here must teach me*, what Reason cannot . . .' (1984, p. 644). And Locke laments the low quality of the results that are derived from mere experience:

> This *way* of getting, and *improving our Knowledge in
> Substances only by Experience* and History, which is all that the
> weakness of our Faculties in this State of *Mediocrity*, which
> we are in in this World, can attain to, makes me suspect,

that natural Philosophy is not capable of being made a science. (1984, p. 645)

Similarly, Hume holds that if we had a rational knowledge of causal connections we would grasp a necessary connection between cause and effect, and we would be able to achieve this by examining the ideas of the items involved. But we cannot grasp this necessity, and we learn about causal connections only through experience:

> 'Tis easy to observe, that in tracing this relation, the inference we draw from cause to effect, is not deriv'd merely from a survey of these particular objects, and from such a penetration into their essences as may discover the dependence of the one upon the other. There is no object, which implies the existence of any other if we consider these objects in themselves, and never look beyond the ideas which we form of them. Such an inference wou'd amount to knowledge, and wou'd imply the absolute contradiction and impossibility of conceiving any thing different. But as all distinct ideas are separable, 'tis evident there can be no impossibility of that kind. When we pass from a present impression to the idea of any object, we might possibly have separated the idea from the impression, and have substituted any other idea in its room.
> 'Tis therefore by EXPERIENCE only, that we can infer the existence of one object from that of another. (1978, pp. 86–7)

In other words, the characteristic feature of rational knowledge is that it provides us with a grasp of necessary connections between the items that concern us, and experience fails to measure up to this demand. It is also worth emphasizing that neither Locke nor Hume is arguing that no necessary connections exist in the world. Rather, their point is that even if such necessity does obtain, the fact that we are incapable of recognizing this necessity shows that our beliefs in these connections are not rational.

This contrast between reason and experience is not peculiar to empiricists; rationalists agree that rationality requires necessity, and that experience does not live up to this requirement. But rationalists also hold that we can grasp a wider range of necessary truths than empiricists will allow, and thus rationalists contend that we can achieve rationality in areas in which empiricists deny that this is possible.

1.3 Rules

In the examples from logic and mathematics discussed above we solved problems by applying rules, and this brings us to a third feature of our classical conception of rationality: the rationality of any conclusion is determined by whether it conforms to the appropriate rules. When we proceed from a starting point to a conclusion in accordance with a set of rules, we free ourselves from the arbitrariness that is characteristic of nonrational decisions. Consider our arithmetical example once again. When we do a long division problem we follow a definite set of rules, and we would be severely hampered if we did not have those rules. We could, of course, guess at an answer, but what makes one guess more reasonable than another? One response is that while no guess is in itself more reasonable than another, we can sort out guesses after they have been made. If, for example, we have learned how to do multiplication but have not yet learned to do division, we could guess the answer to the division problem, and then use multiplication to check this guess. But note what is happening here. We have the rules for multiplication, and the acceptability of a proposed solution to the division problem does not depend on the guess, but on the response we get when we apply these rules. The only solution that we can rationally accept is the one which is shown to be correct when it is tested by means of the rules of multiplication, and the rationality of our procedure rests in the use of the multiplication rules, not in the guesses that we make.

In fact, mathematics provides us with cases exactly like this one. Consider, for example, the difference in the procedures for finding derivatives and integrals. In the former case we have a set of rules that we can apply to any expression in the same straightforward way that we apply the rules of arithmetic, but there is no general procedure for determining the integral of an expression, nor even any general rules for deciding whether an expression has an integral. But an integral is the inverse of a

17

derivative, and however we come up with a proposed integral for an expression, we can determine whether this proposal is correct by finding its derivative. In other words, an expression, *I*, is the integral of another expression, *E*, if and only if, the derivative of *I* is identical to *E*. Thus while we have no rule-governed procedure for finding integrals, we do have a rule-governed procedure for testing whether proposed integrals are correct. The only integrals that we can rationally accept are those which are shown to be correct by differentiation, and the rationality of our decision lies in this second step.

It is important that we be clear on the power of rule-governed procedures. We have no difficulty in conceiving situations in which different people have very different ideas about the solution of a problem, but how do we decide whether we should accept one of these solutions rather than another? Following an impulse or an intuition will not do here because we have competing intuitions, and intuition is not terribly reliable in any case.[5] If we have a set of rules that will allow us to generate or verify answers then we know how to proceed, and it would be difficult to find a clearer model of irrational behavior than that exhibited by a person who refuses to make use of such rules when they are available. Picture someone who refuses to solve division problems by applying the rules, but would rather guess. There is something eminently unreasonable about such behavior.

This point has important applications to a wide range of epistemic situations. We have already seen some of its applications to elementary mathematics, and these ideas apply to deductive sciences generally. Typically, a working mathematician is either looking for an interesting new theorem, or attempting to decide whether an existing conjecture is in fact a theorem. In either case the mathematician establishes her result by providing a proof, and the acceptability of her result depends on the validity of that proof, i.e., on whether the proof conforms to the rules for valid deductions. Modern mathematicians are particularly insistent on the completeness and rigor of proofs since there is considerable historical evidence that even the best mathematicians' intuitions about which steps of a proof can be safely skipped are highly fallible.

A similar analysis applies in the case of empirical science. However they do it, scientists come up with hypotheses, but the fact that someone has thought of an hypothesis does not provide a reason for accepting it. Scientists decide whether to accept an hypothesis by carrying out empirical tests. The rules of scientific method determine which tests are relevant, and whether a body of empirical results is sufficient for accepting or rejecting a proposal, or whether judgement should be suspended pending further investigation. A rational decision is one that is guided by the appropriate rules, and when we come to a decision on the basis of such rules, we understand what we are about.

Thus rules are at the heart of our classical model of rationality: if we have universally applicable rules, then all who begin from the same information must indeed arrive at the same conclusion, and it is these rules that provide the necessary connection between our starting point and our conclusion. Moreover, we can now clear up an ambiguity that has been implicit in our discussion. Consider, first, beliefs. When we speak of a rational belief we are concerned with belief in some proposition. Properly speaking, the rules of logic, mathematics and scientific methodology establish relations between propositions, and when we apply these rules we are assessing a proposition, we are not directly assessing a belief. This suggests that it is propositions that are rational in a fundamental sense, and that the rationality of a belief is derivative. The fact that a proposition follows from, say, a body of evidence on the basis of a set of rules is an objective feature of that proposition, and a rational individual believes only propositions that meet this test. A similar analysis applies for other propositional attitudes. For example, if I decide to pursue some goal, that goal will be expressible in a proposition, and my decision will be rational only if that proposition meets the demands that are encapsulated in an appropriate set of rules. We have also seen that there is a second necessary condition for rational belief, action, etc.: it is not enough that a proposition conforms to the appropriate rules; I must recognize that this is the case. But here too the question of whether the proposition itself is rationally acceptable is fundamental since I cannot recognize that a proposition meets a particular test if it does not in fact meet that test.

1.4 Algorithms

Reflection on Hofstadter's discussion of rationality has led us to the key idea that rationality requires rules; we must now consider just what sort of rules we need. Among the many kinds of rules we can imagine, one class, *algorithms*, stands out. These are rules which, when applied to a problem, guarantee a solution in a finite number of steps. The rules for the various arithmetic procedures, the rules by which one finds the derivative of any function, Venn diagrams, the truth-table test for validity, and most computer programs are examples of algorithms.[6] I want to develop the example of truth-tables a bit further so that we will have a concrete example of an algorithm before us, and then I want to compare the procedures involved in testing an argument for validity by means of truth-tables with those involved in attempting to prove that an argument is valid by deriving the conclusion from the premises in accordance with some predetermined rules of inference.

I will confine this discussion to a case in which we are given a set of premises and a conclusion that are already in symbolic form, and our task is to determine whether or not the conclusion follows validly from the premises. When we use truth-tables we first determine the number of distinct variables in our problem, which can be done by inspection; initially we will need one column for each of these variables. Next we determine the number of rows we need for the table. This is straightforward: given n distinct variables, we need exactly 2^n rows, assuming that we allow for only two truth-values, 'true' and 'false'. If we had, for some reason, a larger number of truth-values, we would need more rows, but for any number of truth-values, m, we will need m^n rows on our table. The number of rows needed is thus definite and calculable; there is no guesswork involved.

Third, we write down all possible combinations of the truth-values. I want to write out a detailed procedure for generating these truth-values since this will give us a succinct example of an algorithm, and an illustration of how algorithms work. We will assume that we are using the two truth-values T and F, and that we have determined that the truth-table is to have r rows. Here is the algorithm:

1. Begin in the leftmost column and set s to equal to $r/2$.
2. Moving down the column, write down s Ts followed by s Fs.
3. If we have reached the bottom row (row r) of the table, go to Step 4; if not, go to step 2.
4. If s equals 1, stop; if s is not equal to 1, go to step 5.
5. Move to the top of the next column to the right.
6. Set s equal to half of its current value.
7. Go to Step 2.

If we follow these rules we will move around a loop until we reach the direction to stop, and we will have the complete set of possible combinations of truth-values for the number of variables at hand. This procedure may take time, and may be boring, but it does guarantee a complete set of truth-value combinations in a finite number of steps. And it guarantees that everyone who follows these rules will end up with exactly the same set of truth-value combinations. Each of the steps involved in constructing a truth-table can be reduced to such an explicit, mechanically applicable procedure, and this guarantees the reliability of truth-tables and the universality of their results. I will not go into such detail again, but I do want to sketch the rest of the procedure.

We now work through our premises and conclusion, one by one, building the column that contains the truth-value of each of these expressions for all possible cases. Here we will have to break up complex expressions into smaller pieces that contain either one variable, in the case of negation, or two variables, for the binary operators. Again a procedure can be written, although it will be considerably more complex than the one above. Note especially that at each stage in the process we will be constructing a column of truth-values. The correct truth-value for each slot in a column will be determined by the truth-values in either one or two other columns in the same row, and by the operator being used. Each operator is itself defined by a truth-table that gives a resultant truth-value for any truth-values we plug in, just as a multiplication table gives the results of multiplying pairs of numbers. We can write a procedure for searching through these tables that is quite as rigid as the one given above for setting up the table, and, in effect, the entire procedure for constructing a truth-table consists of a complex algorithm built up out of simpler algorithms. Finally, we scan the completed truth-table to determine if there is a row that has all true premises and a false conclusion. If such a row is found the argument is invalid, if no such row exists, the argument is valid.

Now compare an alternative approach to this problem: we have a set of valid rules of inference, and we attempt to find a series of steps, each in accordance with one of these rules, that will lead from the premises to the conclusion. We do not typically follow a set of mechanical rules when we attempt to construct a valid deduction. Indeed, for large classes of important problems we cannot generate a proof by following mechanical rules because no such rules are known.[7] Moreover, there is no guarantee that anyone will find a proof in a given case because (among other possibilities) the argument in question may be invalid, so that no proof exists. Truth-tables have a second advantage besides being mechanically applicable: they provide a 'decision procedure', that is, they tell us whether the argument we are examining is valid or invalid. But once we get beyond relatively simple problems there are no decision procedures. We can attempt to prove an argument valid by constructing a valid deduction, and we can attempt to prove it invalid by finding a counter-instance; but we may pursue both options for a long time without finding either. The history of mathematics is full of such cases. Even where the argument is in fact valid, there are no clear procedures to follow in seeking a proof. Different people will proceed in different ways, some will solve a given problem rapidly, and some will never solve it at all. The ability to find a valid deduction is a matter of insight and intuition, skill and luck; we do not have to rely on these when we are constructing truth-tables.

Note, however, that while the ability to discover a valid deduction may be a matter of intuition and skill, the decision as to whether we should accept a proposed deduction as valid does not depend on such unreliable factors. Here our initial list of valid arguments does provide the basis for an algorithm, and the process of *justifying* the claim that a given argument is valid can be reduced to a mechanical procedure. Once we have applied this algorithm to the proposed proof and found it valid we have reasons for accepting the proof as correct. But consider what would happen if we did not even have an algorithm for testing proposed proofs. At what point would we be justified in maintaining that we had adequate reason for accepting a proof? We would have to depend on the skill and intuition of the person who constructed the proof, along with the skill and intuition of those who were convinced that the proof was right. Yet what justification would we have for believing in the abilities of any of these individuals if we had never actually been able to check some proofs and show that these people are reliable?

These questions underline the central role of algorithms in rational decision-making. If we are to have a rational basis for accepting a conclusion we must have adequate reasons for accepting it, but how are we to understand the notion of *adequate* reasons? In the cases we have examined thus far algorithms provide us with an answer. In all of these cases we were given a starting point – a set of premises, a body of numerical data, an expression to be differentiated – and a conclusion; our problem was to determine whether that starting point does indeed adequately support the conclusion. When we can test the relation between starting point and conclusion by the application of an algorithm, the answer will be clear. Not only will the algorithm give a definite response, but all individuals who apply the algorithm correctly will necessarily arrive at the same result. Note especially that algorithms do two jobs for us. When a conclusion is connected to a starting point by an algorithm, then the required relation between starting point and conclusion does in fact obtain; second, when we follow the algorithm we learn that this relation holds. These are the two conditions for rationally believing a proposition that were discussed at the end of the previous section.

1.5 *Induction*

I now want to turn to cases in which we accept a result on the basis of inductive evidence, and I want to consider why induction has long been considered problematic. As in the previous cases, in considering induction we will be concerned with a relationship between some starting point and some conclusion. Typically the starting point will be a finite set of singular sentences that express results of observations and that function as evidence for the conclusion, while the conclusion will be a sentence which has not been, or cannot be, tested directly against observation. To take a well worn example, the evidence may consist of a large number of observations of swans where, in each case, the swan observed was white. The conclusion may be either the claim that some specific swan that has not yet been observed is white, or the universal generalization 'All swans are white'. Formally, we have an argument whose premises are singular sentences, and whose conclusion is either another singular sentence, or a universal sentence; the problem is to determine the circumstances under which the premises provide adequate reasons for accepting the conclusion. Two further examples will help sharpen the problem.

Consider first a case in which a scientist is attempting to make inferences on the basis of a body of data that can be represented as points on a graph, such as the data indicated by the 'x' points in Figure 1. If we were only interested in predicting other data points, we might infer that further testing would confirm the existence of the point labelled 'a'. More ambitiously, we might infer a general relation which would hold for any possible data point we tested. Fitting a curve to the data, e.g., the straight line in Figure 2, amounts to making an inductive inference from a specific body of data to a universal relationship.

But now a question arises: why not adopt the more complex curve of Figure 3, instead of the straight line of Figure 1? Like the first curve, this curve also fits all of the available data points. The decision to choose a particular curve is equivalent to accepting a generalization that is supported by the data, yet the two curves are equally well supported since they both pass through all of the available data points. Yet the curves in Figure 2 and in Figure 3 lead to very different predictions as to what we will find if we make a variety of further observations that have not yet been made. For example, the curve of Figure 2 is consistent with the prediction of point a in Figure 1, while the curve of Figure 3 is consistent with the prediction of point b in Figure 4. Yet if we now return to the case in which we only wished to predict one more point on the basis of the given data, there seems to be no better reason for predicting a than for predicting b.

One more step will complete this line of argument. There is an unlimited number of different curves that will fit any finite set of data points (which is all we ever have), and the data do not seem to provide any basis for choosing one of these curves rather than another. Moreover, if we are only concerned with the prediction

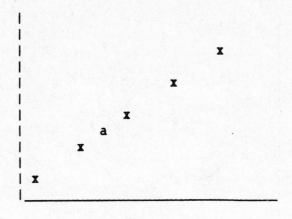

Figure 1

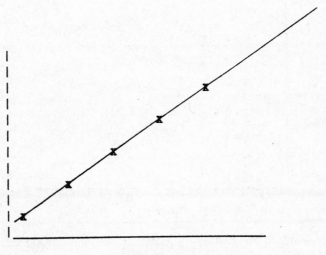

Figure 2

of a single additional data point, the decision to make one prediction rather than another gets what justification it has from the possibility of its appearing on some curve that passes through all of the given data points. But whatever specific prediction we make, it will always be possible to find a curve that passes through that predicted point and the original data points. Thus the given

25

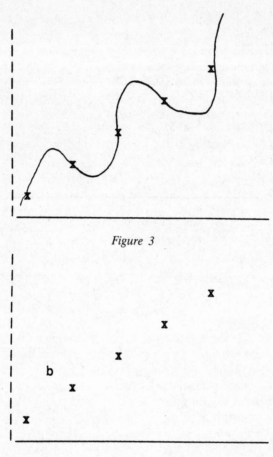

Figure 3

Figure 4

data seems to support any prediction we might make equally well.

Many readers will recognize the above as Nelson Goodman's 'new riddle of induction' (1965). The traditional problem of induction arises when we try to understand the connection between premises and conclusion in an inductive argument, and it turns on a contrast between inductive and deductive arguments. In a valid deductive argument there is a necessary tie between premises and conclusion: it is impossible for the premises to be true and the conclusion false, and there is an algorithm for determining

26

whether the conclusion in question does in fact follow from the premises. In the inductive case it is always possible that the premises are true and the conclusion false. There is no necessary tie between premises and conclusion, and this makes it unclear whether we are ever rationally justified in accepting an inductively supported conclusion. These doubts would be mitigated if we could find an algorithm which would permit us to determine whether a given set of premises inductively supports a given conclusion, and the main line of research in inductive logic has long been the attempt to produce such an algorithm.[8]

This point becomes considerably more pressing when we turn to the sharpened version of the problem that was sketched above. Now we must note that there is not only a problem in understanding the relation between premises and conclusion in a particular inductive argument, but that for any given set of premises, there is always a number, perhaps an unlimited number, of mutually inconsistent conclusions that receive identical inductive support from those premises. This inconsistency will appear in one of two ways. If our concern is to make specific predictions, we will find that mutually inconsistent predictions will be equally well supported by our premises. If we are seeking universal generalizations, we will find that the data supports alternative generalizations that yield mutually inconsistent predictions for at least one case. This is what occurred in our curve-fitting example, and a bit of reflection on the history of science suggests that this does not just occur in artificial cases. For example, Galileo concluded on the basis of a number of experiments that objects fall to the earth with constant acceleration, and he took this to be a general result – he even used it to calculate how long it would take a stone to fall to the earth from the distance of the moon (1967, pp. 221–3). A few decades later Newton found that the acceleration of a falling object varies inversely as the square of its distance from the center of the earth, but that Galileo's observations were not sufficient to distinguish between the two laws. In other words, if Galileo had thought of Newton's more complex law, Galileo's observations would not have provided any grounds for choosing between the two laws – or between these and many other laws that might also have occurred to him.

It will be useful to consider another kind of example, taken from Goodman, since this will show that the point is not restricted to cases involving quantitative relations. Suppose we have come to the conclusion that all emeralds are green on the basis of uniform experience. Goodman suggests that we consider the predicate *grue*, which can be defined as follows (this is simpler than Goodman's definition but it will suffice for present purposes): an object is grue if and only if it is green before time, t, and blue after t, where t is some time in the future. Since t has not yet occurred, and since all of the emeralds that have been examined are green, the available evidence supports the generalization 'All emeralds are grue' to the same extent that it supports 'All emeralds are green'. Yet the latter generalization leads us to predict that, after t, emeralds will still be green, while the former generalization leads us to expect that after t they will be blue. The fact that the latter prediction may strike us as highly unlikely is irrelevant to the question that concerns us: what rational basis does the available evidence about the color of emeralds provide for choosing one of these generalizations, with its attendant prediction about the future, rather than the other? Again, less fanciful illustrations are available. Hume, for example, notes that:

> The Indian prince, who refused to believe the first relations concerning the effects of frost, reasoned justly; and it naturally required very strong testimony to engage his assent to facts, that arose from a state of nature, with which he was unacquainted, and which bore so little analogy to those events, of which he had had constant and uniform experience.
> Though they were not contrary to his experience, they were not conformable to it. (1975, pp. 113–14)

The Indian prince had certainly experienced variations in the temperature of water, and, in Goodman's terminology, he would have projected that water would continue to be liquid as its temperature continued to drop, while he would have no basis for expecting that at some point a drop in temperature would result in solid water. Indeed, Hume emphasizes that 'The operations of cold upon water are not gradual, according to the degrees of cold; but whenever it comes to the freezing point, the water passes in a moment, from the utmost liquidity to perfect hardness' (1975, p. 114, n. 1).

Similarly, before the discovery of radioactivity physicists did not expect that, at some future date, a lump of radium would have largely turned into lead. This last case also suggests an important point about Goodman's example: if at some time in the future we were to discover that our emeralds were blue, we would not have to conclude that time had causal efficacy. We would only have to conclude that we had projected the wrong predicate, and we would be free to seek a deeper explanation for the change we had discovered.

The parallel between these cases and those in which we must decide which curve to fit to the available data should be clear, and it should be equally clear that variations on Goodman's example will be constructible for any prediction that we choose as long as we do not have a necessary connection between our evidence and one conclusion. But if the available evidence can support any prediction whatsoever, the appeal to evidence becomes a sham, and any prediction we make is arbitrary – and an arbitrary decision is the antithesis of a rational decision.

An extended discussion of possible solutions to the problems of induction would take us far from our present concerns, but I do want to consider one attempt to solve the curve-fitting problem, and one attempt to solve Goodman's emerald problem. A standard approach to the former problem is to propose that we always accept the *simplest* possible curve for the given data. When further data becomes available we may find that we have to abandon that choice and pick a new curve, but we will again pick the simplest curve that fits the currently available data. For present purposes, the crucial feature of this proposal is that it *offers us a rule* in accordance with which to make a choice, and a rule is what we need if we are to decide between possible curves on a rational basis. There are objections to this rule, and two of the most common objections will serve to underline my point. First, the notion of 'simplicity' is far from clear, and we will be inclined to ask for some rule for determining which of two curves is simpler; in the absence of such a rule, we still lack a rational basis for deciding between alternatives. Second, we need some assurance that in every given case one and only one curve will turn out to be the simplest. If we find a case in which the criterion of simplicity cannot provide sufficient grounds for choosing between alternatives we will be left, again, with distinct alternatives and no rational basis for our choice, and we will be inclined to ask for some further rule to mediate this choice. In all of these circumstances a rational decision requires that we have a sufficient set of rules to guarantee a unique decision between competing alternatives.

Turning to the emerald example, Goodman notes that if we compare the predicates 'green' and 'grue', we will find that in fact 'green' has a substantial history of being applied to objects and of being used to make successful predictions, while 'grue' has no such history. Thus Goodman suggests the following rule: in cases of conflict, use those predicates that already have a history of successful projection in our language. This proposal too faces problems, but here I wish only to note that we have, again, been offered a rule, and that for this rule to do its job, it must in fact be unambiguously applicable to all relevant situations, and it must succeed in giving a definite solution in all cases in which conflict occurs.

To sum up, the problem with induction is that we do not know what rules to apply in attempting to decide whether to accept inductive arguments. If we are to solve the traditional problem, our classical model of rationality requires that we find a set of rules that will allow us to decide how much support the available evidence gives to what was usually taken to be an obvious conclusion. Goodman sharpened the problem by requiring that we also consider what other conclusions might be supported by the evidence. In both cases, however, it seems that we need rules if our decisions are to be rational, and philosophers have typically sought to solve the problems raised by induction by seeking algorithms that would fill this gap.

1.6 Discovery and justification

The view of rationality we have been examining provides the basis for a classic distinction, originally due to Hans Reichenbach (1938, pp. 6–7), between the *context of discovery* and the *context of justification*; a discussion of this distinction will help clarify the main features of this model of rationality. The point of the distinction is that discovery, understood as the process by which individuals come up with new ideas, is distinct from the procedures by which such ideas are tested and evaluated – and questions of rationality arise only in the latter context. Richard Rudner, for example, focusing on scientific hypotheses, writes:

> Now, in general, the context of validation [i.e., justification] is the context of our concern when, regardless of how we have come to discover or entertain a scientific hypothesis or theory, we raise questions about accepting or rejecting it. To the context of discovery, on the other hand, belong such questions as how, in fact, one comes to latch onto good hypotheses, or what social, psychological, political or economic conditions will conduce to thinking up fruitful hypotheses. (Rudner, 1966, p. 6)

Similarly, Karl Popper tells us that:

> The initial stage, the act of conceiving or inventing a theory, seems to me neither to call for logical analysis, nor to be susceptible of it. The question how it happens that a new idea occurs to a man – whether it is a musical theme, a dramatic conflict, or a scientific theory – may be of great interest to empirical psychology; but it is irrelevant to the logical analysis of scientific knowledge. This latter is concerned not with *questions of fact* (Kant's *quid facti?*), but only with questions of *justification or validity* (Kant's *quid juris?*). Its questions are of the following kind. Can a statement be justified? And if so, how? Is it testable? Is it logically dependent on certain other statements? Or does it perhaps contradict them? In order that a statement may be logically examined in this way, it must already have been presented to us. Someone must have formulated it, and submitted it to logical examination.
>
> Accordingly I shall distinguish sharply between the process of conceiving a new idea, and the methods and results of examining it logically. As to the task of the logic of knowledge – in contradistinction to the psychology of knowledge – I shall proceed on the assumption that it consists solely in investigating the methods employed in those systematic tests to which every new idea must be subjected if it is to be seriously entertained. (1968, p. 31)

Items in the context of discovery are, on this view, nonrational: the processes and circumstances involved in conceiving a new idea are irrelevant to the question of whether we have good reasons for accepting or rejecting that idea. Ideas occur to various people in various situations, and the factors that elicit these ideas can be studied by psychologists, historians, biographers, and so forth, but the results of these studies have no bearing on the question of whether it is rational to accept that proposal. Rational acceptance or rejection of a proposal depends solely on how that proposal fares when it is evaluated in accordance with the appropriate rules.

The career of the Indian mathematician Srinivasa Ramanujan provides a striking example of the point at issue. Ramanujan had an astounding ability to conceive complex mathematical theorems, 'half a dozen new ones almost every day', according to G. H. Hardy (1959, p. 11). How Ramanujan did this is quite unknown. Hardy offers the following description of Ramanujan's range and limits; it is well worth pondering even if some of the mathematical references are unfamiliar:

> The limitations of his knowledge were as startling as its profundity. Here was a man who could work out modular equations and theorems of complex multiplication, to orders unheard of, whose mastery of continued fractions was, on the formal side at any rate, beyond that of any mathematician in the world, who had found for himself the functional equation of the Zeta-function, and the dominant terms of many of the most famous problems in the analytic theory of numbers; and he had never heard of a doubly periodic function or of Cauchy's theorem, and had indeed but the vaguest idea of what a function of a complex variable was. His ideas as to what constituted a mathematical proof were of the most shadowy description. All his results, new or old, right or wrong, had been arrived at by a process of mingled argument, intuition, and induction, of which he was entirely unable to give any coherent account. (Hardy, 1927, p. xxx)

Yet impressive as Ramanujan was, none of his proposals could be accepted simply because he pronounced it. This is particularly clear when we note that Ramanujan was not always right. (See, for example, Hardy, 1927, xxiv; 1957, p. 15.) But even if Ramanujan never made an error, we could only know this because mathematicians had verified his results, i.e., had constructed proper proofs from established principles. And if we were to decide on the basis of past experience that Ramanujan is always right, and that we would henceforth accept all of his pronouncements without question, we would in effect be accepting his new proposals on inductive grounds. In either case, the key point is that we have rational grounds for accepting a proposal only if we have justified that proposal.

An analogous point holds for empirical science, although here the testing process depends ultimately on observational results, not just on formal proofs. Even the most brilliant scientists are fallible. Kepler thought he could prove that there must be exactly six planets; Galileo denied that the sun and moon play any role in causing the tides, and developed a theory which held that tides are caused by the motion of the earth; Newton worked at least as hard at alchemy as at physics; Einstein spent a large part of his life in an unsuccessful attempt to develop a unified field theory – many other examples could be cited. Once we recognize that even the greatest thinkers are fallible, we must also recognize that proposals carry no rational weight unless they have been subjected to independent tests, and that it is the outcome of these tests that determines the appropriate stance toward any hypothesis. And even if we did not have a history of human fallibility, a point that was made above holds again: we could not know that previous thinkers were uniformly correct unless we had verified their claims. In general, a rational response to a proposal requires relevant reasons, and items in the context of discovery are not relevant reasons.

It is also worth noting that the set of procedures to be found in the context of justification may be very limited. For example, the process of constructing a deductive proof is often as difficult and as unpredictable as the process of thinking up a new theorem, and both fall in the context of discovery. Properly speaking, a proposed proof is as much an hypothesis as is the conclusion that the proof is intended to demonstrate, and a proposed proof can be fallacious. It is only when we are testing the validity of a proposed proof against the laws of logic that we have entered the context of justification, and at this point we are engaged in a process that is completely governed by a set of algorithms. Those proofs which our logical algorithms show to be correct are rationally acceptable, and those which do not pass these tests are not rationally acceptable, no matter who invented them. If this seems restrictive, its importance must not be underrated, for it is only by appeal to an algorithm that we get an unequivocal answer to questions of the sort, 'does evidence *E* provide adequate grounds for accepting conclusion *C*?' In the absence of an algorithm, the relation between our premises and our conclusion remains indeterminate, and we are in the position of the person who accepts the results of a long division problem on the basis of intuition.

Analogous points apply, again, in empirical contexts. There is a long tradition, running from Francis Bacon in the seventeenth century to John Stuart Mill in the nineteenth century, which holds that induction provides a set of rules that allow us to generate new discoveries automatically from data, but it is now generally recognized that no such procedures exist. Carl Hempel sums up the situation thus:

> Induction is sometimes conceived as a method that leads, by means of mechanically applicable rules, from observed facts to corresponding general principles. In this case, the rules of inductive inference would provide effective canons of scientific discovery; induction would be a mechanical procedure analogous to the familiar routine for the multiplication of integers, which leads, in a finite number of predetermined and mechanically performable steps, to the corresponding product. Actually, however, no such general and mechanical induction procedure is available at present; otherwise, the much studied problem of the causation of cancer, for example, would hardly have remained unsolved to this day. Nor can the discovery of such a procedure ever be expected. (1966, p. 14)

But Hempel is more optimistic about the possibility of finding algorithms which will allow us to assess hypotheses against evidence, and he concludes that 'any "rules of induction" will have to be conceived, in analogy to the rules of deduction, as canons of validation rather than of discovery' (1966, p. 18).

1.7 The value of rationality

One virtue of the model of rationality we have been discussing is that it provides an answer to the perennial question 'Why be rational'? What point is there to making rational decisions or adopting rational beliefs, rather than choosing on the basis of impulse or emotion, or even at random? Part of the answer to this question derives directly from the point that when we are trying to answer a question, whether in mathematics, in empirical science, or in our everyday lives, one of our aims is to get a *reliable* result, and rational procedures provide reliable results. Again the case of arithmetic is particularly clear. Why, for example, should I use the rules of arithmetic to balance my checkbook instead of simply intuiting an answer, or waiting for one to come to me in a dream? The answer is that I do not want to write down just any balance in my checkbook, but rather the correct balance, and the rules of arithmetic provide the surest way of getting the correct balance. The situation is similar in other fields. We often want to know whether some conclusion is supported by a particular body of information: given the axioms of Euclidean geometry, does it follow that all plane triangles have 180 degrees? Given that people with streptococcus infections are usually cured by taking penicillin, should I too take penicillin when I have such an infection? Given the available evidence, is special relativity worthy of belief? Rational procedures allow us to arrive at nonarbitrary answers to these questions.

But this is not the entire story, because it is not enough just to get the right answer: we must also be able to *recognize* that an answer is correct if we are to have a basis for accepting it. To see what I am after here, note that someone who attempts to balance a checkbook by trying to guess the answer may get the right result – nonrational procedures do not guarantee error. Similarly, we may imagine a new Ramanujan who, in a moment of intuition, writes down a physical theory that no contemporary physicist will accept, but which will be recognized as a major achievement 500 years from now. Do we really want to reject such correct results just because we do not now have *rational* grounds for accepting them? Unfortunately, our answer must be 'Yes', exactly because we have no way of recognizing that this result is correct, and thus we have no way of distinguishing it from a multitude of incorrect claims that we are also unable to evaluate. A different example will help to clarify the point. Suppose I write a number of distinct declarative sentences on strips of paper, being sure that for every sentence in the set I also include its contradictory, and I put the strips of paper into a hat. I can be certain that I have a good deal of truth in the hat – exactly half the strips of paper hold true sentences – and if I pick a strip at random, I may indeed have a true sentence. Unfortunately, picking a sentence does not tell me if it is true, and if I have no way of knowing whether this sentence is true, I am in no better position than I was before I picked it out of the hat. What I need is not just a true sentence, but some way of being able to recognize true sentences, and this is what rational procedures allow us to do: they provide not just a conclusion, but a reason for accepting that conclusion. The procedures of arithmetic do not just give an answer to a problem, nor even just a correct answer; they also provide grounds for believing that the answer is correct. A valid argument gives me reasons for accepting its conclusion, however I may have arrived at that conclusion in the first place. Empirical evidence for a scientific hypothesis provides grounds for believing and acting on that hypothesis. In other words, the trouble with the intuitive physicist's theory is that while it may be true, at the present state of the development of physics we have no reasons for accepting it, and indeed we have no more grounds for accepting this theory than for accepting any of a number of other hypotheses that are inconsistent with it.

This discussion also provides a basis for understanding why it has long been customary to contrast reason with authority and faith. When we are asked to accept, say, a religious claim, on faith, we are asked to accept it without being given any reasons, and this makes it rather difficult to know if the claim is worthy of belief – especially when we are faced with incompatible competing claims. We would be able to sort out and assess these claims if we could find some evidence for preferring one of them over the others, and many religious thinkers have pursued this task, but now we are proposing to rely on reason instead of faith.

The situation is a bit more complicated in the case of authority. All of us accept important claims that we have not tested for ourselves on the authority of scientists, engineers, physicians, automobile mechanics, and others, and we cannot avoid doing this because we simply do not have the time and knowledge required to evaluate every claim. Even an experimental scientist who is testing an hypothesis will make use of claims that she has not tested herself, but accepted on the authority of other scientists, when she is designing her equipment, and evaluating her results. Still, physicians, scientists and automobile mechanics do make their decisions on the basis of information that is in principle available to me, and a competent professional can usually provide some basis for her recommendations even to a lay person. Moreover, I can get a second opinion, or learn the necessary skills myself. This kind of authority stands in striking contrast to the kind of claims to authority that we sometimes encounter in religious contexts, where we are asked to accept the authority of a revelation that is only available to certain individuals. We cannot test their claims under the best of circumstances, and no second opinions are allowed. Nevertheless, strictly speaking, whenever I accept a decision on the basis of authority I am not being fully rational, although the model of rationality we have been examining does suggest an approach to making such decisions rational without our having to become authorities on every subject – we might be able to develop rules for distinguishing reliable authorities from those who are not reliable.

Finally, we can also see why it is desirable to increase the range of problems that can be resolved on a rational basis. In the absence of adequate rules we regularly find ourselves unable to determine how to act and what to believe. This is particularly striking in matters of public policy and international politics, as well as in intellectual matters and cases concerning personal practical decisions. If we could find a set of algorithms for resolving such issues, then we would actually know what we are doing. Perhaps the most ambitious expression of this goal is due to Leibniz, who envisioned a 'universal characteristic', i.e., a symbolism analogous to arithmetic which 'will reduce all questions to numbers, and thus present a sort of statics by virtue of which rational evidence may be weighed' (1951, p. 24). If such a characteristic were available, it would allow us to settle philosophical and religious disputes, questions of war and peace, and all other human difficulties, 'with the clarity and certainty which was hitherto possible only in arithmetic' (1951, p. 23). Such a technique is not now at hand, and perhaps Leibniz was a bit too optimistic about its prospects, but we can see why he would consider it desirable.

CHAPTER II

Foundations

In chapter I I described a familiar model of rationality, and I attempted to show that it embodies a set of powerful and plausible ideas. Nevertheless, when pressed, that model faces serious problems, problems that make it difficult to see how any belief can in fact be rational.[1] To see how these problems arise, recall that rational beliefs must be based on reasons. On the classical model of rationality,[2] reasons are provided by the information we begin with, along with the rules that establish the connection between this information and the proposition believed. But as soon as the model is put this starkly, two questions arise – or, rather, the same question arises in two contexts: on what basis do we select the information from which to begin, and on what basis do we select our rules? If a belief is to be genuinely rational, it must be rational on both of these counts. There would not be much point in claiming that a conclusion had been arrived at in a rational manner if we arrived there on the basis of an impeccable algorithm from randomly chosen premises, or if we proceeded from appropriate premises in strict accordance with ridiculous rules. The classical model requires that we begin from an appropriate starting point and use appropriate rules. I will discuss rules in the final section of this chapter; most of the chapter will be concerned with the premises from which rational justification must begin.

Examples such as Hofstadter's problem, or a textbook problem in logic or mathematics, become misleading if we dwell on them too long since in these problems the premises are given and we are only concerned with getting from those premises to a conclusion. But this leaves out a major part of the problem of rationality, a part that becomes quite pressing once we leave the textbook realm. Here we cannot focus only on the inference, we must be equally concerned with the reasonableness of the premises from which we make that inference. Thus we are led to ask what makes a premise rationally acceptable. The obvious answer is that a premise will be rationally acceptable just in case it has been accepted on the basis of the appropriate rules, but we require premises before we can apply those rules; the problem has only been pushed back a step, and we face the threat of an infinite regress of premises invoked to justify other premises. Roderick Chisholm develops this problem, and leads us to the traditional solution:

> We consider certain things that we know to be true, or think we know to be true, or certain things which, upon reflection, we would be willing to call *evident*. With respect to each of these, we then try to formulate a reasonable answer to the question, 'What justification do you have for thinking you know this thing to be true?' or 'What justification do you have for counting this thing as something that is evident?' (1977, p. 17)

But the obvious answer leads on to further questions:

> In many instances the answers to our questions will take the following form: 'What justifies me in thinking that I know that *a* is *F* is the fact that it is evident to me that *b* is *G*'. . . . Such an answer, therefore, presupposes an epistemic principle, what we might call a 'rule of evidence.' The rule would have the form: If it is evident to me that *b* is *G*, then it is evident to me that *a* is *F*. . . .
>
> This type of answer to our Socratic questions shifts the burden of justification from one claim to another. For we may now ask, 'What justifies me in counting it as evident that *b* is *G*?' or 'What justifies me in thinking I know that *b* is *G*?' And possibly we will formulate, once again, an answer of the first sort: 'What justifies me in counting it as evident that *b* is *G* is the fact that it is evident that *c* is *H*'. . . .
>
> We might try to continue *ad indefinitum*, justifying each new claim that we elicit by still another claim. Or we might be tempted to complete a vicious circle: in such a case, having justified '*a* is *F* by appeal to '*b* is *G*,' and '*b* is *G*' by reference to '*c* is *H*,' we would then justify '*c* is *H*' by reference to '*a* is

F.' But if we are rational beings, we will do neither of these things. For we will find that our Socratic questions lead us to a proper stopping place. (1977, pp. 18–19)

On the classical model of rationality we must find this stopping place if any belief is to be rational, and the attempt to find it has generated one of the most persistent problems of philosophy. This stopping place must consist of a set of propositions that are rationally justified without their justification being dependent on other propositions. In other words, we need propositions that are *self-justifying*. Just as in some theologies a self-caused being is invoked to break the regress of causes and effects, so a set of self-justifying propositions will break the regress of propositions justified by appeal to further propositions, and will do so without introducing a nonrational element. Now the most common way of seeking self-justifying propositions has been to look for propositions that are *self-evident*, i.e., propositions that are true, and whose truth is clear to anyone who properly understands them.[3] It is clear that self-evident propositions will provide the required stopping place, i.e., that self-evidence is a sufficient condition for self-justification: we are justified in believing propositions that are self-evidently true, and this justification does not require that we appeal to other propositions. Thus it is not surprising to find that many philosophers have attempted to discover a set of self-evident truths that would provide a foundation for all rational justification. These attempts have not been successful, and I want to examine some of the most important of these attempts from the history of philosophy, and some of the reasons why they have failed.[4] After doing so, I will consider whether self-evidence is a necessary condition for self-justification, and then discuss one attempt to defend the classical model of rationality without a self-justifying foundation. Finally, I will discuss the problem of finding the rules that are required to establish the rationality of those beliefs that are not self-justifying.

2.1 Plato

We can begin with Plato's discussions of mathematics and dialectic in Book VI of *The Republic*. Recall that Plato first argues that knowledge is not possible in the realms of art and sense perception, while knowledge may be possible in the purely intellectual disciplines of mathematics and dialectic. Now important as mathematics is to Plato, he offers two reasons why mathematics does not provide knowledge in the full sense of the term. The first, which need not concern us here, derives from the claim that mathematics must make use of sensory images. The second reason, which does concern us, is that in mathematics the mind carries out its investigations 'by means of assumptions from which it proceeds not up to a principle, but down to a conclusion' (510b; 1961, p. 745). But no matter how firm our reasoning, if we start from assumptions, then any conclusion we arrive at lacks a rational basis. Perhaps we might have started from different assumptions and arrived at a contrary conclusion, and even if no other starting point is possible, we do not know this as long as we are working from an assumption. We may have arrived at a correct result, but we do not have an adequate grasp of why it is correct. If we are to achieve knowledge we must find a starting point which is not just an assumption, and Plato maintained that dialectic – the Socratic process of question and answer – can bring us to this starting point, since in dialectic the mind 'advances from its assumption to a beginning or principle that transcends assumption' (510b; 1961, p. 745).

Typical applications of dialectic occur when we attempt to grasp the meaning of a concept. We begin with a formulation of that meaning, and, through the process of criticism and redefinition, we move to better definitions until we eventually reach a correct understanding of the concept in question. It is only when that goal has been reached that we have knowledge.[5] Now the claim that there is one correct understanding of any concept is founded on Plato's theory of forms, while the thesis that we are able to reach that understanding through dialectic is based on Plato's theory of learning as recollection; these are widely discussed views, and I will not consider them here. There is, however, a crucial question that is germane to our present inquiry: how do I recognize when I have achieved an adequate grasp of a form? This cannot be based on an argument from some set of premises, since that would leave us in the same unsatisfactory situation that Plato thinks we are in in the case of mathematics. The goal of dialectic is to bring us to the fundamental level from which all rational argument must begin.

Plato's answer turns on an appeal to a kind of intuition – when we get there we simply know it: 'at last in a flash understanding of each blazes up, and the mind, as it exerts all its powers to the limit of human capacity, is flooded with light' ('Seventh Letter', 344b; 1961, p. 1591).[6] In other words, when we finally grasp a form, it is self-evident that we have done so, and we need not appeal to any external considerations to justify our sense that we have grasped that form. Without this intuition the process of dialectic might never end, and it is this intuition that provides a starting point that transcends assumptions.

Now in one respect Plato's concerns are different from those that arise in the classical model of rationality, since Plato is concerned with grasping concepts rather than with grasping propositions. Still, Plato's discussion illustrates a pattern that is pervasive in the history of philosophy: he has diagnosed a potential infinite regress of justifications, and has appealed to intuition in order to block that regress. Moreover, this seems to be the only way to break this regress. Yet this appeal to intuition should give us pause. On Plato's view it is extremely difficult to grasp a form, and there certainly are cases in which individuals sincerely, but mistakenly, believe that they have achieved this goal – yet there is no way of checking intuitions, since this would open up the very regress that intuitions are supposed to block. But what makes my belief that I have succeeded in grasping a form any more reliable than Ramanujan's mathematical intuitions? In terms of the classical model of rationality, intuition should be taken as an occasion to enter the context of justification and begin the process of rational evaluation, not the terminus at which further rational evaluation is no longer required. We are in a genuine bind here. There must be some self-justifying foundation if justification is to be possible at all, and the search for this foundation has driven philosophers working in many different intellectual traditions to invoke a self-evident starting point that is established by intuition as the ultimate foundation of rational knowledge. Aristotle's analysis of scientific knowledge will provide us with a second example.

2.2   Aristotle

Unlike Plato, Aristotle is deeply interested in knowledge of the
sensible world; but like Plato, Aristotle insists that such knowledge, which he calls 'scientific knowledge', must be knowledge of
eternal truths. According to Aristotle, scientific knowledge is
arrived at by syllogistic demonstration from previously accepted
principles, but this immediately raises the question of the nature
of our knowledge of those principles. At some point we must have
principles that are not derived from demonstrations, and these
first principles must be known if the conclusions that are derived
from them are to be known. Moreover, Aristotle maintains that
these principles must be *better known* than the conclusion if they
are to provide a justification for that conclusion. We approach
these truths through induction: we examine objects, formulate
hypotheses about their natures, test these hypotheses by further
examination, adjust our hypotheses, and so on. Aristotle summa-
rizes the relation between demonstration and induction in his
discussion of the intellectual virtues in Book VI of the *Nicomachean Ethics*.

> Now what scientific knowledge is, if we are to speak exactly
> and not follow mere similarities, is plain from what follows.
> We all suppose that what we know is not even capable of
> being otherwise; of things capable of being otherwise we do
> not know, when they have passed outside our observation,
> whether they exist or not. Therefore the object of scientific
> knowledge is of necessity. Therefore it is eternal: for things
> that are of necessity in the unqualified sense are all eternal;
> and things that are eternal are ungenerated and imperishable.
> Again, every science is thought to be capable of being taught,
> and its object of being learned. And all teaching starts from
> what is already known, . . . for it proceeds sometimes
> through induction and sometimes by syllogism. Now induction
> is the starting-point which knowledge even of the universal
> presupposes, while syllogism proceeds from universals. There
> are therefore starting-points from which syllogism proceeds,
> which are not reached by syllogism; it is therefore by induction
> that they are acquired. (1139b; 1941, pp. 1024–1025)

Unfortunately, this is not enough. The inductive procedures

that lead us to first principles do not yield anything beyond well founded hypotheses; if our first premises are to be known with certainty, something more is required. According to Aristotle, 'it is intuitive reason that grasps first principles' (1141a; 1941, p. 1027). In the *Posterior Analytics* Aristotle describes this as an innate ability of the mind to grasp fundamental truths after induction has done the necessary preparatory work:

> We conclude that these states of knowledge are neither innate
> in a determinate form, nor developed from higher states of
> knowledge, but from sense-perception. It is like a rout in
> battle stopped by first one man making a stand and then
> another, until the original formation has been restored. The
> soul is so constituted as to be capable of this process. (100a;
> 1941, p. 185)

Again we find intuition being invoked as a source of first principles from which rational demonstrations must proceed. Moreover, although we are now working in the realm of sense-perception, the same problems that we encountered in Plato's intellectual realm appear here as well. If intuition is to provide a foundation for rational justification, it must yield self-evident propositions. But if the propositions in question cannot be justified on the basis of independent evidence, it is difficult to know how we can mediate competing claims to have achieved self-evidence, and how we distinguish cases in which an intuitive grasp of a proposition has been achieved from cases in which we mistakenly believe that we have achieved this grasp. Again we are in a bind: if we allow reasons, we reopen the regress that our foundational propositions were supposed to block; and if we do not allow reasons, it is difficult to see how claims to self-evidence can be rational. The classical model of rationality has continually pushed philosophers into this dilemma. Let us jump ahead several centuries.

2.3 Descartes

Although in different ways, rationalists and empiricists both appeal to intuition in order to establish a foundation for rational knowledge. In the case of rationalism, intuition is supposed to provide a variety of fundamental truths which do not need further justification, but which are required if rationality is to be possible at all. Descartes's *cogito* provides a prime example. Presumably the truth of this most basic claim of Descartes's philosophy is grasped by intuition; at least this reading of the 'Second Meditation' eliminates one common criticism. For, as has been frequently pointed out, if we view Descartes as constructing a deductive argument that moves from the premise 'I think' to the conclusion 'I am a thinking thing', the argument is invalid: the premise only refers to a momentary thought, while the conclusion invokes a thinking thing that exists through time. On the alternative interpretation this is not intended as a deductive argument at all. Instead, the step from premise to conclusion takes place by way of an intuitive grasp of the relation between momentary acts of thought and the thing that thinks. Moreover, this reading is consistent with Descartes's methodology after the *cogito* has been established. For while the *cogito* is intended, in some sense, to provide the foundation on which all further knowledge is to be built, it does not provide a foundation in the sense of a premise from which deductions can be made. Descartes's first concern after establishing the *cogito* is to rescue mathematics from the dubitable status that hyperbolic doubt has temporarily conferred on it, but Descartes makes no attempt to do this by deducing mathematical results from the *cogito*. Rather, Descartes reflects on the procedure that led to the *cogito*, and asks how he can be sure that this result is true.[7]

> I am certain that I am a thinking thing. Do I not therefore
> also know what is required for my being certain about
> anything? In this first item of knowledge there is simply a clear
> and distinct perception of what I am asserting; this would not
> be enough to make me certain of the truth of the matter if it
> could ever turn out that something which I perceive with
> such clarity and distinctness was false. So I now seem able to
> lay it down as a general rule that whatever I perceive very
> clearly and distinctly is true. (1985, vol. 2, p. 24)

Thus clear and distinct perception ('perception' is being used in a broad sense that includes what we could call 'conception') guarantees truth. Once this state is reached, we have the best possible grounds for believing a claim, and no further rational justification is required.

In the detailed working out of Descartes's epistemology this appeal to clarity and distinctness actually occurs in two contexts, and it is worth considering both even though the second will take us beyond the question of foundations. First, we accept specific propositions because we clearly and distinctly see that they are true. In addition to the *cogito*, we accept the first premises that lie at the basis of the various deductive sciences, e.g., the axioms of Euclidean geometry, because they are self-evident. But Descartes contends that only 'simple' truths can be grasped in this direct, intuitive manner; in other cases intuition must be supplemented by demonstrations in which theorems that we cannot grasp intuitively are justified by deduction from propositions that we can know by intuition.[8] Now a deduction consists of a series of propositions, each of which follows from previous propositions in accordance with a principle of logic, but what justifies us in accepting a particular step as valid? Descartes's answer is that each step in a proof is certified by intuition: we simply 'see' that the present step follows from previous steps; this is the second place at which intuition enters into the construction of a body of knowledge. On this view, deductive proofs replace a logical gap that is too great to be crossed in a single intuition with a series of smaller gaps, each of which can be handled in a single intuitive step. This is an intriguing view, and there seems to be something essentially correct about it. We find a proof convincing when we can grasp the connections between the steps, and when we cannot grasp one of these connections we seek further intermediate steps. At the same time, this view raises some troubling problems that we must explore.

Assume, to begin with, that a theorem, T, does in fact follow from a set of axioms, A, and that this has been demonstrated by a lengthy proof. In the course of this proof a large number of laws of logic will be invoked, but it is possible to replace this series by a single complex law that validly takes us immediately from A to T. Suppose, moreover, that Ramanujan reappears, and insists that the detailed proof is quite unnecessary, since he can grasp the connection between A and T directly. Should we dispense with the intermediate steps? There are two reasons for insisting that we retain the longer proof. First, on Descartes's analysis, the proof is supposed to carry the mind from the premises to the conclusion in intuitive steps, and for most of us Ramanujan's proof will not do this job. Second, we know that Ramanujan's pronouncements are fallible, while genuine intuitions are not fallible; thus some of Ramanujan's pronouncements are not based on intuition, even when he thinks they are. This suggests that there must be some criterion for deciding what counts as a legitimate step in a proof, and this criterion would also allow us to distinguish genuine intuitions from apparent intuitions. Further, if this criterion were directly applicable to the connection between steps in a proof it would not involve the introduction of any additional propositions whose rational acceptability is in question. Descartes does seem to have such a criterion: intuitions must involve only simple steps, and whether a step is simple is an objective matter, not a question of individual preference. On this view, Ramanujan did not have the ability to grasp intuitive connections that the rest of us cannot grasp. At his best, Ramanujan should be compared to a fast runner who can cover the same distance more rapidly than a slower runner, but who must still pass through all of the space that anyone else must traverse. Presumably Ramanujan made mistakes because he did not always follow all the simple steps, but sometimes took illegitimate short-cuts. Moreover, his abbreviated proof is not a legitimate proof exactly because it involves a leap from premises to conclusion that is not simple.

An analogous point holds for the premises from which proofs begin: premises whose truth can be grasped by intuition must involve only simple connections between ideas, else we would be required to demonstrate their truth by means of a deduction from more elementary premises. But now an obvious question arises: how are we to determine when the required simplicity has been achieved? There is a troubling interaction here between the notions of intuition and simplicity: each of these supports the other, but how do we break out of this circle and establish a set of simple premises, or a list of simple inferences? If we are to rely on intuition to decide what is simple, then we will be hard put to explain why Ramanujan's presumed intuitions should not be accepted at face value. But if we appeal to simplicity to determine what counts as a legitimate intuition, we are back to wondering how we determine which axioms and which inferences are simple.

There is an interesting parallel between Cartesian intuitions and the intuitions that yield the final grasp of a Platonic form. In both

47

cases the intuitions are supposed to be reliable because they are not just 'states of mind', but have an objective foundation. In Plato's case it is the forms that provide this foundation; in Descartes's case we can only achieve clarity and distinctness when the ideas and the connections we are dealing with are truly simple. Yet people make mistakes, and they sometimes sincerely but incorrectly believe that they have achieved an intuitive grasp of a fundamental truth, or of the connection between steps in a deduction. Thus we must be able to recognize when we not only think we have a proper intuition, but actually have one, and the introduction of an objective basis for intuitions does not automatically solve this problem; we still need a way of deciding when we have met the conditions embodied in this objective basis. In other words, if intuition is to provide the foundation we require, it must not only certify truths, it must also certify itself. It is not enough that self-evident truths be true, it must not be possible for us to be mistaken about whether we have achieved self-evidence. If we admit second-order doubts, we face again the very threat of an infinite regress that intuition was supposed to end.⁹ Indeed, this is exactly the situation that we encounter when Descartes addresses the possibility of error in his 'Fourth Meditation'. Here he insists that we cannot be mistaken as long as we achieve clarity and distinctness, and then attempts to account for human fallibility by maintaining that we can be wrong about *whether* our ideas are in fact clear and distinct. Presumably something like this happened to Ramanujan on a number of occasions. Yet this leaves us hanging in midair. We have a criterion for recognizing self-evident truths, but it is not self-evident whether this criterion has been properly applied. We need a meta-criterion to guide our application of this criterion, and no such meta-criterion has been forthcoming. Yet without this meta-criterion we can never complete the process of rationally justifying any belief. Once again we find that a philosopher has appealed to intuition in order to close the justificatory regress, but it is difficult to see how intuition can do the job.

2.4 Empiricism

Rationalists such as Descartes and Spinoza appeal to intuition to establish a variety of general propositions that provide axioms from which further results can be derived by deductive reasoning alone.[10] Empiricists reject the claim that we can come to know universal truths about the world in this *a priori* manner, and insist instead that the foundations of knowledge rest on the least general propositions that we know, i.e., on claims about specific items we perceive. One problem that arises on this approach is that we seem to need induction to explain how we get from claims about specific objects or events to claims of any degree of generality, and even to explain how we can predict what will occur in a specific situation that we have not yet examined. I will leave problems associated with induction aside in the present chapter, and concentrate on our knowledge of those observation statements that are supposed to provide the basis for all of our knowledge of the world. These statements are accepted as a result of sensory experience, rather than on the basis of reasons. Indeed, observation statements cannot be justified by appeal to reasons – I cannot establish the claim that there is a table here in front of me by argument, but this does not make that claim nonrational since no such argument is required. Rather, I see the table and feel it, and it is difficult to know what better grounds I could have for believing that there is a table in front of me than the fact that I see and feel it. I believe the proposition 'There is a table in front of me' on the basis of observation, and when the proper observational conditions obtain, that proposition is self-evident.

We do, however, need to be careful here. We are seeking foundational propositions about whose truth we can be certain, and we are not just interested in a subjective feeling of certainty. Rather, as in the cases of intuition that we have already discussed, we are concerned with claims that are objectively certain, i.e., claims that are not properly subject to doubt. But once we are clear on this, we must back up a bit and consider more carefully what we are to count as an observation. It has long been argued that phenomena such as illusions show that perception does not yield self-evident propositions: while perception may make the belief that there is a particular physical object in front of me psychologically compelling, it is still possible that this belief is false. Macbeth did not have a dagger before him, and the claim that there is a table in front of me is not beyond all doubt. My perceptual awareness of the table may in fact derive from any of a number of complex illusions, or from some malfunction of my mind or brain. Empiricists have recognized this problem, and have adjusted their concept of observation accordingly. To see what adjustments are needed, let us consider how I might discover that I was wrong in believing that a table was before me.

There is a crucial aspect of physical objects such as tables that must be taken into account: they exist through time. As a result, I could discover that I was mistaken about the table if further investigation showed that there was no table out there after all. For example, further inquiry might reveal that the item in question was a cleverly designed mock-up of a table front, with no back; or that I only seemed to see a table because of a trick with lights and mirrors. But even if this were to occur, there is another point that must not be ignored: at the moment at which I mistakenly believed that there was a table in front of me, I was perceptually aware of something, and that item of perceptual awareness provided the basis for my belief about the table. The proposition 'There is a table in front of me' goes beyond the actual contents of my perceptual awareness, and if I had restricted myself to believing a proposition that describes the contents of perceptual consciousness, I would not have gone wrong. Another example will help to clarify the point. Suppose I see what I take to be a pink piece of paper but that, after closer examination, I notice that the paper is in fact covered with a series of red and white dots. Had I originally concluded that the paper was pink, I would have been mistaken. Yet however things are with the paper, when I first examined the paper I was visually aware of pink, and nothing that I see as a result of a later examination of the paper can negate that fact.

The point here is that we must not take physical objects and their properties as the items of perceptual awareness. The paper, like the table, is a physical object spread out in time, and it can be examined and re-examined. As I re-examine a physical object I may change my mind about its properties, but at each stage of this examination I am perceptually aware of something, and any beliefs I arrive at concerning a physical object are based on that perceptual awareness. New perceptual experiences may lead me to revise my beliefs about a physical object, but they cannot alter my earlier state of perceptual consciousness. In other words, unlike physical objects, items of immediate perceptual awareness are not spread out in time. Rather, they are transient and limited to a 'moment' of awareness, and beliefs that are strictly proportioned to these items of immediate awareness cannot be shown to be mistaken by further evidence. As long as we restrict ourselves to describing what we actually perceive we cannot be mistaken because no future evidence would be relevant to showing that we are mistaken.

This approach raises a host of problems, but I only want to pursue one of them here. Note, first, that epistemic notions such as 'truth' and 'certainty' do not become relevant to matters of perceptual experience if we do no more than contemplate the items we perceive. If perception is to play an epistemic role it must lead to beliefs, and if these beliefs are to enter into the logical process of justifying and evaluating claims, they must become expressed in propositions, since logical relations hold only between propositions. This has been recognized by twentieth-century empiricists who have typically located the foundations of empirical knowledge in a set of 'observation reports', but we are now in an odd situation. Even granting that there is some item that we are immediately, intuitively, indubitably aware of when we perceive, this item is not a proposition – the proposition 'This is pink' may spontaneously occur to me when I am aware of pink, but it need not do so. Empiricists have generally held that a child who has not yet learned enough language to entertain the proposition 'This is pink' can still be conscious of the color pink, and that this prelinguistic awareness of a sensation is a necessary precondition for the child's being able to learn the word 'pink' in the first place. Yet it is not the sensation, but the proposition, that must serve as the basis for the rational justification of other propositions. If perception is to provide the way out of the regress of justifications, perception must provide us with self-evident propositions. The characteristic empiricist thesis that concerns us here is that these foundational propositions derive their self-evidence from their association with sensations; we must examine this association.

We can begin by considering some possible relations between a sensation and a proposition. The proposal that the sensation provides evidence for the proposition can be dismissed at once. If sensations provided evidence then the resulting propositions would not be self-evident, and, in any case, on the view we are discussing, evidential relations hold only between propositions;

our problem is to understand how we get from a sensation to a self-evident proposition. It might be suggested that the sensation causes us to entertain the proposition, but this also will not do. If the relevant sensation can occur in a child without the proposition, then the sensation alone does not cause us to entertain this proposition, and while it might be argued that there is still a causal connection in the adult, this complicates the situation in an unacceptable way. For this new causal connection can only appear in the adult as a result of some difference between the child and the adult, and this difference will presumably involve, at least, the fact that the adult has learned a language. But it is a common theme in empiricist writings that the introduction of learned elements brings along the possibility of error. One reason for focusing on perception as a source of certainty is that our basic perceptual abilities are presumably independent of anything we may have learned.[11]

A less obvious suggestion will take us closer to the position that early empiricists implicitly, and twentieth-century empiricists explicitly, maintained. The idea here is that, along with whatever sensations occur when we perceive, there is also a special body of language, often called an 'observation language', that is applicable to our sensations in an especially perspicuous manner. This language will be composed of a set of simple property terms such as 'hot' and 'hard' and 'pink' which we apply to momentary objects of perception, and do so in a way that entails nothing about any future perceptual experience. Thus, the argument goes, learning notwithstanding, the application of these terms to our sensations is not subject to error, and propositions that are expressed in the observation language can be indubitable. This requires some discussion.

In most cases our use of a term to describe some item is subject to reconsideration. We have already noted that this can occur in the case of material object claims because further evidence might show that our description of an object was mistaken. There is, however, a more general reason why our application of a term may be subject to revision. To see what this reason is, consider how we decide whether a particular term is applicable to some item. One common and plausible answer is that we do so on the basis of rules, rules that are embodied in the definition of the term. In some cases this is obvious. If I want to determine whether a particular polygon is a dodecagon I count the sides, since, by definition, a polygon is a dodecagon if and only if it has twelve sides. In other cases this is not quite as obvious. I can, for example, recognize at once whether a figure is a triangle without having to count the sides. But, the argument goes, this case is not as different as it seems. There is a rule for determining whether a figure is a triangle, I can state that rule, and I learned that rule when I learned the word 'triangle'. Thus the fact that I can distinguish triangles much more rapidly than I can distinguish dodecagons does not show that my recognition of triangles is not rule-governed. In other cases we cannot formulate a satisfactory rule. It is rather difficult to state exactly what makes an object a chair or a game or a work of art, but, again, it is argued that the difficulty in formulating the rule does not show that there is no rule implicit in our linguistic behavior. One task of linguists and linguistic philosophers is to formulate such rules.

Now I have introduced the notion that the application of terms is rule-governed only in order to point out a contrast, for whatever the case may be for other terms, our application of the terms of the observation language must *not* be rule-governed. This is because the application of observation terms must be indubitable, but rule-governed activities are subject to error: anyone who follows a rule may make an error in its use. To be sure, algorithms offer protection from error in one sense, because the power of algorithms lies in the fact that, as long as they are followed properly, they guarantee a correct response. But even with this guarantee, we human beings can still fail to follow an algorithm properly – we do make mistakes in arithmetic and logic, and we presumably fail to follow a rule when we misspeak ourselves. Yet if rule-governed procedures are intrinsically dubitable, while our application of observation terms must be indubitable, it follows pretty clearly that the latter is not rule-governed. But what is the alternative? The only one that seems available is yet another appeal to some form of intuition: we do not apply observation terms by means of rules, but simply *recognize*, under the appropriate circumstances, that a term applies. In other words, the empiricist attempt to found knowledge on observation seems to require two intuitions: sensory experiences simply appear to us without any rational mediation, and the language that we use to report a particular sensory experience must also just pop into our minds.

What are we to make of this? First, we can note that the empiricist attempt to find a foundation also leads to an appeal to intuition. Yet we have also arrived at a position that is seriously at odds with other aspects of empiricist philosophy. Recall that one of the striking differences between sensations and statements in the observation language is that the latter always involve learned predicates, and that empiricists have typically been wary of the introduction of learned concepts into the foundations of knowledge exactly because they held that learned elements bring along the possibility of error. Moreover, this last concern seems to be well founded. It is no secret that we are capable of making mistakes in attaching terms even to the most basic sensations. I can, for example, mistake a sensation of orange for a sensation of red, or a sensation of cold for a sensation of heat; similarly, it has been reported that people commonly confuse sour with bitter and that this can be attributed 'to differences in skill in naming the sensation rather than to differences in sensitivity' (Amerine and Roessler, 1983, p. 49). But we do not have a proposition until we name the sensation. Thus the view that applications of learned abilities do not yield indubitable results would seem to be correct, and since observation reports presuppose learned linguistic abilities, these reports do not provide an unquestionable, self-evident foundation for knowledge. Again we find philosophers appealing to intuition to establish a foundation, and again we find that this appeal does not give the foundation we require.

2.5   Modest foundationalism

We have seen that the classical model of rationality requires that there be some self-justifying propositions, and philosophers have most commonly attempted to meet this demand by seeking propositions that are self-evident, but this project does not seem very promising. This leads us to ask whether there is any other way to establish self-justifying propositions. The thesis that rational knowledge may be founded on propositions that are self-justifying without being self-evident is known as 'modest foundationalism';[12] I want to consider whether this approach can provide a sufficiently strong foundation for the needs of the classical model of rationality.

According to the classical model we should only believe propositions that are justified, and in the absence of sufficient justification we must suspend belief. As a result, there are two cases in which it would be irrational to believe *p*: those in which we have sufficient evidence for believing not-*p*, and those in which we do not have sufficient evidence for choosing between *p* and not-*p*. Neither of these can occur in the case of self-evident propositions, and our present question is whether we can ever have sufficient grounds for believing a foundational proposition in the absence of self-evidence; there are two arguments against this option that are already in the literature. The first argument is due to John Pollock:[13]

> Suppose *P* is an epistemologically basic proposition that is not incorrigible. For example, *P* might be 'I am appeared to redly'. As it is not incorrigible for *S* that he is appeared to redly, *S* could believe that and be mistaken. But then it is presumably possible for *S* to have reasons for thinking that he is mistaken in believing that he is appeared to redly. To continue to believe the epistemologically basic proposition in the face of such reasons would be to believe it unjustifiably, and hence it is not incorrigibly justified. (1979, p. 95)

Indeed, I think we can take a somewhat stronger position here. If I contemplate a proposition and find that it is not self-evident, then I recognize that there are considerations which could show that it is false. The classical model requires that I suspend belief until I eliminate those considerations, but when I seek to eliminate these sources of doubt, I will be supplying reasons to justify believing *p*. Yet a proposition that requires such justification is not self-justifying, i.e., it cannot break the regress of propositions justified by appeal to other propositions.

The second argument is due to Hilary Kornblith (1980, pp. 605–6). Kornblith considers two men, Moe and Joe, who are looking at a bowl of fruit; as a result of what they see, both believe that there is an apple in the bowl. But Joe, unlike Moe, also believes that he is sufficiently myopic that he would be unable to distinguish an artificial apple from a real apple at this distance. As a result, Joe's belief that there is a real apple in the bowl is unjustified, and it is unjustified because of one of Joe's background beliefs. This could not occur if the proposition believed were self-evident, and Kornblith's point is that as long as *p* lacks self-evidence, other propositions must be taken into account in assessing whether my belief in *p* is justified. Again, this is sufficient to show that *p* cannot block the regress of propositions whose justification requires appeal to other propositions:

> It has sometimes been suggested that some beliefs, though not incorrigible, are justified independently of their relation to other beliefs. This cannot, however, be true. As long as a belief is not incorrigible, its justificatory status will vary not only with changes in the process responsible for its presence but also with changes in background beliefs. Thus, for any given belief-forming process, there will always be background beliefs that would make that process inadequate for justification. *All nonincorrigible beliefs are thus justified, in part, in virtue of their relations to other beliefs.* (1980, p. 606)

Now one striking feature of Pollock's and Kornblith's arguments, as well as of the argument against foundationalism developed in the body of this chapter, is that they turn on difficulties in knowing when we have achieved a self-justifying foundation. A number of philosophers have attempted to undercut such arguments by maintaining that this condition need not be met. For example, William Alston has distinguished two forms of foundationalism:

> Simple Foundationalism: For any epistemic subject, *S*, there are *p*'s such that *S* is immediately justified in believing that *p*.

and

> Iterative Foundationalism: For any epistemic subject, *S*, there are *p*'s such that *S* is immediately justified in believing that *p* and *S* is immediately justified in believing that he is immediately justified in believing that *p*. (1976, p. 171)

Alston maintains that arguments of the sort we have been considering are only effective against iterative foundationalism, and that simple foundationalism is sufficient to stop the justificatory regress.

But our concern here is with *rational* belief, and in this context simple foundationalism is not sufficient, for I cannot believe *p* rationally if I do not recognize that my belief in *p* is rational. Some of Alston's own examples will help to make this point. Alston writes:

> I may be justified in believing that Louis IX reigned in the thirteenth century, since I acquired that belief on excellent authority, but not now be able to specify that authority, much less *show* that it is reliable. (1976, p. 178)

In other words, Alston claims that the fact that the authority is reliable is sufficient to justify my belief irrespective of any beliefs I might have about that authority – presumably I need not even remember that it is a reliable authority. Yet the fact that we are dealing with a belief that is based on authority makes this case particularly problematic. Many sources present themselves as authorities, and the propositions they put forward as worthy of belief typically include competing contraries. At a minimum, rationality requires that we believe only those claims put forward by genuine authorities, not those put forward by impostors, and we must justify the claim that a self-styled authority is a genuine authority if we are to accept its pronouncements on a rational basis. Moreover, we need not actually have competing claims to be in this position. No claim that is accepted because of its source is rationally justified unless we have reasons for believing that this source is indeed reliable.

Another of Alston's examples will help us see that this conclusion is not limited to beliefs derived from authority. Alston writes:

> Can't I prove a theorem in logic without being able to prove that I have proved it? The former requires only an ability to wield the machinery of first-order logic, which one may possess without the mastery of the metalogic required for the second. (1976, p. 177)

For the moment, let us leave aside the question of just how much metalogic I must invoke in order to be justified in accepting a proof. This much, I think, is clear: if *I* am to be justified in accepting a proof as valid, some other conditions must be met besides the fact that the proof is valid. I must at least recognize that it is a valid proof, and in order to do that, I must know something about validity and about first-order logic, and I must have examined the proof in the light of that knowledge. An illiterate individual could not be justified in accepting a printed proof as valid, nor could a logician who produced the proof in a trance without any grasp of what was going on. In general, even if there are propositions that are intrinsically worthy of belief, I am not justified in believing any of those propositions unless I can recognize when one is before me.[14]

Again a regress threatens. If, for example, rational acceptance of a proof requires a metalogical proof, then I am going to need a higher-order proof that my metalogical proof is indeed a proof, and so on; if I need criteria for picking out genuine authorities, then presumably I must also be able to justify those criteria by appeal to other criteria, and so on again. The classical model of rationality requires that we either find a foundation in each case that is not only justified, but that shows itself as justified, or give up any hope of achieving rationality.

The upshot of this discussion, then, is that foundational propositions must be self-evident. But there are no grounds for believing that there exists a body of self-evident propositions that will allow us to justify substantive beliefs, and foundationalism fails. Moreover, if, as I argued at the beginning of this chapter, the classical model of rationality requires a foundational epistemology, the classical model fails too: without self-evident foundational propositions, we cannot actually arrive at any rational beliefs. There is, however, one more option we should explore before we reject the classical model of rationality, for there is still one way in which we might be able to overcome the absence of a foundation. Recall that the central idea of the classical model is that rational beliefs are justified on the basis of rules, and it was reflection on rules that led us to the demand for a foundation. Suppose, however, that we could find a set of rules that would allow us to assess the rationality of a belief *irrespective of the starting point*. In this case, the propositions from which we began would drop out of our final assessment of the rationality of a belief, and the fact that we began from unjustified propositions would be irrelevant. This is the strategy of critical rationalism, which I want to consider next.

2.6 Critical rationalism

Critical rationalism derives from the work of Karl Popper, and although it has been developed into a general theory of rationality, Popper's original concerns were with the philosophy of science, thus I will focus on scientific knowledge in the following discussion. Popper sums up the difficulties that we have been examining in terms of a trilemma that he attributes to J. F. Fries:

> He taught that, if the statements of science are not to be accepted *dogmatically*, we must be able to *justify* them. If we demand justification by reasoned argument, in the logical sense, then we are committed to the view that *statements can be justified only by statements*. The demand that *all* statements are to be logically justified (described by Fries as a 'predilection for proofs') is therefore bound to lead to an *infinite regress*. Now, if we wish to avoid the danger of dogmatism as well as an infinite regress, then it seems as if we could only have recourse to *psychologism*, *i.e.* the doctrine that statements can be justified not only by statements but also by perceptual experience. (1968, pp. 93–4)

Popper's use of the term 'psychologism' in this passage is somewhat idiosyncratic, but I will adopt that usage here and apply the term to any view which holds that a proposition can be justified by an experience. Thus all appeals to intuition will be instances of psychologism, not only those that invoke perception. Fries' first two alternatives are incompatible with the classical model of rationality, and we have seen that the third option has long been pursued unsuccessfully. Popper attempts to find his way out of this trilemma by giving up the demand that rational knowledge requires justification.

Popper rejects the traditional rationalist view that we can establish *a priori* foundations for knowledge, and develops his position in an empiricist framework. But Popper is also convinced that the problem of induction is insoluble – thus he attempts to build an empiricist philosophy of science without reliance on induction. Popper's central thesis is that while insuperable logical difficulties appear when we attempt to use statements that describe observations as evidence in *support* of a scientific claim, no comparable difficulties arise when we use such statements to *refute* scientific claims, since the latter only requires deductive logic. This is because any scientific claim must entail some propositions describing observable situations, and when observation shows us that one of these claims is false, we can invoke the elementary deductive argument *modus tollens* to show that we began from a false premise. Thus, according to Popper, scientific claims are never proven, but always stand as hypotheses subject to further testing. An hypothesis that has been tested and not refuted is 'corroborated', and we are justified in continuing to accept it, subject to later reconsideration. Popper introduces the new term 'corroboration' to underline the difference between this notion and the more common idea of empirical confirmation. On Popper's view, the rationality of our current beliefs does not depend on their being corroborated, but on our continued commitment to their empirical testing, and on our readiness to reject beliefs that are refuted.

This is a major departure from traditional epistemology. Instead of having to establish our foundations before we can begin, Popper contends that we can begin the development of science anywhere as long as we treat our starting point as a conjecture, and seek evidence that will refute this conjecture. When we find such evidence we reject our present conjecture and replace it with a new one, but there are two important constraints on further conjectures. I want to introduce some special terminology that will be useful in discussing these constraints. Let O stand for a description of an observable situation, and consider a case in which O has been deduced from a set of premises in which the hypothesis under test plays an essential role.[15] Popper calls propositions such as O 'basic statements' in order to distinguish them from the presumably indubitable 'observation statements' of other empiricists; we will discuss the reasons for this distinction shortly. Popper accepts the common empiricist view that the deduction in question constitutes an explanation of O, and although there is much to be said about that claim, I will adopt it here since it will allow us to express Popper's points rather concisely. Suppose, now, that an hypothesis that provides the basis for explaining a number of basic statements is refuted, requiring that we seek a new explanatory hypothesis. Popper's first constraint is that *the new hypothesis must explain all the basic statements that the original hypothesis explained, plus those basic statements that led us to reject the old hypothesis*. If the new hypothesis entailed the negation of any of these basic statements it would be immediately refuted, but a new hypothesis might have no entailment relations with one of our basic statements, i.e., it might entail neither O nor its negation. An hypothesis of this sort would either leave some previously explained basic statements unexplained, or leave us without an explanation of the new discovery that led us to reject our earlier hypothesis, and Popper's first constraint forbids the introduction of such hypotheses. In addition, Popper imposes a second constraint: *the new hypothesis must lead to the deduction of new basic statements that could not be deduced from its predecessor*. To understand the point of this condition, we must explore another of Popper's key ideas; I want to work up to that idea from a new direction.

One of Popper's goals is to eliminate the customary tie between the notions of 'science' and 'truth'. According to Popper, the characteristic feature of a scientific claim is that it is amenable to testing and possible falsification, and Popper uses this feature as a criterion for distinguishing science from nonscience – subjects such as metaphysics and theology which are presumably built on propositions that are not subject to empirical refutation are not sciences.[16] Many of the claims that are accepted by current science are in fact false, and we will eventually discover that they are false when a refutation appears, but they are still scientific claims, and will continue to be scientific claims even after they have been refuted. Similarly, refuted claims from past science are still scientific hypotheses, although we no longer accept them. But this is not to say that science is uninterested in truth.[17] Popper insists that the discovery of true claims about the world is a central aim of science, and one reason why we might find it difficult, try as we might, to refute a particular hypothesis is because that hypothesis is true. Still, Popper contends, we can never be *certain* that we have achieved truth, and the only rational way of dealing with our current beliefs is to be prepared to test them further and withdraw belief from those propositions that we can refute.

Now Popper recognizes that there are cases in which we can achieve truth quite easily, e.g., when we accept a tautology, or simply summarize our data without making any generalizations or predictions. In these cases we protect ourselves from accepting falsehoods by restricting the content of the propositions we accept.

In a similar way, we can reduce the chances of being mistaken by being as vague as possible when we do go beyond the data. If I say that the air contains one or more gases, then it is less likely that I will be wrong than if I say that the air contains 21% oxygen and 78% nitrogen. But while the latter claim is risky it also contains more information than the former claim. Popper argues that this is not coincidental, and that the number of ways in which a proposition can go wrong provides a measure of its empirical content. To determine the empirical content of a proposition, p, we consider the set of basic statements that, if false, would result in p's falsification; call these p's 'potential falsifiers'. The larger the set of a proposition's potential falsifiers, the greater the proposition's empirical content. Tautologies, which have no potential falsifiers, are forever safe from empirical refutation, but they have zero empirical content, and thus tell us nothing about the world.

This might seem a surprising turn-about. One might think that we should identify the content of a proposition with the set of true statements that can be deduced from it, but this would rapidly get us into trouble. Given any true consequence of a statement, we can easily generate further true consequences by trivial logical maneuvers – and there are serious problems about how we decide if a proposition is true. Moreover, Popper's suggestion does capture our sense that a statement which generalizes over instances is both riskier and says more than a statement that simply reports those instances; and that a highly specific claim tells us more than a vague claim, even though we take a greater risk of being wrong when we make a more specific claim.[18]

We can now return to Popper's second constraint on new hypotheses: they must yield some new predictions. This amounts to a demand that a new hypothesis have some potential falsifiers not possessed by the hypothesis it replaces. Now one consequence of Popper's first constraint is that the new hypothesis must share all of its predecessor's potential falsifiers. Taken together, the two constraints require that, after a refutation, we must introduce a new hypothesis that has *greater empirical content* than the one that was rejected. In other words, science aims not just at truth, but at true propositions with high empirical content. Since we can never be certain that a proposition with any empirical content is in fact true, we seek refutations, recognizing that if we cannot know when we are right, we can at least know when we are wrong.

After each successful refutation we move to a new hypothesis of greater empirical content, and Popper pictures science as a series of conjectures of ever-increasing empirical content, and refutations of those conjectures. Moreover, this is a rational enterprise because rationality lies in the process by which we criticize and replace our beliefs.

There is much that is attractive in this view of rationality. Note, however, that Popper is working in the framework of the classical model of rationality, and is thus seeking a set of rules that will govern rational decision-making. His key idea is that *modus tollens* provides us with an algorithm that allows us to determine when an hypothesis should be rejected, while all attempts to find a comparable algorithm for deciding when to accept an hypothesis have failed.[19] It is this rule that allows the critical process to be rational, and induction is not rational because there are no rules to guide it. Unfortunately, a closer examination will show that Popper fails to provide an adequate set of rules for making critical decisions, and that in fact we are left without any rules at three crucial junctures.

The first of these arises when we encounter a false consequence derived from a serious scientific theory. The application of *modus tollens* is straightforward when we deduce a false statement from a single hypothesis, but scientific predictions cannot be derived from one hypothesis. Popper's basic statements are singular sentences which describe such things as the reading on a particular instrument or the observation of a specific item at a specific time and place. Such statements cannot be deduced from universal propositions alone, although they can be deduced from a combination of universal and singular propositions. Thus the actual deduction of a basic statement from a scientific theory will require at least two premises, and in practice many more will usually be required. For example, the prediction that a given planet will be found at a particular point in space at a particular time does not follow just from Newton's law of gravitation. In order to make this prediction we also need Newton's laws of motion, along with a great deal of information about the planet and the planetary system in question. For a rough determination of the planet's orbit we need to know the planet's mass, its distance from the sun at some definite time, its tangential velocity with respect to the sun at that time, the mass of the sun, and the value of the universal gravitational constant; for a more precise calculation we must also know the masses and locations of the other planets in the system. In addition, to get the actual position of the planet at some time, we must know its location on its orbit at some other time.

Now suppose that we have all of this information, calculate the planet's location, and find that it is not where we predicted. Application of *modus tollens* does indicate that something in this complex of propositions is incorrect, and in this respect refutations are logically clearer than confirmations. But *modus tollens* does not tell us which of the propositions we began with has been refuted, nor how many. It may be that Newton's gravitation law is wrong; but perhaps one or more of Newton's laws of motion is at fault, or it may be that we are wrong about the mass of the planet or the sun, or any of the other items involved, or some combination of them, or maybe all of them. Thus the application of *modus tollens* is only the first step. If we are to make a rational decision about which hypotheses we should reject we need some further rules, and none have been supplied.[20] This is the first point at which Popper's rules are not sufficient to guide a rational decision. But pressing as this problem is, it only arises after we have recognized that a basic statement deduced from our theory is false, and it would be hasty to assume that this recognition is itself unproblematic. Let us examine basic statements in a bit more detail.

Basic statements are singular sentences that describe particular matters of fact, but Popper does not view them as having the certainty that other empiricists attributed to observation statements, and Popper reminds us of this point by giving them a special name. Now it is central to Popper's epistemology that all empirically significant propositions are subject to critical examination and rejection. But this raises a problem for the idea of a refutation, since falsification always involves *acceptance* of a basic statement. For example, if the hypothesis we are testing leads to the prediction that, under present experimental conditions, the dial in front of me ought to read '17', but in fact it reads '28', I have grounds for considering the hypothesis falsified. In effect, I have accepted the basic statement 'This dial does not read 17', and I have done so because I have accepted another basic statement, 'This dial reads 28', that is logically inconsistent with 'This dial reads 17'. Yet the basic statement I have accepted is falsifiable, and this provides grounds for denying that the hypothesis has been refuted; I can attempt to protect my hypothesis by seeking a refutation of the troublesome basic statement. Thus we not only lack a rule that determines which members of a set of hypotheses are to be rejected, but, in spite of first appearances, we also lack a rule to determine when the set of hypotheses has encountered a refutation. This makes all scientific decisions uncertain, and while this uncertainty may seem consistent with the spirit of Popper's theory of knowledge, it also runs counter to one of the major driving forces of that theory: the search for rules that will allow us to determine what attitude we can rationally take toward a proposition. In fact, Popper provides no rules for determining when we have a genuine refutation, nor even any rules for determining whether we have adequate reasons for deciding, tentatively, that we can treat the theory as refuted for the present. But the situation is even more serious than this.

Although Popper sets out to replace what he takes to be a nonexistent logic of theory acceptance with a well understood logic of theory refutation, we have just seen that any refutation requires that we accept some basic statement. On what grounds do we decide to accept a basic statement? It might seem that the answer is obvious: we accept a basic statement because of an observation, e.g., I conclude that the meter in front of me reads '28' because I see it. But this response immediately runs foul of another of Popper's central concerns – the desire to avoid psychologism. The claim that I can evaluate the epistemic status of a proposition on the basis of what I see is a paradigmatic psychologistic claim, one that violates the central principle that propositions can only be evaluated by reference to other propositions. This is not a quibble. One of the virtues of Popper's work in epistemology is that he recognizes many of the problems that the classical model of rationality faces, and attempts to solve them. The present instance is no exception; Popper maintains that basic statements are accepted by agreement among the investigators. He writes:

> Every test of a theory, whether resulting in its corroboration or falsification, must stop at some basic statement or other which we *decide to accept*. If we do not come to any decision, and do not accept some basic statement or other, then the test will have led nowhere. But considered from a logical point

of view, the situation is never such that it compels us to stop
at this particular basic statement rather than at that, or else
give up the test altogether. (1968, p. 104)

And two pages later: 'Basic statements are accepted as the result
of a decision or agreement; and to that extent they are conventions' (1968, p. 106). Popper also maintains that, 'The decisions
are reached in accordance with a procedure governed by rules'
(1968, p. 106), but he never provides an algorithm for deciding
what basic statements should be accepted. He does offer some
rules of thumb, e.g., that we should accept only basic statements
which are 'especially easy to test', (1968, p. 104) but that we
should not accept 'stray basic statements' (1968, p. 106), i.e.,
basic statements that arise from circumstances that cannot be
reproduced. This is surely good advice, but these maxims lack the
clarity and precision that we find when we do arithmetic, construct
truth-tables, or invoke *modus tollens*. Popper is aware of this
difficulty, and seems to suggest that it is resolved pragmatically
by considerations derived from the context in which we are
working (see, for example, 1968, p. 106), yet it is striking that
Popper explicitly rejects such appeals when they are made on
behalf of a traditional empiricist view. Indeed, Popper does not
even consider the demand that we should make observations to
be sufficiently clear and precise for methodological purposes:

> Thus the real situation is quite different from the one
> visualized by the naive empiricist, or the believer in inductive
> logic. He thinks that we begin by collecting and arranging our
> experiences, and so ascend the ladder of science. . . . But if
> I am ordered: 'Record what you are now experiencing' I shall
> hardly know how to obey this ambiguous order. Am I to
> report that I am writing; that I hear a bell ringing; a newsboy
> shouting; a loudspeaker droning; or am I to report, perhaps,
> that these noises irritate me? (1968, p. 106)

Now the kinds of contextual considerations that Popper invokes
in attempting to explain how we come to accept a basic statement
are equally appropriate in attempting to answer these questions.
But once such pragmatic considerations come into play, we have
stepped outside the constraints of the classical model of ration-

ality, and Popper does not succeed in providing us with a view of rationality that meets the demands of that model.

It is important that we be clear on the significance of Popper's conclusion that basic statements are accepted by convention. There is an approach to the philosophy of science known as 'conventionalism' that Popper is especially concerned to reject. To see what is at issue, consider a problem that arises when we attempt to test a fundamental scientific claim such as Newton's first law: objects move with a constant velocity unless acted upon by an external force. In order to test this hypothesis we would presumably observe objects with no forces acting on them, and measure their velocities. But if we do this, and find a case of varying velocity, we have a number of available options besides rejecting Newton's law. We could reconsider whether this object in fact has no forces acting on it, and possibly postulate a previously unknown force. Or, since measurement of velocity requires measurement of time, and measurement of time requires some periodic phenomenon, we might wish to reconsider the adequacy of our means of measuring time. Other options are available, and we have here a further illustration of the limited guidance we receive from deductive logic in the face of an apparent refutation. Now conventionalists argue that this logical situation allows us to choose some claims that we will permanently protect from refutation by agreeing always to apply the force of a counter-instance against some other hypotheses. One motivation for this proposal derives from the familiar concern to avoid infinite regresses of justification; conventionalists attempt to avoid such regresses by urging that we agree that certain fundamental principles shall not be subject to refutation. This results in a foundationalist view, with conventionally accepted propositions providing the ultimate foundation of knowledge. Thus Newton's first law can become a principle that we need never reconsider, and that needs no further justification – not because it has been proven once and for all, but because we have agreed to treat it in this way.

Popper views conventionalism as a serious attempt to solve a serious problem, but it is also a paradigm case of the sort of dogmatism that he wishes to avoid. Thus one of Popper's major methodological doctrines is that we should avoid 'conventionalist stratagems', i.e., that we should take it as a fundamental epistemological principle that all empirical propositions are capable of being put in jeopardy, and that this is to apply especially to universal claims. In other words, Popper proposes that we adopt a policy of not protecting general propositions, even though it is logically permitted that we protect them. Yet Popper ends up accepting a version of conventionalism himself, since basic statements are accepted by convention. Popper argues that this is a significantly mitigated conventionalism for two reasons: it is the least general propositions in the epistemic edifice, rather than the most general, that are accepted by convention; and even here, reconsideration is never permanently debarred. Still, conventionally accepted basic statements are the keystone of Popper's critical structure. Even if we do reject one of these conventions, we can only replace it with another convention, and all rational appraisal rests on conventions. Moreover, conventions enter in at another even more striking point, and this brings us to the last of the three crucial junctures at which Popper fails to provide us with an adequate set of rules for making rational decisions.

Popper's main goal in developing a philosophy of science is to produce a set of methodological rules, i.e., a set of guidelines for conducting the search for knowledge. Suppose, however, that we ask why we should accept his guidelines rather than some other set. Hopefully we can get a rationally acceptable answer to this question, but Popper appeals, once again, to conventions: 'Methodological rules are here regarded as *conventions*' (1968, p. 53, see also pp. 37–8, pp. 49–50, *et passim*). If we press for a reason why we should accept these conventions rather than some others, we get the following response:

> As to the suitability of any such convention opinions may
> differ; and a reasonable discussion of these questions is only
> possible between parties having some purpose in common.
> The choice of that purpose must, of course, be ultimately a
> matter of decision, going beyond rational argument. (1968,
> p. 37)

Once again, when the question is pushed far enough, we find that the entire structure of rational analysis rests on a nonrational foundation. By now it should be clear that this is a recurring symptom of the classical model of rationality.

Let us back up for a bit and ask how Popper's philosophy of

science stands with respect to Fries' trilemma. Popper's own view is that he has solved it. Clearly he has avoided the regress of justifications since he holds that no empirical propositions are justified, in the sense intended by Fries. He also believes that he has avoided psychologism since, whatever role experience may play in motivating our acceptance of a basic statement, experience is not invoked to *justify* that acceptance. Finally, Popper acknowledges that our acceptance of basic statements is dogmatic in the sense that basic statements are accepted without proof, but he maintains that, 'this kind of dogmatism is innocuous since, should the need arise, these statements can easily be tested further' (1968, p. 105). I want to suggest, however, that this solution is not quite as neat as it might seem, and that Popper is in fact left suspended between dogmatism and psychologism in a way that he should not find comfortable. For his escape from dogmatism requires that we not accept any basic statements that we might agree to, but only those that are properly motivated by perceptual experience. It is, for example, not appropriate to accept the claim that the meter reads '28' without anyone having looked at the meter; and once we have examined the meter, we are constrained to conclude that it reads '28', not '17'. What is the nature of this constraint? Popper never tells us, yet the constraint is crucial, because without it, our decision to accept one basic statement rather than another would be not only dogmatic, but thoroughly arbitrary. Yet if our perceptual examination of the meter somehow legitimates our acceptance of a basic statement, we have fallen back into psychologism. A. J. Ayer develops a similar line of argument and concludes that:

> we have to reject the view that statements can be justified only by one another; and once this view has been rejected, there seems to be no good reason why we should not regard our experiences as directly justifying, not only sense-data statements, but the sort of statements which Popper treats as basic. We cannot hold that they verify them conclusively; but this is not a bar to our holding that they give us an adequate ground for accepting them. (1974, p. 689)

Clearly Popper cannot accept this conclusion, and for the moment I want to note that Popper's difficulties here derive from his acceptance of the view that justification, like falsification, is a matter of logical relations, along with the recognition that logic only deals with relations between propositions. In other words, Popper's unsatisfactory account of the role of experience in empirical knowledge is a direct consequence of his following out the demands of the classical model of rationality with uncommon consistency.

2.7 Appropriate rules

Much of the discussion in this chapter has been concerned with the need for premises from which the process of rational evaluation can begin, but even if we had a set of foundational propositions, we would still need rationally acceptable rules before we could justify nonfoundational claims. It will be instructive to consider how we determine if a rule is appropriate. We can begin by noting that there are different kinds of rules that are introduced for different purposes. For example, the rules of baseball or of chess define a game; the rule that requires drivers to stop at red lights aims to achieve a presumably desirable end. I will be concerned here only with rules of the latter sort, and in particular, with rules that lead to rationally acceptable conclusions. We typically evaluate those rules which aim to achieve a goal by assessing their success in leading us to that goal, but this raises a problem in the present context. For we seem to require rationally acceptable rules before we can determine which are the rationally acceptable conclusions, and any attempt to appeal to conclusions in order to evaluate our rules will end in a vicious circle. An alternative would be to invoke a set of meta-rules for evaluating rules, but these meta-rules must also be rationally acceptable, and the familiar threat of an infinite regress now appears with respect to rules. If we are to avoid this new regress in the framework of the classical model of rationality we need foundational rules in addition to foundational propositions.

There is a second problem about rules that will also concern us: we often encounter alternative rules, and have to decide which of these is rationally appropriate. Suppose, for example, that I endeavor to balance my checkbook by multiplying the amount of the check I have just written by the previous balance, instead of subtracting the former from the latter. We can agree that this would be absurd, but note that I am acting in accordance with an algorithm when I multiply, and indeed, in accordance with an algorithm which it is rational to use in some circumstances. Similarly, we can imagine a mathematician or a scientist who attempts to deduce interesting consequences from a set of premises by continually adding disjuncts. Each step is licensed by a valid rule that is rationally applicable in some circumstances, yet we would not accept this as a sane procedure. These examples suggest that proceeding in accordance with a rule, even a rule of arithmetic or logic, is not sufficient for rationality. In order to be rational we must proceed in accordance with *appropriate* rules, and we must be able to choose these rules in a rational manner. But how do we determine which rules to choose? Again the obvious proposal is that we use a meta-rule, but we might well find competing meta-rules, and will have to seek higher level meta-rules to choose between them. The threat of an infinite regress appears in yet another guise, and again it seems that rationality requires foundational rules.

There is one further difficulty concerning rules that should be mentioned: rules can be misapplied, so even if we have an appropriate set of rules, we must still know how to apply those rules. For example, a common error among introductory logic students is to attempt to infer 'not-*p*' from 'not-(*p* and *q*)', and to justify this by appeal to the rule that permits us to infer '*p*' from '*p* and *q*'. This is clearly a misapplication of a valid rule, but how do we correct the student's error? One way would be to provide the student with another rule, a rule for applying the rule in question, but there is no reason to expect that this new rule will be any more self-applicable than the original rule; thus the problem can arise again, and we are now on our way to an infinite regress of rules and rules for the applicaion of rules. We have already encountered this problem in discussing Descartes: clarity and distinctness were supposed to provide a rule for recognizing true propositions, but we saw that there are problems in knowing when we have applied this rule correctly. One way out of this difficulty is to suppose that anyone who adequately understands a rule knows how to apply that rule, but the above examples suggest that this will not do. Our confused student understands that it is legitimate to detach a conjunct, and she may even be able to recognize all expressions to which this rule applies, but not be able to distinguish *only* those expressions to which the rule applies.

Something is lacking in her grasp of the rule, yet it would be odd to say that she simply does not understand the rule.

But perhaps all these worries are misguided. Perhaps at some point we actually do encounter a set of rules whose adequacy is self-evident, and which we are able to apply once we understand them; and perhaps it is these rules that provide the basis for all of our rational decision-making. Elementary logic provides the clearest examples of rules that have seemed beyond the pale of reasonable doubt, and I want to explore the status of these rules. On examination we will find that it is not self-evident which rules of logic we should accept. Rather, these rules are subject to reconsideration, and require justification. Let me emphasize, however, that my concerns are strictly epistemological, i.e., I am going to argue that our beliefs as to which are the appropriate rules of logic are fallible. This is compatible with the view that there is only one correct logic, and that logicians endeavor to discover it; and it is compatible with the possibility that we have already discovered some of the rules of that logic. My point will be that it is not indubitably obvious when we have discovered such rules, and thus that the claim to have discovered one of these rules requires justification if that rule is to be rationally acceptable.

The most direct way to argue for the dubitability of logic is to exhibit cases in which we have in fact been wrong; subalternation provides a striking example. It was long held as an obvious principle of logic that everyday sentences of the *I* form 'Some S are P' are validly deducible from sentences of the *A* form 'All S are P'. Lewis Carroll's discussion of existential import provides a good illustration of the certainty with which first-class logicians took this to be a valid inference. Carroll notes that to a large degree there is no fact-of-the-matter as to which propositions do, and which do not, carry existential import for their terms, and that 'every writer may adopt his own rule, provided of course that it is consistent with itself and with the accepted facts of Logic' (1955, p. 166). The validity of subalternation is one of the 'accepted facts of logic' that plays a central role in Carroll's discussion (1955, pp. 165–71). Nevertheless, most modern logicians reject this inference as invalid: the invalidity of subalternation follows directly from the analysis of *A* sentences as hypotheticals, while the corresponding *I* sentences are analyzed as conjunctions, for we cannot validly infer a sentence of the form 'S and P' from one of the form 'If S then P'.

What are we to make of this? Whatever view we may take as to the relative merits of modern and classical logic, we must conclude that many excellent logicians have been mistaken about the validity of an elementary inference. And this is enough to make the point that concerns me: it is not self-evident which are the correct rules of logic. However we decide what the correct principles of logic are, these decisions can be mistaken. This, in turn, suggests that as long as we are working in terms of the classical model of rationality, we cannot accept the validity of a rule of logic without justification, but it is not at all clear where that justification is to be found.

Let us consider another example. The principle of excluded middle says that every statement must be either true or false; this is one of the oldest principles of logic, and one of the traditional 'laws of thought'.[21] In spite of its venerability, and its inclusion in most contemporary systems of logic, a number of philosophers and logicians have raised serious questions about its validity, and developed systems of logic in which this principle is not valid. One line of objection comes from intuitionist philosophy of mathematics. Proponents of this view hold that we have no grounds for asserting the truth of a mathematical proposition unless we have a proof, and no grounds for asserting the falsity of a mathematical proposition unless we have a disproof. This leaves open the possibility that there are some mathematical propositions which can be neither proven nor disproven, and intuitionists hold that such propositions are neither true nor false. This rejection of excluded middle brings along a partial rejection of the law of double negation. On an intuitionist interpretation, to assert 'p' we must have a proof of 'p'; to assert 'not-p' we must have a disproof of 'p'; and to assert 'not-not-p' we require a disproof of 'not-p'. Now a proof of 'p' provides a disproof of 'not-p', and thus a proof of 'not-not-p'. As a result, intuitionist logic permits us to infer from a proposition to its double negation. But the converse inference must be rejected, since a disproof of 'not-p' does not amount a proof of 'p', and no proof of 'p' may be possible. Many familiar inferences that involve moving from a sentence of the form 'not-not-p' to one of the form 'p' are thus rejected as invalid. For example, we can still move validly from 'if not-p then not-q' to 'if not-not-*q* then not-not-*p*', and this can be reduced to 'if *q* then not-not-*p*', but a further reduction to 'if *q* then *p*' is illegitimate. (See Dummett, 1977, for a detailed discussion.)

Intuitionism is a highly controversial view, but it is not the only source of doubts with respect to excluded middle, even among logicians. For example, Frederic Fitch (1952) has developed a different logic without excluded middle for a different purpose. I want to consider some of the differences between Fitch's system and intuitionism. Note, first, that while neither of these systems permits us to write down '*p* or not-*p*' for any sentence whatsoever, in each system it is often possible to prove this for specific sentences, and when this occurs, each system permits all inferences that are valid in standard logic. The key differences between Fitch's system and intuitionist logic derive from their treatment of two inferences. I already noted that intuitionists reject the inference from 'not-not-*p*' to '*p*'. At the same time, they permit full blown *reductio* proofs, i.e., if we can derive a contradiction from '*p*' we can assert 'not-*p*'. Similarly, if we can derive a contradiction from 'not-*p*' we have a proof of 'not-not-*p*' – but the latter is not equivalent to a proof of '*p*'. Fitch's system includes the full double negation rule, but only allows *reductio* proofs for those cases in which '*p* or not-*p*' can be established. Thus each of these systems of logic restricts the set of valid inferences in a different way. To add some further examples, intuitionist logic only permits certain forms of De Morgan's laws, while Fitch's logic permits all of the familiar De Morgan inferences (see Fitch, 1952, pp. 61–2 for a summary); but Fitch only permits the inference from 'if *p* then *q*' to 'if not-*q* then not-*p*' for those cases in which we can establish '*p* or not-*p*'. This inference is always valid in intuitionist logic.

Fitch's reasons for rejecting excluded middle are also different from those of the intuitionists. Intuitionists reject this principle because of views they have about the nature of mathematical proofs; Fitch rejects excluded middle because he can then construct a system of logic in which the paradoxes that led to the theory of types do not arise. For example, the liar paradox can be blocked by denying that the troubling sentence, 'This sentence is false', has a truth-value (1952, p. 8); and the argument that generates Russell's paradox turns out to be invalid. These results allow us to dispense with the theory of types (1952, pp. 109–10), and Fitch considers this to be highly desirable. For the theory of types prevents paradoxes by outlawing self-referential claims, while Fitch maintains that the generality sought by philosophers requires self-reference. For example, a general theory of theories is itself a theory, and must be self-referentially correct if it is to be adequate. Indeed, Fitch notes that the claim 'No proposition may be self-referential' is a self-referential proposition, and that we cannot state a universal theory of types without self-reference. (See Fitch, 1946, reprinted as Appendix C of Fitch, 1952.) What is particularly intriguing here is that there are trade-offs between accepting certain rules of inference and achieving other cognitive goals, and once this is recognized, we can no longer accept the claim that familiar inferences require no justification.

Another line of objection to the principle of excluded middle arises when we consider the nature of concepts, and the role they play in classifying items that we encounter. For a given concept, C, excluded middle requires that every sentence of the form 'x is C' must be either true or false. This, in turn, requires that every concept be fully determinate, i.e., that every concept have a complete set of necessary and sufficient conditions. If this were not the case, then there might be an item, a, which could not be classified as either C or not-C, and the sentence, 'a is C', would be neither true nor false. But psychologists studying the ways in which people categorize items, and the ways in which they relate concepts to one another, have generated a substantial body of evidence that is extremely difficult to explain on the hypothesis that all concepts have necessary and sufficient conditions, but which can be explained much more readily on alternative hypotheses. (See Smith and Medin, 1981, for a review of the evidence and the competing hypotheses.) Moreover, if we do not think of concepts as *a priori* givens, but as means of classification that people develop as they interact with the world,[22] it would be surprising to find that every concept is completely determinate. Rather, it is more reasonable to expect that we will build into our concepts what we need to deal with the situations we have encountered, and that we may encounter items that we have not envisaged, and whose status will be unclear. Such items would have some of the features we require for a C, but it would remain unclear whether they have enough exactly because we have never faced this question before. For example, many people are now unclear about whether they would count a telephone as furniture

(Smith and Medin, 1981, pp. 38–9), and there is no guarantee that there must be an answer to this question that we can find if we only reflect on our concepts hard enough. The concept of furniture is considerably older than the concept of a telephone; there is no reason to assume that an answer to this question must have been built into the earlier concept; and the question may not be of sufficient interest outside of the psychological laboratory for us to have come to a decision since telephones have appeared on the scene. This point can also be illustrated in science, where concepts are usually considerably more precise than in everyday life, e.g., 'there is no uniform agreement among biologists as to whether *Euglena*, a mobile organism that manufactures chlorophyll, should be classified as an animal or a plant' (Smith and Medin, 1981, p. 31). This question, like the question of whether a virus is to be considered a living organism, arose at a particular point in the history of science, and presented us with possibilities that had not been thought of previously. Thus there need not have been any answers to these questions already built into our existing concepts. Note again that our assessment of the acceptability of a principle of logic can be affected by results in a variety of different fields, and that we do not seem to have any direct insight into even the most elementary laws of logic.[23]

I want to consider one more example of a law of logic that has been called into question, but this time a case in which it has been explicitly maintained that a familiar law of modern logic has been empirically refuted. The law in question is the distribution of conjunction over disjunction, i.e., the inference from 'p and (q or r)' to '(p and q) or (p and r)'. (The converse inference is not being questioned.) The supposed empirical refutation comes from quantum theory, and although it arises in several ways, I will only discuss one case that is strikingly clear (see, for example, Putnam, 1969; Finkelstein, 1972; Jammer, 1974, ch. 8).

Consider an electron that is confined in a long, narrow box, and let the box be divided into a number of small cells. Since we know that the electron is in the box, we also know that it is located in one of these cells, but we do not know which cell. Let all the cells be of the same width, and label the cells $x_1, x_2, \ldots x_n$; if we were to determine which cell the electron is in, the uncertainty in its location would be equal to the width of the cell. Now Heisenberg's 'uncertainty principle' tells us that there is a relation between the uncertainty in the electron's position and the uncertainty in its momentum such that the product of these two uncertainties must be larger than a particular number. In other words, the greater the precision in our determination of one of these parameters, the greater the uncertainty in our determination of the other. Suppose, then, that we determine the electron's momentum, p, with sufficient precision that we would be violating the uncertainty principle if we were also to know in which cell the electron is located. Our knowledge of the momentum, along with the fact that the electron is located in one of the cells, can be expressed as:

p and $(x_1$ or x_2 or $\ldots x_n)$.

The distribution principle permits us to infer:

$(p$ and $x_1)$ or $(p$ and $x_2)$ or $\ldots$ or $(p$ and $x_n)$.

The premise of this inference is true, but the conclusion is false since the uncertainty principle entails that each of its disjuncts is false. The overwhelming empirical support for quantum theory provides excellent reasons for accepting the uncertainty principle, and we seem to have a counter-instance for the inference, i.e., a case in which the premise is true and the conclusion false. This is a standard way of showing that an inference is invalid. There is much controversy over the claim that the distribution rule is invalid, and I am not endorsing any position on this topic. My only concern is to illustrate some of the ways in which commonly accepted principles of logic can be questioned.

I have argued in this chapter that the classical model of rationality faces serious problems when it is consistently developed. The model requires that rationally acceptable claims be justified, and that the justification proceed from rationally acceptable principles in accordance with rationally acceptable rules. Each of these demands leads to an infinite regress unless we can find some self-evident principles and rules from which to begin, but these have not yet been found, and there is no reason to expect that they will be forthcoming. The upshot of this discussion is well captured in the following passage from Herbert Simon:

Modern descendants of Archimedes are still looking for the fulcrum on which they can rest the lever that is to move the whole world. In the domain of reasoning, the difficulty in finding a fulcrum resides in the truism 'no conclusions without premises.' Reasoning processes take symbolic inputs and deliver symbolic outputs. The initial inputs are axioms, themselves not derived by logic but simply induced from empirical observations, or even more simply posited. Moreover, the processes that produce the transformations of inputs to outputs (rules of inference) are also introduced by fiat and are not the products of reason. Axioms and inference rules together constitute the fulcrum on which the lever of reasoning rests; but the particular structure of that fulcrum cannot be justified by the methods of reasoning. For an attempt at such a justification would involve us in an infinite regress of logics, each as arbitrary in its foundations as the preceding one. (1983, pp. 5–6)

It is interesting to note that even though the crux of the classical model of rationality lies in the demand for rules, current doubts about this model have been largely generated by the failure to establish foundational principles on which the rules can operate. Indeed, having made the pessimistic declaration quoted above, Simon goes on to discuss reason on the assumption that standard rules of reasoning are adequate, and that given rules without foundations, it follows that:

reason is wholly instrumental. It cannot tell us where to go; at best it can tell us how to get there. It is a gun for hire that can be employed in the service of whatever goals we have, good or bad. (1983, pp. 7–8)

But if the rules of inference are also open to question, then there is no more basis for viewing reason as a gun for hire than for viewing it as a marshmallow for hire. Of course, we may want to interpret the outcome of this discussion differently – we may want to reconsider the idea that rationality is captured in rules. Before taking up this option, I want to press the classical model of rationality further by considering a field in which it has often seemed especially strong: science and the rules of scientific method.

CHAPTER III

Rationality and Science

An adequate model of rationality should be exemplified by those disciplines that we take to be paradigm cases of rational ende- avors. To be sure, our present views as to which disciplines are rational are not infallible, and we might be led to reconsider these views as a result of further reflection on the nature of rationality. Still, our understanding of rationality is in part a function of the paradigm cases to which we apply this concept, and a model that preserves these central instances is *prima facie* preferable to one that forces us to abandon them. In the case of rationality, science provides a crucial test case, since science, and particularly physical science, currently stands as our clearest example of a rational enterprise; if a model of rationality were to entail that science is not rational, we would have good reason for questioning the adequacy of that model.[1] Moreover, proponents of the classical model of rationality have typically considered science to be a clear instance of rationality in action. Now the classical model demands that rational activities be rule-governed, and one standard task of philosophy of science has long been the attempt to formulate the rules in accordance with which scientific hypotheses are to be accepted or rejected. Recent work on the history and philosophy of science has, however, cast considerable doubt on the existence of the sorts of rules that philosophers have sought. These doubts derive from a mixture of logical and historical considerations. The main logical points have already been made in our discussions of induction and critical rationalism, and in this chapter I want to sharpen some of these logical points, and weld them to the relevant historical data. I will then introduce an alternative view of science which rejects the thesis that science is governed by the kinds of methodological rules that philosophers have sought. By the time we are done it should be clear that there is serious conflict between the classical model of rationality and scientific practice.

3.1   The rules of scientific method

The search for an inductive logic constitutes the oldest and long-est-running attempt to formulate rules for evaluating scientific hypotheses. It is important that we be clear on two points about this project. First, as we saw in Chapter I, inductive logic, like deductive logic, is concerned with the evaluation of arguments in which the premises and conclusion are given. In the typical inductive case the premises consist of a set of singular sentences describing observational data, and the conclusion is a scientific hypothesis. Most discussions of inductive logic assume that the premises are known to be true; for the present I will accept this assumption and focus on the rules used to evaluate hypotheses, given the observational data. Second, deductive logic has typically provided the model for attempts to construct an inductive logic: inductive logicians have sought purely formal rules for evaluating inductive arguments, while assuming that in a properly constructed inductive argument there would be a necessary connection between premises and conclusion, just as there is a necessary connection between premises and conclusion in a valid deductive argument. The difference between induction and deduction would then lie in the fact that the rules would be different in the two cases. This last point requires some further discussion.

Historically, the central role that the demand for necessity has played in discussions of induction becomes especially clear when we note how easy it has been for philosophers to display the failings of induction. Hume, for example, could argue that we have no rational basis for accepting any inductive argument simply by pointing out that in such arguments it is always *possible* for the premises to be true while the conclusion is false. In other words, Hume took the existence of a necessary tie between prem-ises and conclusion, which is the characteristic stamp of a valid deductive argument, as a requirement for every rational argu-ment, and this criterion was long accepted by those who would defend induction. When the proposition 'All swans are white', a claim that had long stood as a textbook example of a universal proposition that had been proven by induction, was refuted by the discovery of black swans in Australia, John Stuart Mill insisted that the argument to this conclusion 'cannot have been a good induction, since the conclusion has turned out erroneous' (1950, p. 184). This is just what we should expect on the classical model of rationality: it was universally agreed that the premises were correct (cf. Mill, 1950, p. 184), and in such cases the classical model requires that the conclusion be derived from those premises by means of universal, necessary rules. Had this been done, only a true conclusion could have resulted.

Mill's response to the discovery of black swans underlines his conviction that correct rules' for induction do exist, and that it is the logician's task to formulate these rules. We do not yet have an explicit set of rules for induction, and this may account for the fact that we sometimes accept erroneous inductive arguments as correct, but it does not prevent us from also constructing correct inductive arguments. Mill cites the propositions that 'Men's heads grow above their shoulders and never below', and that 'A straight line is the shortest distance between two points . . . even in the region of the fixed stars' (1950, p. 185) as examples of true conclusions that have been proven by induction. In Mill's day, Newtonian mechanics seemed to stand as an overwhelming example of an important scientific theory that had been inductively established. Newton's three laws of motion and his law of gravitation provided the basis for an enormous number of correct predictions in both celestial and terrestrial mechanics, and scientists, along with scientifically informed lay people, were generally convinced that Newton had said the final word in physics. As late as the 1890s, bright young men were being advised by physicists not to study physics, since all of the important work had been completed. (See, for example, Feuer, 1982, pp. 254–6.)

Yet in spite of the powerful evidence on its behalf, we now have overwhelming evidence that Newton's principles, taken as a description of the physical world, are false: they give incorrect results when they are applied to objects moving at high velocities, to complex gravitational fields, and to objects of atomic and sub-atomic dimensions. They do not even permit us to calculate the orbit of Mercury correctly, although the ability to get the planetary orbits right was once the strongest argument for Newtonian mechanics. True, in many situations Newton's mechanics does give results that are sufficiently accurate for practical purposes, but it does so for the wrong reasons. As Thomas Kuhn has pointed out, this use of Newtonian results is analogous to the surveyor's use of an astronomy in which the earth stands still and the heavens move (1970c, p. 102). In both cases an incorrect theory yields correct results in a relatively simple way, and we have a good idea of how far we can get away with using the simpler theory, but we are in fact taking advantage of a well known logical phenomenon: that we can validly deduce true conclusions from false premises.

It would be difficult to overstate the seriousness of the problem that the failure of Newtonian physics poses for the view that the rules for evaluating scientific hypotheses can be captured in an inductive logic of the sort we are currently considering. The degree of empirical support that had accrued to this theory far exceeded that which had been developed for any previous theory, yet this support was not sufficient to prove the theory true or to prevent it from being superseded. Of course this does not show that there are no rules for induction; we may just have another case in which we applied the unformulated rules of induction improperly. But another option seems more reasonable: we can give up the demand that an acceptable inductive argument must be capable of proving its conclusion, and replace it with the notion that an inductive argument must only show its conclusion *probable*; twentieth-century inductive logicians have devoted much energy to this project. On this view, massive inductive evidence only conferred a high degree of probability on Newtonian physics, and a high probability is compatible with the eventual failure of the theory. We must make this proposal more precise, and the natural way to do that is by using the mathematical theory of probability. Moreover, this move will solve the main problem that has been worrying us, the problem of what rules we are to apply when we attempt to assess an hypothesis against the evidence. The required rules are now provided by probability theory, and like the rules of any mathematical theory, the inferences they license are all *deductive*: they permit us to deduce a conclusion that makes a claim about probabilities from a set of probabilistic premises. For example, given that the probability of a head on a single toss of a particular coin is .5, it follows necessarily that the probability of two heads on two tosses is .25. If the coin is unbalanced so that, e.g., the probability of a head on a single toss is only .4, then it follows deductively that the probability of two consecutive heads is .16. In general, given the probability of a head for a single toss, the mathematical theory of probability allows us to compute the probability for any specified combination of heads and tails, and an analogous result holds for more complex examples.

Note especially that we are now working only with deductive rules of inference, and it is difficult to see how any other kind of rule would be acceptable as long as we adhere to the classical model of rationality. Unfortunately, the problem of how we are to establish the appropriate premises for these deductive arguments now returns. Previously we were able to avoid this problem as long as we accepted the view that there are discrete observations which provide the premises for nonprobabilistic inductive arguments. But deductions using the probability calculus require premises that include probabilities, and these cannot be derived from discrete observations. Rather, we must use sets of observations to establish our premises, and when we consider how this is done, the old problem of induction reappears, and does so in a particularly difficult guise. If, for example, we wished to determine, by observation, the probability of throwing a head on a particular coin, we could toss the coin and determine how often heads came up. This process must stop after some finite number of tosses, but we might find that the percentage of tosses yielding a head was tending towards a definite ratio as the number of tosses increased. We could take this ratio as the probability of a head, but in doing so we would be drawing the conclusion that the percentage of heads would continue to tend towards this ratio as the number of tosses continued to increase. Yet this is an inference that attempts to project a feature of past experience into the future, i.e., it is an inductive inference. The classical model of rationality requires that we have rules for assessing the legitimacy of such inferences, and the problem we attempted to solve by introducing probability reappears. At the same time, it is harder to assess the relation between an observed ratio and a probability claim than it is to assess the relation between discrete observations and a universal hypothesis. For example, it is relatively clear that a counter-instance raises a problem for a universal claim, and that this problem must be addressed; problems cannot be generated quite so easily for a probabilistic claim. The claim that an outcome has a particular probability in a population is compatible with our finding a substantial range of different percentages of occurrence of that outcome in a sample taken from the population. Thus the fact that heads occurred on forty percent of the tosses made thus far does not contradict the claim that the probability of a head is .38 or .5. Again the classical model of rationality urges that we seek rules for deciding what to do in such cases, and the introduction of probabilities seems to require more complex rules than we required before we took this tack. Note also that we have not even begun to approach the problem that originally concerned us. Probability theory provides a tool that can be used to assess the truth or falsity of probabilistic claims, but our concern was to assign a probability value to such universal claims as Newton's law of gravitation. Here the relevant evidence consists of observations that confirm or contradict the law. Presumably, one contradictory observation drops the probability of the law to zero, but we have no clear idea how to assign a probability to a universal law on the basis of a set of instances that confirm it.

There is a variation on the probabilistic approach, based on Bayes' law, that attempts to solve some of these problems. Bayes' law follows by deduction from the axioms of probability theory, and provides an algorithm for adjusting our estimates of the probabilities of a set of competing hypotheses as new information becomes available. To apply this algorithm we need the following: (a) a set of competing hypotheses; (b) initial estimates of the probabilities of the competing hypotheses; (c) a body of evidence that is relevant to the choice between these hypotheses; and (d) for each hypothesis, an estimate of the probability of the evidence on the basis of that hypothesis. In its general form, Bayes' law specifies the following procedure for calculating the adjusted probabilities: for each hypothesis multiply the initial probability by the probability of the evidence given that hypothesis, let H_i be the resulting number for hypothesis h_i. The adjusted probability for hypothesis h_i is H_i divided by the sum of the H_i's for all of the competing hypotheses. Typically, requirements (a) and (c) will not be problematic. The probabilities needed for requirement (d) can usually be determined by deduction (I will illustrate this below). The obvious sticking point is (b): where are these initial probabilities to come from? Proponents of Bayes' law often adopt the view that these are individual estimates, based on a personal assessment of the odds one would require before betting on the hypothesis. These probabilities cannot be chosen at random, since it can be shown that if the choices do not conform to the axioms of probability theory, it is possible to set up a sequence of bets on which one would lose no matter what the outcome. But this is a very weak constraint, and in any given case there will be an enormous number of alternative probability assignments that meet it.

In the context of the classical model of rationality the selection of the initial probabilities would seem to involve an arbitrary choice. We might think that this is sufficient to show that any results derived from the application of Bayes' law will not be rationally acceptable, and problems with the choice of initial probabilities do provide one of the most common lines of objection to the use of Bayes' law to solve the problem of induction. But we should be careful here. For a substantial range of cases the initial probability assignments are relatively unimportant because other factors involved in the law overwhelm these choices, with the result that we get fairly rapid convergence to a single conclusion whatever initial probabilities we choose. Let me illustrate this with an extremely simple example. Suppose we wish to determine whether a coin is a normal coin with a head and a tail, or a two-headed coin, but the only evidence we have is the result of a series of tosses of the coin. One tail will show that the coin does not have two heads, but assume that every flip gives a head; at what point should we conclude that the coin has two heads? In this case the probability of the evidence given each hypothesis can be determined by deduction: if the coin has two heads, the probability of any sequence of heads, no matter how long, will be one; if it is a normal coin, the probability of n consecutive heads will be $.5^n$. If we begin with the initial probability that one coin out of every thousand has two heads, Bayes' law will raise the probability that this coin is two-headed above .5 after 10 consecutive heads, and will raise it above .9 after 14 consecutive heads. If we reconsider and decide that only one coin in ten thousand has two heads, it will now take 14 consecutive heads to lead us to the conclusion that this is more likely to be a two-headed coin than a normal coin; and 17 consecutive heads to raise this probability above .9.

The strategy of using Bayes' law is, in one respect, analogous to the strategy of critical rationalism: given the right sorts of rules, we may be able to evade the problem of establishing our premises. If we can show that the starting point loses its significance when we apply our rules, then the fact that our starting point was, strictly speaking, arbitrary becomes of no importance.[2] Unfortunately, there are serious problems with the attempt to apply Bayes' law to crucial cases that arise in science. Recall that we are not concerned here with applications of Bayes' law to statistical hypotheses, but with attempts to use this law to assess the probability of a nonstatistical hypothesis against a body of evidence. Here we face a variation on a problem that we have already encountered: beginning with a nonstatistical hypothesis we deduce a prediction, and when the prediction is verified, we still must find a means of generating the probabilities required by Bayes' law. I want to develop this point in the context of one standard problem, which Glymour calls 'the old evidence/new theory problem' (1980, p. 86); this will then provide the basis for a somewhat deeper insight into the difficulties involved in attempting to use Bayes' law to evaluate the degree of verification of universal hypotheses.

Sometimes a new theory is proposed in an existing scientific field. In this case there will often already be an established body of data that is relevant to the new theory, and the theory must be able to account for that data. For example, special relativity had to account for the already existing evidence regarding physical phenomena at low velocities; if the new theory had been inconsistent with this evidence, we would have had grounds for rejecting that theory. In fact special relativity gave a completely satisfactory account of this evidence, and this provided some empirical support for the new theory. If Bayes' law provides an adequate account of the impact of evidence on the probability that a theory is correct, it should allow us to assess this impact in the present case. Now Bayes' law only provides a means of adjusting initial probabilities, so we should think of the present example in the following way: a new theory has some initial probability before we consider a particular piece of old evidence, and we use Bayes' law to calculate an adjusted probability in the light of this evidence. Philosophers who seek to apply Bayes' law to this case often make use of a simple form of the law. In this form, to determine the adjusted probability of our hypothesis we multiply the initial probability, $P(h)$, by the probability of the evidence given the hypothesis $P(e,h)$ and divide by the probability of the evidence $P(e)$:

$$P(h,e) = \frac{P(h) \times P(e,h)}{P(e)}$$

Since we are only concerned here with the case in which the hypothesis entails the evidence, $P(e,h) = 1$ and this term drops out of the equation. As a result, once we have decided on the initial probability of the hypothesis, its adjusted probability is completely determined by the probability we assign to the old evidence. Yet whatever probability we assign, we get odd results.

The obvious proposal is to assign the evidence a probability of one since the evidence is already available, and the sentences describing that evidence are thus known to be true. But if we set the denominator of Bayes' law equal to one it also drops out of the expression, and the new probability of the hypothesis is equal to the initial probability. In other words, the evidence has no impact at all on the probability of the hypothesis; this is not acceptable. Alternatively, we can argue that we are dealing with empirical evidence, and that no sentence describing empirical evidence is ever certain. Thus we should set the probability of the evidence equal to some value less than one. But this also leads to unacceptable results. One advantage of automatically assigning a probability of one to the evidence is that, in effect, we have a rule that dictates our assignment. There is no available rule that will tell us what probability assignment we should make if we consider the evidence to be uncertain. Somehow we must make a decision, and the adjusted probability value we arrive at will depend on this decision. But this introduces a second subjective factor into the application of Bayes' law, in addition to that involved in choosing our initial probabilities, and this raises new doubts about whether we are likely to achieve convergence to a single final probability for our hypothesis. In addition, we must now face the possibility that different bits of evidence will be assigned different probabilities, but when we plug these probabilities into Bayes' law, we find that lower probabilities yield larger adjustments of our initial probability. In other words, evidence of low probability is more significant than highly probable evidence. We might try to evade this result by restricting the application of old evidence, requiring that we only use the single piece of evidence that has the highest probability value, but there are no good reasons for accepting this proposal. Since we have no algorithm for assigning probabilities to evidence, we can expect disagreement as to which bits of available evidence are most probable. Moreover, where a variety of evidence is available, there is no guarantee that the evidence that scientists consider the most significant will also be the most probable. Finally, increased significance for less certain evidence arises in a second way. Recall that we are concerned here only with nonstatistical hypotheses that entail the evidence. In this case, the probability of the hypothesis cannot exceed the probability of the evidence, and if our initial probability estimate for our hypothesis is higher than the probability we assign to a piece of evidence, we must lower that initial probability estimate. But here too the adjustment we must make will be greater for less certain evidence than for more certain evidence. Indeed, the probability of our hypothesis cannot exceed the probability of the least certain piece of evidence it entails. Again, this does not seem to be right, and it does not capture the way scientists assess new hypotheses against old evidence.

I think we can get some insight into the underlying source of these difficulties if we compare the way Bayes' law is used in the situations we have been examining with the way it is used in doing probability calculations. Note that when we are evaluating nonstatistical hypotheses, the hypothesis we are evaluating plays no role in determining the probability we assign to the evidence; this probability must be determined independently of that hypothesis. From one point of view this is most desirable, but it involves a significant departure from the paradigm applications of Bayes' law in probability theory. There we do not make use of the simple form of Bayes' law. Rather, we use the general form in which it is clear that Bayes' law always involves a comparison of alternative hypotheses, and in which the denominator is explicitly dependent on these competing hypotheses. For example, a typical case in which we might use Bayes' law for a probability computation would be one in which we have two urns, each with a known distribution of red and white balls, and in which our evidence consists of the result of drawing a number of balls from one of these urns. Bayes' law permits us to determine the probability that our outcome is the result of drawing from each of the urns. In order to apply Bayes' law, we first use probability theory to calculate the probability of the known outcome for each of the competing hypotheses. We then multiply each of these probabilities by the initial probability we have assigned to that hypothesis, and the denominator of Bayes' law is the sum of these weighted probabilities. If we change our hypotheses, e.g., by adding another urn to the set of possible sources for our outcome, the value of the denominator may change as well, while the evidence remains unaltered. In those applications of Bayes' law to confirmation theory that we have been considering, the probability of the evidence has nothing to do with the hypotheses under examination.

Thus the attempt to use Bayes' law as a means of analyzing the confirmation of nonstatistical hypotheses involves significant departures from the paradigmatic uses of this law. In the context of the classical model of rationality this extension of the law is extremely tempting exactly because Bayes' law provides us with an algorithm. At the same time, it returns us to a problem that we encountered when we first discussed the attempt to assign probabilities to universal hypotheses: the need to determine the probabilities that we are to plug into our confirmation theory. Let me emphasize this point: once the initial probabilities of our hypotheses are given, the denominator of Bayes' law can be calculated when we are working within probability theory; it must be supplied from some external considerations in confirmation theory.

The discussion in this section will serve to underline a peculiar interplay between deductive and inductive methodologies. One clear advantage of deduction is that we understand what sorts of rules we need, and to a large degree we are confident that we know the rules. Attempts, such as those of the classical rationalists, to capture science in a deductive methodology failed because they could not provide the premises they required. Traditional proponents of an inductive methodology were able to solve the latter problem by holding that the premises for inductive reasoning are provided by observations, but they were unable to specify the rules needed to evaluate inductive arguments. Contemporary proponents of probabilistic confirmation theory have adopted the traditional solution to the problem of finding rules: the mathematical theory of probability provides them with a set of deductive inference rules, but the problem of finding the probabilistic premises required for these inferences reappears. Thus far this problem has been intractable.

3.2   More on critical rationalism

The above discussion illustrates some of the major reasons for doubting that inductive reasoning can be captured in a set of rules analogous to the rules of deductive logic. This does not mean that it is nonrational to accept inductively supported scientific claims, but the discussion does suggest that the rationality of doing so cannot be captured in the framework of the classical model of rationality. Still, the development of an inductive logic is not the only way in which philosophers have attempted to elaborate a philosophy of science that meets the demands of the classical model. We saw in chapter II that critical rationalism was a direct response to the failures of induction, and that Popper sought to meet the requirements of the classical model of rationality by eschewing proofs, and relying on deductive arguments for determining when an hypothesis has been refuted. We also saw that Popper failed to provide the required rules, and I want to cite some examples from the history of science in order to emphasize just how difficult it is to develop a set of rules that will guide us in the face of apparent refutations.

Many of the examples that concern me are familiar from the literature in history and philosophy of science of the past 30 years, and they can be cited briefly. Perhaps the oldest case is that of Aristarchus. In the third century B.C. Aristarchus proposed that the sun is at the center of the solar system, and that the earth rotates daily on its axis, and revolves around the sun in the course of a year. Now the annual motion of the earth around the sun should be reflected in a change in the apparent relative locations of at least some stars; this is known as 'stellar parallax'. Careful observation revealed no such change, and Aristarchus' proposal seemed to be refuted, although Aristarchus was not convinced.

Rather, he noted that the amount of parallax is inversely proportional to the distance to the stars, and that if the stars were far enough away, the earth could move without our being able to detect any parallax. This is an interesting proposal, and we now have excellent reasons for believing that Aristarchus was correct, and that the distance to the stars is vastly greater than anything his contemporaries had imagined. In fact, the parallax is so small that it was not detected until the 1830s, long after the motion of the earth had been accepted. But in Aristarchus' day there was no way to test this new hypothesis. Taken in its historical context, Aristarchus' claim about the distance to the stars provides an illustration of the kind of move that Duhem envisioned and that Popper wished to declare illegitimate: the introduction of an untestable hypothesis in order to evade the refutation of a favored thesis. In Popperian terms the only reasonable decision to make at the time was to reject Aristarchus' proposal, and this is exactly what Aristarchus' contemporaries did. Yet the refutation itself was rejected at a later stage in the development of astronomy.

In one respect this need not trouble Popper since he has noted from time to time that refutations are no more permanent than confirmations; but I want to argue that in another respect it is deeply problematic. Let me set the stage for that argument by noting that today we have many examples of overturned refutations. In chapter V I will discuss some of the massive evidence that contradicted the thesis that the earth moves when that thesis was revived by Copernicus, but the Copernican view eventually prevailed. In the mid-nineteenth century, after many decades of debate between wave and particle theories of light, an experiment was done that seemed, finally, to have refuted the particle theory. Nevertheless, in 1905 Einstein revived the particle view in order to account for the newly discovered photoelectric effect. (See Brown, 1975, for further discussion of the above examples.) Einstein's new theory was vigorously resisted, and for a time the experimental evidence seemed to refute it; but the burden of evidence shifted, and Einstein's theory was eventually accepted (Stuewer, 1970). In the late nineteenth century, the physicist Kelvin put forth an especially powerful argument against Darwin's theory of evolution: on the basis of the best available physical theories, the sun could not have been burning long enough to provide the necessary time span (Burchfield, 1975). When nuclear processes were discovered this objection evaporated.

An especially interesting situation is provided by cases in which new evidence seems to contradict a well established theory, but instead of rejecting that theory, scientists introduce new hypotheses in order to bring the old theory into conformity with the evidence. This strategy is not always fruitful, but it has led to a number of major discoveries, e.g., the planets Neptune and Pluto. Early in this century there was a body of evidence that seemed to contradict a number of fundamental conservation laws in physics, including conservation of energy. One response was to postulate a new particle, the neutrino, which had the properties required to save the conservation laws. When it was originally postulated, this particle was believed to be non-observable, although a method of observing it was eventually developed, and it was detected some 30 years after it had first been proposed. Today neutrinos are routinely observed, and they play an important role in testing scientific hypotheses (see Brown, 1987, section 3.4 for details). This approach is common in modern high energy physics. Here physicists have encountered several cases in which existing theory leads one to expect that a particular decay will occur, but that decay is not observed, and physicists have responded by postulating previously unknown conservation laws that would be violated if the decay in question were to occur. Several important conservation laws that later received independent confirmation were discovered in this way. (Cf. Davies, 1979, ch. 5 for a popular discussion.)

Einstein's introduction of special relativity provides an important variation on this theme. This theory rests on two main postulates: that the laws of nature are the same for all observers moving with constant velocities, and that the velocity of light is the same for all observers. Other physicists before Einstein recognized that there was strong support for these two hypotheses, and that they might provide the foundation for a new physics; but they rejected this proposal because it can be shown, in the framework of classical physics, that the two hypotheses are mutually inconsistent. Einstein noted this problem early in his first relativity paper, and stated that he would show that this is only an apparent inconsistency. He then argued that the inconsistency does not derive from this pair of propositions alone, but from the pair in conjunction with a third proposition – that measurements of time are independent of the motion of the observer; and Einstein provided reasons for rejecting this third claim. Apparently, before Einstein no one had considered this to be an hypothesis that was subject to reconsideration, and Einstein's rejection of this claim required a radically new analysis of the concept of time. But note what has happened here. Instead of an empirical refutation, we have a logical inconsistency. Something is clearly wrong somewhere in the body of propositions we are working with, but even if we had a rule that picked out one of the hypotheses before us for elimination, it would not be sufficient in this case since the problem lay with a proposition that was not generally viewed as an hypothesis that could be reconsidered. Thus the range of responses to the strongest sort of refutation has expanded, and now includes the possibility of undertaking new conceptual analyses with the aim of turning the refutation in a totally new direction. Moreover, Einstein's surprising move should provide a warning to those who think that we at least have a comprehensive list of all the possible moves that might be undertaken. We do not have any such list, and we do not know what further options will appear as a result of further scientific development – recall our discussion in chapter II of the proposal that we turn a refutation against a law of logic.

All of this leaves us in a highly uncertain methodological situation. The history of science does not provide any clear grounds for believing that science is more likely to progress if we follow a policy of rapid elimination of hypotheses in the face of contrary evidence than if we follow a policy of tenacious protection of apparently refuted theories, while we search for supplementary hypotheses that will allow us to protect those theories. Nor is there any reason to believe that we can put clear limits on how long it is legitimate to seek a means of protecting an hypothesis. Positive evidence for Aristarchus' claim about the distance to the stars did not appear for many centuries. Again, my aim here is not to question the rationality of any of these scientific decisions, but rather to question the claim that if these decisions were rational, they must have been governed by some unstated rule. It is clear that refutations are more revealing than confirmations since a refutation shows that there is something wrong somewhere in the set of propositions that generated the refutation, but it is not at all clear how we should proceed when we face an apparent refutation. Should we reject the hypothesis? Should we seek some new hypothesis that will protect the current theory and perhaps yield an important new discovery? Should we assume that there was something wrong with the procedures that produced the new evidence, and simply wait for the experimenters to correct themselves? All of these options have been pursued in the history of science, sometimes successfully and sometimes unsuccessfully. Note especially that we are in a different position from our predecessors on this issue exactly because we have more information about the development of science than they had. It may have been rational for Aristarchus' contemporaries to reject his apparently untestable hypothesis out of hand, but it is not clear that it would be rational for us to respond in the same way in an analogous situation. To be sure, we might specify a set of rules which all scientists could adopt, and which would have the effect of ensuring that scientific decisions would be made in a rule-governed manner. But it is difficult to avoid the impression that this decision would be arbitrary, and we would face, again, a situation that we have already encountered several times: we would have the appearance of a rational, rule-governed activity, resting on a nonrational foundation.

This discussion might suggest that science should be an extremely unstable enterprise, and it makes one wonder why scientific research is not totally chaotic. It also makes it difficult to understand how anyone could have taken science to be a model of a nonarbitrary, rule-governed activity. One possible response is that there are relevant aspects of science that have so far been left out of our discussion, and in recent years a number of historians and philosophers of science have attempted to provide a new picture of science that includes such aspects. The most influential of these studies is due to Thomas Kuhn, and I will approach this topic by examining and assessing Kuhn's analysis of the way science develops. This will provide us with new answers to some of the questions raised in the above discussions, but will do so in a way that will generate even more pressing problems for the classical model of rationality.

3.3 Paradigms

Kuhn maintains that the history of science can be divided into three types of periods, and that only two of these approach the kind of chaos that would seem to follow from the lack of sufficient rules. I want to focus first on the nonchaotic periods. Kuhn calls such periods 'normal science' because he believes that, in the developed sciences, these are the periods in which professional scientists typically spend their working lives. The characteristic feature of normal science is that there is wide agreement on fundamentals in the research community; this permits scientists to avoid disputes about foundations, and get on with the business of research. These points of agreement are embodied in what Kuhn calls a 'paradigm'. This is a complex and not always clear notion. One aspect of this idea explains Kuhn's choice of the term 'paradigm': a paradigm is, first and foremost, a specific scientific achievement that provides a *model* for work in the discipline. For example, Newton's solutions for a set of physical problems provided the paradigm for classical physics in the sense that physicists adopted Newton's methods as a model for solving new scientific problems. I will return to this point in chapter V; here I want to focus on a different aspect of paradigms, one that is, for Kuhn, derivative, but still important.

One consequence of our discussion thus far is that we lack a sufficient set of general methodological rules for the practice of science. But in accepting a paradigm, scientists accept an additional set of rules for the practice of research in their discipline (cf. Kuhn 1970c, pp. 38–42); these rules supplement the rules provided by logic and methodology, and go a long way towards closing the methodological gaps that we have been concerned with. As a result, normal scientific research presents a close approximation to research in accord with the classical model of rationality. For example, if a scientist working in the Newtonian framework encounters an accelerating object with no apparent forces acting on it, she will not have to consider the possibility of revising Newton's first law, even though this is logically permissible. In a period of normal science the paradigm is not being tested and evaluated; instead it provides guidelines for dealing with the relevant portion of nature. Thus our scientist will proceed under a clear injunction to seek the missing force, and a failure to find this force would not count as evidence against Newton's first law, but rather as an indication of the limited skill of this particular scientist. Phenomena which do not fit the expectations generated by the paradigm become *puzzles* to be solved by the proper application of the paradigm. Kuhn uses the term 'puzzle' here to indicate one parallel between normal scientific research and such activities as solving jigsaw or crossword puzzles: we assume that a solution exists, and that our ability to find that solution is a test of our skill. Similarly, normal scientists assume that problems can be solved in the context of the paradigm, and that their task is to find those solutions, not to raise questions about the adequacy of the paradigm. This is a significant departure from the common picture of the scientist who always questions everything, but it does give us some indication of how scientists can get on with the task of studying nature in a coherent manner. Moreover, if paradigm-guided research is as common as Kuhn thinks it is, we can understand why science has so often seemed to present a clear picture of a rational endeavor that meets the demands of the classical model. The paradigm indicates which aspects of nature should be studied, what questions should be asked, and what kinds of answers should be sought, and normal scientific research is tightly constrained by rules.

Consider some of the principles that have played this methodological role in the history of science. Ancient astronomers agreed that all celestial motions are circular, and they spent much effort and ingenuity attempting to show how motions that look noncircular to us could be produced by compounding circular motions. A similar role has been played at various times by conservation of matter and of energy, by Newton's laws, by the thesis that biological species are fixed, and by the claim that no physical process can exceed the velocity of light. Let me take a recent example to illustrate the way that the last of these operates in contemporary research. For several years radio astronomers have been observing the quasar 3C 273, along with a small blob of matter that is moving away from the quasar. Observations made over a three-year period between 1977 and 1980 seem to indicate that the distance between the blob and the quasar has increased by 25 light years, yielding a velocity that is several times the velocity of light. Logical considerations alone provide no grounds for deciding whether to seek an account of this motion, or take it as a basis for questioning special relativity. In fact the scientists who made this observation have pursued the former option, and their decision to do so is supported by the central role that special relativity plays in contemporary physics. (Cf. Redhead 1982, pp. 59–60; Henbest and Marten 1983, pp. 229–31.)[3] As the example illustrates, the attempt to understand scientific practice solely in logical terms leaves too many options open, and the principles provided by a paradigm promote coherent research by restricting those options.

The suggestion that we cannot understand science unless we recognize that substantive claims about nature carry methodological force has an important forerunner in Kant's synthetic *a priori* principles (cf. Brown 1975, 1979b, pp. 101–6); it will be useful to recall why Kant introduced these principles. Kant was also interested in situations in which scientists refuse to treat an observation as evidence against a principle, even though it could stand as a counter-instance from the point of view of formal logic. Suppose, for example, that an event occurs with no apparent cause. It seemed clear to Kant that scientists are not free to take this as evidence against the causal principle; rather they must seek a cause for that event, and continued failure to find a cause, even after a long and diligent search, would still not provide evidence against the causal principle. Instead, this failure would indicate the limited skill of these scientists, or reflect on the state of their art. Other synthetic *a priori* principles, such as that there is something that remains constant in every change, work in a similar fashion. Here is one of Kant's rare examples:

> A philosopher, on being asked how much smoke weighs, made reply: 'Subtract from the weight of the wood burnt the weight of the ashes which are left over, and you have the weight of the smoke.' He thus presupposed as undeniable that even in fire the matter (substance) does not vanish, but only suffers an alteration of form. (1963, p. 215)

The possibility that we might have lost some matter in this case need not be considered.

Now Kant was working in the framework of the classical model of rationality, and it is interesting to note that he was not content simply to propose that certain principles played a foundational role in science. Rather, Kant attempted to assimilate his synthetic *a priori* principles to principles of logic by inventing 'transcendental logic'. This new logic is, in a sense, a formal logic, but it deals with the general form of objects of experience, instead of the form of propositions. Thus Kant contends that while there is no logical inconsistency involved in the claim that a particular event has no cause, we cannot actually conceive of an experienced event as uncaused. It is transcendental logic that provides this additional constraint, and Kant even attempted to derive the principles of this new logic from the principles of formal logic. But the principles of transcendental logic must not be viewed as having a second-class epistemic status. As long as we are concerned to act in, and understand, the world that we experience, the rules of transcendental logic are just as inviolable as the rules of formal logic.

There is, then, one important parallel between principles provided by a Kuhnian paradigm and Kant's synthetic *a priori* principles: for Kuhn, a paradigm provides a set of rules that supplement the rules of formal logic and that are inviolable for the normal scientist. On the other hand, the examples that have already been cited also indicate one key way in which the principles derived from a paradigm differ sharply from Kant's synthetic *a priori* principles: the principles derived from a paradigm can be reconsidered and rejected. Indeed, all of the examples mentioned above except the constancy of the velocity of light, which is a relatively recent addition to the list, have been rejected. Principles provided by a paradigm guide research in a discipline for a time, and Kuhn maintains that any paradigm will eventually face anomalies that cannot be resolved within its framework, and will thus become subject to reconsideration and replacement. Note, however, that once the adequacy of a paradigm is questioned, the rules it provides can no longer simply be accepted, and scientists will find themselves in a situation in which they lack a sufficient body of rules to meet the demands of the classical model of rationality. I will discuss such periods shortly, but before doing so it is important to note that Kuhn's picture of normal science is highly controversial; how much of this analysis must we accept for our purposes here?

Kuhn's description of normal science has been vigorously attacked on a number of grounds. For example, Kuhn often writes as if a paradigm is accepted by all the scientists in a discipline, and that those who do not conform cease to be members of the research community, but it is not clear that science is quite so monolithic. Others find a considerable lack of clarity, and even of consistency, in Kuhn's descriptions of paradigms, and of the way they operate in science; Popper (1970) considers the very existence of normal science to be an effect of bad education. Fortunately, we only need one key idea from Kuhn's analysis, one for which there is substantial evidence: that many scientists do spend their professional lives solving problems within the framework of an accepted theory such as special relativity, or quantum theory, or evolutionary biology. They use these theories as a basis for their work, and do not consider themselves to be under a methodological injunction to test or to attempt to falsify these theories. It is worth noting that some of Kuhn's strongest critics agree on this point, and have attempted to improve on Kuhn's account of the nature of these accepted principles, and the way they operate in science. It will be instructive to consider two of these alternative proposals, due to by Imre Lakatos and Larry Laudan.

According to Lakatos (1970), the extra-logical guiding principles that organize scientific research are provided by a 'research programme'. This is a set of hypotheses that guides research in a discipline much the way that a Kuhnian paradigm does, but these hypotheses are explicit propositions that are divided into sets that do different jobs. One of these sets embodies what Lakatos calls the 'hard core' of the programme. This is a set of claims about nature that form the heart of the programme, and any alteration of this hard core amounts to the abandonment of that programme. But other, less central, claims are also involved in the detailed development of any research programme; these function as auxiliary premises that can be sacrificed without abandoning what is characteristic of the programme; they form the 'protective belt'. When problems arise, scientists seek to protect the hard core by modifying some of the claims in the protective belt. In addition, a research programme provides a 'positive heuristic' and a 'negative heuristic'. The former is a set of suggestions as to how to proceed in deploying the programme as a means of understanding nature. The negative heuristic is a set of injunctions as to how we should *not* proceed in developing the programme, and seems to amount to the general methodological demand that the hard core shall be protected.

Some brief examples may help clarify what Lakatos is up to here. Ancient astronomy may be viewed as a research programme for understanding and predicting planetary motions with two theses constituting its hard core: that the earth is stationary, and that all planetary motions are circular. In addition, there were a number of other principles that were added to this hard core at various times, and that were modified or abandoned as astronomers attempted to account for the observed planetary motions. For example, in early versions of the programme it was often assumed that the earth was at the center of all planetary motions, but attempts to develop a quantitatively correct version of the programme led astronomers to introduce departures from this hypothesis (i.e., epicycles and eccentrics, see Kuhn, 1959, ch. 2, for details), while maintaining the key assumptions that the earth is stationary and that all of the motions involved are circular. Copernicus' abandonment of a stationary earth was a much more radical departure, one that amounted to rejection of this programme. In a similar way, the hard core of Newton's research programme included the three laws of motion, and the existence of a central force law of universal gravitation. But the exact mathematical form of the gravitation law was not a part of the hard core. At various times small modifications of the gravitation law were proposed, e.g., adding an inverse fourth power term to handle a problem with the motion of the moon. Einstein's rejection of the idea that gravitation is to be understood as a *force* attacked the hard core, and amounted to the abandonment of the Newtonian programme.

Clearly a Lakatosian research programme does one key job that a Kuhnian paradigm does: it provides a guide for pursuing research and for dealing with observational results that significantly restricts the set of options available to the research scientist. Lakatos even maintains that as long as a scientist is pursuing the programme set out by the positive heuristic, she need not pay attention to apparent refutations (1970, pp. 134–8). Lakatos also maintains that a research programme will generate a series of different theories in the course of its history, and the hard core of the programme provides a set of common criteria for the acceptability of these theories. These criteria remain in force as long as researchers are working in that programme, but there are different hard cores, and thus different criteria for evaluating theories, in different disciplines, and in a single discipline at different points of its history. Thus Lakatos and Kuhn are in agreement on the crucial point that concerns me here: much scientific research is organized around substantive claims about some aspect of nature that function, for a time, as methodological principles not open to empirical refutation.

Now consider those portions of Laudan's (1977) approach that are relevant to the present discussion. Like Lakatos, Laudan argues that research is typically guided by a set of principles that transcends the particular theories in a discipline. Laudan calls these 'research traditions', and argues that they are less specific, and more capable of change, than a Lakatosian research programme. For Laudan, a research tradition is *a set of onto-logical and methodological "do's" and "don'ts"* (1977, p. 80) that become instantiated in a (possibly long) sequence of theories, and that can undergo change as the discipline develops. A research tradition lacks the unchanging hard core that Lakatos attributed to a research programme. Rather, as each new theory that falls under this tradition is proposed, some features of the tradition may be altered, but enough will remain unchanged so that we can consider ourselves to be dealing with a new avatar of the same tradition, rather than with a new research tradition. Two snap-shots of the same tradition taken far enough apart in time may not have a single item in common, but we will be able to trace a continuous development from the first version of the research tradition to its latest version. Again the key point that concerns me here is that scientific research requires such additional principles if it is to proceed in a coherent manner. Laudan allows for consider-able competition between research traditions at a given point in time, as well as for the possibility that a research tradition will be abandoned and replaced, and the considerations that come into play when scientists must choose between research traditions are very different from those involved in choices made within a single research tradition.

Let us return to Kuhn and consider the problems that arise when scientists are not working within a paradigm; we can approach these problems by considering the two remaining periods that Kuhn distinguishes in the history of a science. The first of these, which Kuhn refers to as a 'pre-paradigm period', occurs in a discipline before a first paradigm has been accepted. Such periods do not exhibit the kind of organized research that is characteristic of work when there is agreement on fundamentals. Instead, there are competing groups of scientists, each with their own ideas about the principles on which the field should be built; Kuhn describes the research of each group as scientific, but suggests that the net outcome of all the research occurring in the field is less than science (1970c, pp. ix, 13). In terms of the classical model of rationality, the work of individuals may be sufficiently rule-governed to conform to the demands of rationality, but cooperation between scientists is extremely difficult since they are, to a significant degree, operating in terms of different sets of rules. A pre-paradigm period comes to an end when one of these competing approaches is sufficiently successful for researchers to decide to give up their individual foundations and accept this approach as a basis for further research, thereby generating the first period of normal science in that discipline. Kuhn is convinced that the advantages of paradigm-governed research are so great that, once a paradigm is achieved, researchers in a field will never quite return to the chaos of the pre-paradigm period. Thus each scientific field passes through only one pre-paradigm period.

Note, however, that this first paradigm is accepted as a result of a decision on the part of people working in the field. It is not *proven* to be correct, and there does not exist a sufficient body of rules for deciding which approach should be accepted as a paradigm, or when this decision should be made. From the point of view of the classical model of rationality, such decisions are not rational, and Kuhn seems to be sufficiently under the allure of this model to describe the acceptance of a first paradigm as including an 'arbitrary element' (1970c, pp. 4–5). Two consequences of this description are important. First, if the choice of an initial paradigm is indeed arbitrary, it means that, appearances aside, the classical model of rationality requires that we consider the period of normal science that arises as a result of this decision as nonrational. We have already seen that once we accept a starting point and a set of rules, we can proceed in a rule-governed manner, but this is only a sham display of rationality if our starting point and rules are chosen arbitrarily. I will argue in chapter V that Kuhn denies that crucial scientific decisions are, on his view, nonrational, but he has certainly provided those who read him as an irrationalist with some textual basis for that interpretation.

Second, given this 'arbitrary element' in paradigm choice, along with the point that the paradigm guides research directed at a world that is not created by the paradigm, we should expect that this first paradigm will not be eternally adequate for dealing with all problems that arise.[4] Eventually, Kuhn thinks, a body of problems will appear that will prove sufficiently intractable for scientists in the field to begin to question the paradigm and to consider possible replacements. We now enter a period of 'revolutionary' or 'extraordinary' science, a period that has much in common with pre-paradigm science because foundations are again at issue, and there is no longer a sufficient set of rules for proceeding in a rational manner, as this has been classically conceived. Moreover, once a science enters into a revolutionary period, no previously accepted principles are sacrosanct. There is no sharp divide here between principles of methodology or even logic, on the one hand, and principles peculiar to the paradigm now in question. Rather, as scientists consider what can be preserved, and what must be abandoned, any previously accepted principles can come up for reconsideration. For example, the principle that every event must have a cause, and the long accepted assumption that Euclidean geometry describes the physical world (two of Kant's synthetic *a priori* principles) have been called into question; and we have already encountered a case in which a law of logic has been questioned in the service of substantive scientific results. More complex changes also occur. For example, the methodological thesis that scientific claims must be tested against observation has remained a constant, but what counts as an observation has undergone considerable development, both because of new technologies, and because of new constraints provided by scientific theories. I will return to this last example as we discuss scientific revolutions in the next section.

3.4 Scientific revolutions

According to Kuhn, a scientific revolution is a transition from a period of normal science based on a particular paradigm to a new period of normal science based on a different paradigm. As a result, new questions may be asked, new kinds of answers may be accepted, data may be interpreted in strikingly new ways, previously accepted observations may be rejected as inappropriate, new kinds of observations may be introduced, and more. In other words, the rules that guide scientific practice in the field undergo a sweeping transformation. I will refer to the periods through which such a transition takes place as periods of 'revolutionary science'; the key feature of these periods that concerns me here is that failures of rationality seem to threaten wherever we look.

Let us begin by considering the circumstances that might motivate scientists to enter a period of revolutionary science. Kuhn maintains that this occurs because important unsolved anomalies accumulate, and scientists begin to doubt the ability of the current paradigm to provide solutions; the field faces a crisis, and scientists begin to re-examine accepted foundations. Now this is a tricky idea. Kuhn maintains that there are always anomalies in every field, that these anomalies are a major source of research problems for normal science, and that much normal scientific research consists of attempts to show how these anomalies can be handled within the accepted paradigm.[5] In the course of normal research, some of these anomalies get resolved, some are shelved for reconsideration when the field is more advanced, and others become part of the fund of anomalies that eventually generates a crisis. From the point of view of the classical model of rationality, questions now come pouring in. When, we are impelled to ask, is an anomaly sufficiently serious to justify doubts about the paradigm? How long must a problem remain unresolved before it can legitimately contribute to such doubts? How many of these unresolved problems must we have before we enter a crisis period? What we want, of course, are rules for answering these questions, but Kuhn maintains that there are no rules. Logic and standard methodologies do not provide these rules, and paradigms do not include rules for deciding when they should be considered dubious. Either the decision that we are facing a crisis is ultimately nonrational, or, once again, something is amiss with the classical model of rationality.

Although I have taken Kuhn's views as the basis for raising the question of when it is legitimate to begin considering radical new alternatives, it is not necessary that Kuhn's analysis be correct in detail for this problem to arise. All we need in order to generate this question is the recognition that fundamental changes do occur in the development of science, along with the point that we do not have a sufficient set of rules for deciding when such changes are in order. Let me press this point by considering one important criticism of Kuhn's view that fundamentally new ideas are only introduced in response to crises generated by anomalies. By way of contrast, several writers have argued that revolutionary new ideas are often introduced without a crisis, and even that they sometimes appear during periods of complacency. This seems to have been the case in physics in the late nineteenth century, just prior to the appearance of relativity and quantum theory (see e.g., Feuer, 1982, pp. 252–68), as well as in biology prior to the emergence of Darwin's theory of evolution (Greene, 1980). In fact, this point seems to hold for two revolutions that Kuhn himself has studied in considerable detail: Copernican astronomy and early quantum theory. In discussing the former case Kuhn (1959) notes the reasons Copernicus gave for introducing a radical new hypothesis, but he provides no evidence for the kind of deep, widespread discontent that is supposedly characteristic of a crisis. After Copernicus, radical new proposals such as those due to Tycho Brahe and Kepler did begin to appear, and we can accept this as an example of the proliferation of theories that, according to Kuhn, we should find once we have entered a crisis period. But Copernicus' theory was one of the events that generated this crisis. Note also that Copernicus published his new theory in 1543, and that it posed a challenge to existing theological doctrines, but the Catholic Church did not suspend Copernicus' book until 1616 – six years after Galileo's telescopic discoveries provided important support for the new astronomy. A crisis mentality may have developed among adherents of traditional astronomy, but it did so only after the appearance of reasons for taking Copernicus' new theory seriously.

In the case of quantum theory, not only was there no perceived crisis when Planck introduced his new radiation law in 1900, but Kuhn argues that the radical significance of Planck's work was not recognized for many years. Thus Kuhn tells us that,

Only after Lorentz's Rome lecture [1908] does the physics profession at large seem to have been confronted by what shortly came to be called the ultraviolet catastrophe and thus by the need to choose between Jeans's theory and a non-classical version of Planck's. (1978, p. 195)

Kuhn goes on to note that it was another two years before 'Planck was at last firmly and publicly committed to the entry of discontinuity and the abandonment of some part of classical theory' (1978, p. 200). Planck's work was not a response to crisis, although it helped to generate a crisis.

New ideas may also precede the discovery of anomalies; this point has been pressed by Feyerabend on methodological grounds. Feyerabend argues that in many cases scientists only seek the evidence that casts doubt on an existing theory after a new proposal has led them to consider a new set of observations as worth making. In addition, Feyerabend notes that a direct empirical refutation of the second law of thermodynamics is 'beyond experimental possibilities' (1981, vol. 1, p. 72), but that this law has been refuted by Einstein's theoretical account of Brownian motion (1981, vol. 1, pp. 71–2).

I have introduced this alternative view only in order to note that the classical model of rationality leads to the same sorts of questions here as arise on Kuhn's analysis. At what point, we might ask, is it reasonable to begin proposing radically new ideas? Under what circumstances should scientists attend to new ideas, rather than getting on with the business of normal research? Should scientists continually seek new theories, as Feyerabend proposes, or should they avoid new theories and work in the existing paradigm as long as possible, as Kuhn thinks? Again we lack a sufficient set of rules for answering these questions, and it is difficult to see how these decisions could be rational on the classical model of rationality.

Now let us turn to revolutionary science itself, and consider what occurs once normal research has broken down. According to Kuhn, different individuals and groups will offer different proposals for a new foundation, and these proposals must be evaluated. But if a paradigm has been brought into question, the rules that it provides are also now in question. Thus we should expect that different proposals will, to some degree, embody sets of rules for the evaluation of proposals that differ from those of competing proposals, and from those provided by the old paradigm. Moreover, as was noted above, the debate may extend to issues that go beyond the specific content of the previous paradigm. Once fundamental questions are opened up, *any* aspect of the previous framework may be questioned, including theses that were accepted before that paradigm came on the scene, and theses that are currently central to other disciplines. Thus we have a dispute in progress in which one of the subjects at issue is what rules are to be used in settling the dispute. If we turn to the classical model of rationality for guidance, we will ask for a set of meta-rules to mediate between these competing rules. But this request is futile, and in order to recognize why it is futile, we need only accept Kuhn's historical point that fundamental changes do take place in science, along with the failure of foundationalism. The collapse of foundationalism with respect to both premises and rules forces us to recognize that there is no stage at which questioning *must* stop, no stage to which we can eventually retreat to find a sufficient set of truths and rules to mediate every dispute. Yet this might have been no more than an interesting possibility. The failure of foundationalism is an epistemic failure; it underlines a point about the limits of our knowledge of the truth of our premises and the adequacy of our rules. This epistemic failing is, however, completely compatible with our having in fact discovered a satisfactory starting point. If the history of science provided us with a steady accumulation of truths, with no major revolutions, then we would have strong grounds for believing that we had in fact stumbled onto such a starting point. It is the occurrence of the major revolutions that shows most clearly that, even in science, we have not achieved the universal basis for mediating disputes that the classical model of rationality requires. Thus, again, we must either reconsider the rationality of science, or reconsider the classical model of rationality. It will be useful to press this point by taking some examples of just how deeply scientific revolutions cut.

We have already noted that one of the pervasive nonlogical principles that guided research in classical physics was the thesis that every event must have a cause, a principle that Kant included among the synthetic *a priori* truths, yet this principle has been rejected in quantum theory. Our current understanding of the radioactive decay of a material such as radium provides a clear example of the methodological significance of this rejection. If we were working in classical physics we would attempt to discover what causes a particular atom of radium to decay at a specific time, and an account of radioactive decay that did not achieve this end would *ipso facto* be inadequate. But this criterion of adequacy is rejected in quantum theory. Quantum theory permits us to calculate the percentage of atoms in a quantity of radium that will decay in a given period of time, but it does not permit the determination of which atoms will decay, or of why one atom decays rather than another. Moreover, this is not a failing from the point of view of quantum theory. Classical physics and much philosophy notwithstanding, it is central to quantum theory that no such calculation is possible: all atoms in a sample of radium are identical prior to the radioactive decay of one of these, and there is just no reason why one of the atoms decays instead of another one.

If this sounds odd, it serves to emphasize that scientific revolutions involve deep transformations in the way we deal with an aspect of nature, including changes in the rules we use to evaluate the acceptability of an hypothesis. From the point of view of classical physics, an equation that allows us to determine accurately the number of radioactive decays per unit of time would be acceptable and interesting, but it could not be considered a complete solution to the problem of radioactive decay; in the framework of quantum mechanics it is a complete solution. But now consider a debate between a proponent of the causal principle and someone who thinks quantum theory is quite fine as it stands. The former might insist that there *must be* some deeper, underlying cause that accounts for the decay of a particular radium atom, and that scientists are required to search for that cause. The latter finds that no such search is needed, and might ask why she should look for hidden causes when she already has a theory that adequately predicts an enormous number of empirically testable phenomena. Whatever we might make of this, it is clear that it would be inappropriate to respond by insisting that every event must have a cause, and to do so would be on a par with insisting that Kepler's and Newton's views of the shapes of planetary orbits must be wrong, since these orbits are necessarily circular.

Let me take another example. One of the basic principles of special relativity is that no physical process can take place at a velocity greater than that of light. In order to be clear on what this means in the context of a theory which holds that all velocity is relative velocity, consider the following situation: you are standing on the ground and, by whatever method, you determine the velocity, v, of a passing jet. As the jet passes over your head it fires a missile in the forward direction, and this missile moves away from the jet at a velocity that the jet's pilot measures to be u. Problem: if you were to measure the velocity of the missile, what velocity would you find? It might seem obvious that the answer is $u + v$, and classical mechanics agrees, but this cannot be the correct answer in the framework of relativity. If, for example, v is half the speed of light, and u is three fourths the speed of light, their sum is greater than the velocity of light, which is forbidden. Of course, relativity does not leave the matter there; the principles of the theory entail a different rule for adding velocities. According to this rule, $u + v$ must be divided by the square root of $1 + (uv/c)$, where c is the velocity of light. Note that this formula will never give a velocity greater than the velocity of light, e.g., if the velocities to be combined are both equal to c, the formula predicts that the net velocity is also c. Note also that the velocity of light is enormous, and we require velocities in the neighborhood of half the velocity of light before we get an easily measurable difference between the relativistic prediction and the results of simple addition. We do not normally encounter such large velocities and it requires fairly recent technology to produce them in the laboratory; thus we can understand why the discrepancy was not noticed for so long.

What is especially interesting about this example is that before the advent of relativity people did not think of the velocity addition formula as internal to a particular physical theory and as subject to empirical reconsideration. Rather, it was considered obvious. But it would be a mistake to insist that the simple addition formula is intuitively correct, and that special relativity must, therefore, be wrong. Indeed, to argue that relativity must be wrong because it rejects an obviously correct addition formula is to enter into just the sort of debate that we have been considering: one in which we evaluate a proposal on the basis of criteria that advocates of that proposal reject. A proponent of relativity can just as well argue that classical mechanics must be wrong exactly because it retains the simple addition formula.

Note also that it would be wrong to insist that the older formula must be correct as a matter of simple arithmetic. Just as we have had to learn that there are different geometries, and that we cannot decide *a priori* which of these fits the physical world, so there are different arithmetics, i.e., different rules for combining numerical quantities, and we cannot decide *a priori* which rules apply to which empirical situations. To take another example, suppose we have an electric circuit with pairs of similar circuit elements connected in series, and we wish to replace certain pairs with a single equivalent element. If we seek to replace two resistors, it turns out that the equivalent resistance will in fact be equal to the sum of the two original resistances; but the equivalent replacement for a pair of capacitors must be determined by a different rule, and it will be less than the capacitance of either of our original capacitors. In all cases the correct rule for combining physical quantities into a single equivalent must be determined by experience, and even when there is much evidence supporting the adequacy of a particular formula, further experience may lead us to conclude that a different formula is correct. This is just another example of the limitations of induction, but it is worth emphasizing because of the ease with which we tend to forget that familiar results are based on induction, and come to believe, instead, that we have some sort of intuitive insight into their truth.

Throughout the preceding discussion I have taken it as a given that observation plays a central role in choosing between scientific hypotheses. Observational data has long been viewed as providing a basis for evaluating theories that is independent of the content of any theory, and one powerful reason for maintaining that what we sense is independent of the theories that we hold derives from the fact that our sensations are determined by the biology of our sense organs and by the stimuli that impinge on them. But even if this claim about our sensations is correct, it does not establish that what we observe is independent of the theories that we hold; bare awareness of sensations does not constitute scientific observation. To see why, recall our previous example of the quasar and the blob that appear to be moving away from each other at a velocity in excess of the velocity of light. If the astronomers who encountered this phenomenon were working in the framework of classical physics they would have simply reported an observation of one object moving away from another object at a particular velocity with no further analysis; and they might have taken this to be a theory-neutral description. But the apparent theory-neutrality of this description dissolves as soon as we contrast the relativistic case, where this cannot be an acceptable observation report – at least not in the sense in which we test theories against observation reports. Instead, scientists will look for an account of what is occurring that meets the demands of relativity, and then describe what they have observed in terms of this account. In other words, the observation reports that are appealed to in the process of evaluating scientific theories cannot be identified with theory-independent descriptions of what we sense.

Let us consider another example. According to special relativity, a moving object contracts in the direction of motion; suppose we attempt to test this claim by taking an object that is spherical when it is at rest, and observing it as it moves by at a high velocity. We might think we could carry out this observation by looking at the moving object, perhaps with the aid of binoculars, but this is a mistake, although it is one that many physicists once made (cf. Weisskopf, 1972, pp. 238–47). The problem derives from the fact that relativity only permits us to make observations at the point in space at which we are located, but not observations of distant objects – this is a direct consequence of the rejection of simultaneity at a distance. In order to test the claim that the moving object contracts, this contraction must be measured in a frame of reference that coincides with the object's path. We might, for example, set up a measuring rod along that path, and a series of synchronized clocks along the rod. We can now measure the length of the sphere by recording the coordinates of its two extremities at a single time as shown by these clocks. If we do this, we will find that the length of the object, as indicated by the difference between the two coordinates, is less when the sphere is in motion than the distance measured in the same way when the sphere is at rest. But this does not entail that the object will look foreshortened to a distant observer. In order to determine what we might see, we must trace the paths of light rays from the moving object to the observer's eye, and when this is done it turns out that the sphere will look spherical. There is no inconsistency here since looking at a distant object is not a legitimate form of observation in the context of relativity. In other words, while the appeal to observation may in fact be a universal feature of science, *what counts as an observation can change when*

111

our theoretical framework changes. There is a vast body of 'data' that was considered observational in classical mechanics, but that does not count as observational in a relativistic framework, because relativity imposes much tighter constraints on observation than does classical mechanics. The classical model of rationality suggests that we seek rules to determine what counts as an observation, but any set of rules that we propose can be challenged by a scientific theory, and these rules do not transcend the content of science. (For further discussion see Shapere, 1982; Brown, 1987.)

Let me summarize the key point of this long discussion. What I have been trying to show is that the rules in accordance with which scientific decisions are made change as science develops. From one point of view this should not be surprising, for there is no more reason to assume that we know how to study nature before we begin, than for assuming that we can know nature itself *a priori*. Still, the fact that the rules change shows that they do not meet the conditions of universality and necessity imposed by the classical model of rationality, and thus that science does not meet the conditions for a rational activity embodied in that model. We now have several options before us. We can conclude that science is not rational, and a small number of philosophers have accepted this conclusion. Or we can continue to search for the rules that will allow us to maintain both the classical model and the rationality of science – after all, we have not proven beyond a shadow of a doubt that no such rules will ever be found. Many philosophers of science have opted to carry on this search. Or we can conclude that the classical model of rationality must be replaced. I will argue in chapter V that this is the conclusion Kuhn has drawn, and this is the option that I will develop here. Before doing so, however, there is one more issue that should be considered.

One consequence of our discussion of science is that it opens the door to a number of forms of relativism. Some degree of relativism is clearly involved in scientific decision-making if this analysis is correct, but it would certainly be a mistake to jump from a rejection of the classical model of rationality to the conclusion that no important scientific decisions can be made in a nonarbitrary manner. The issues involved here cannot be fully considered until we have an alternative model of rationality, but there is one form of extreme relativism that should be discussed before we proceed. Proponents of this view argue that the rules which govern science are internal to science, and that there are other human activities that are also governed by rules internal to them. But if this is the case, there may be no legitimate grounds for taking science, rather than one of these other activities, e.g., religion or business or magic, as a test case for a model of rationality. I want to develop and assess this line of argument.

3.5 *Social relativism*

The most extreme forms of relativism hold that each individual can assess cognitive claims however she may choose; no two individuals need share any standards of evaluation, nor need a single individual apply the same standards from moment to moment. Such a view verges on incoherence. The very notion that there might be 'standards of evaluation' loses its point if these standards can be chosen arbitrarily, and this view would seem to be incompatible with any notion of rationality. Nor does our discussion in this chapter suggest this sort of relativism. At most our discussion suggests that standards for evaluating scientific claims vary between different scientific *communities* at different stages in the development of science, and this points to a variety of *social relativism*. On that view there are indeed criteria for the acceptability of knowledge claims, and individuals must behave in accordance with those criteria, but these criteria are internal to a culture or a social group, and can vary from one group to another.[6] To revert to an earlier example, classical physics and quantum theory do not use the same standards for evaluating scientific claims, and a scientist working within one of these frameworks must evaluate claims in terms of the standards of evaluation appropriate to that framework. A social relativist will maintain that each of these frameworks has its own criteria of rationality, and that there is no independent basis for deciding whether one framework is more rational than the other.

Social relativism originally developed in the course of attempts to understand how values vary between social groups, but I will not be concerned with values here. In recent years the social relativist view has been extended to cognitive matters, and in particular to science. If the standards for evaluating scientific claims change across a scientific revolution, it follows that science is not built on a universal foundation that stands independently of the specific beliefs that groups of people hold. This has been seen as an opening wedge for arguing that science itself is only a feature of modern Western society. On this view, all societies build cognitive structures that explain the world around them and guide them in their dealings with that world. Modern Western science is one such cognitive structure, and as such is no better or worse than those developed by other societies in other parts of the world, or by Western societies at other periods of history, or than a number of other structures that coexist with science.

If this view is correct, there is something fundamentally wrong with the project of this chapter and this book. My aim in this book is to develop a model of rationality that will have application beyond the culture in which I happen to live, and part of the basis for this claim will be that the view of rationality that we eventually arrive at will capture those features of science which make it a paradigmatically rational enterprise. If, as social relativists claim, 'scientific rationality' is just different from, say, 'magical rationality', while each of these is equally 'rational' when taken on its own terms, then the attempt to use science as the central test case for a trans-social model of rationality must fail.

In this section I will argue that there is something fundamentally wrong with the relativist view of science and with the arguments on behalf of that view. In the final chapter, after we have developed a new model of rationality, I will return to this question and offer positive reasons for holding that while science did indeed develop in the Western world, there are still powerful grounds for maintaining that scientific procedures and results have a significance that transcends the particular culture in which they appeared. I want to emphasize that I will *not* be arguing that *only* science has trans-social significance; as far as the discussion in this book is concerned, it will remain an open question whether other human endeavors also have such significance, and if so, which they are. But I will be arguing for one instance of a thesis that might have wider application: that while human thinkers always operate in terms of concepts and criteria that appeared in a particular culture, they are nonetheless capable of discovering results that transcend their culture.

I will develop the argument of the present section in three stages. First, I will present the case for social relativism with respect to knowledge in general, and science in particular. Second, I will attempt to show that there are fundamental defects in the arguments for this position, as well as in the position itself. Third, I will argue that both the apparent plausibility of social relativism, and the source of its major defects, lie in the tacit acceptance by its advocates of the classical model of rationality. We will then, finally, be ready to begin developing an alternative model of rationality.

There are two major, but interlocking, lines of argument for the social relativist thesis: the first derives from the results of cultural anthropology, the second from considerations of the nature of language and its role in human cognition. I will begin with the former.

We all grow up and learn to think in a particular society, and it seems common for us to assume that the manners and mores we are familiar with are 'natural'. This is not surprising, given that many of us never encounter widely different ways of life, and that we are often in fact unable to imagine sane people who live and think in very different ways from us. For many tribal people, the term in their language for members of their tribe and the term for 'human being' are identical, with the implication that outsiders are not fully human. From this perspective, extended encounters with other cultures can be rather sobering. An early example of this in the Western world was provided by the medieval crusades, which brought Western Christians into contact with the Moslem world, and which eventually forced a grudging recognition among some that it was indeed possible for there to be non-Christians who had a sophisticated, functioning culture. Cultural anthropology regularly brings its practitioners into extended contact with people from other cultures, and anthropologists have expended considerable effort in attempting to come to terms with these people. Early anthropologists tended to assume that non-Western, non-technologically developed people were intellectually inferior to us, and that this accounted for their multifarious differences. One version of this view had it that tribal peoples were at an earlier stage on an evolutionary scale than us, and were, in effect, our 'contemporary ancestors'. Another version, due to Levy-Bruhl, maintained that there is a 'primitive mentality', characterized by a 'pre-logical' mode of thought, which explains why these people believe in magic, and why they failed to develop modern science and technology on their own.

These views have generally been rejected by contemporary anthropologists, and Levy-Bruhl has retracted his views on primitive mentality. There is simply no reason for believing that tribal people differ from us either intellectually or in evolutionary terms. Moreover, these people generally have rich, complex cultures, even though these cultures are very different from our own, and there is every reason for believing that if you or I had been brought up in, say, an African tribe, we would have learned and accepted their culture just as we have learned and accepted our own. There is an important parallel here between cultures and languages, for different as languages may be, any normal human infant will learn the language of the society in which she grows up. This has led to a fundamental methodological principle for the practice of anthropology: ethnocentrism – the habit of evaluating other cultures on the basis of how they compare with our own culture – must be avoided. A major aim of anthropology is to provide detailed descriptions of various cultures, and in doing so, it is argued, anthropologists must refrain from making judgements based on norms that the people being studied do not share. This is particularly true in dealing with cognitive matters: anthropologists attempt to understand how these people experience the world they live in, even if they do so in terms of concepts that are alien to a scientific world view, and it becomes extremely difficult to achieve this understanding if we are continually judging their views on the basis of our own. Yet once we suspend the judging eye, it becomes clear that there are many long-lived societies which deal with the world around them quite successfully, even though they do so in very different ways from us. Moreover, these people often have great stores of knowledge that we lack – as anyone who contemplates attempting to survive on her own in the arctic or the bush will quickly realize.

As a methodological principle this is unobjectionable, and it is not difficult to see how the line of argument that has taken us this far can easily lead us one step further. Suppose we wish to maintain that, at least in science, we have created a body of knowledge that is not just different from those beliefs that developed in other cultures, but cognitively superior. It would seem to be very difficult to avoid the charge of lurking ethnocentrism here. For although we would like to claim that our scientific beliefs are objectively founded, we are in the uncomfortable position of claiming that this objectivity accrues to an item from our own culture. It is not clear how, as members of this culture, we arrive at a position from which we can objectively assess these claims for science, and it seems to be a good general rule that we should be especially sceptical of any supposedly objective comparison between cultures that leads to the conclusion that what is familiar is superior to what is unfamiliar. Unfortunately, members of other cultures are in no better position in this regard. All cognitively developed individuals are members of some culture, and deal with the world in terms of the norms and concepts that are character-istic of their society. Thus it seems difficult to make good on the claim that an objective assessment of science is possible. What grounds do we have, then, for holding that some beliefs from our culture have a different status from those we find in other cultures? Presumably, the cognitive superiority of science would not seem so obvious had we been brought up in another culture, and it becomes difficult to locate any clear difference between claiming that our science transcends our culture, and claiming this for our religions or our choice of foods.

We can develop this point in another way by considering the difficult notions of 'reality' and 'truth'. One standard account of the special status of science turns on the claim that scientific results are true, and that their truth consists in the fact that they correctly describe a reality that is independent of any of our beliefs. But how do we determine whether a claim does in fact accord with reality? Recall here one result of our earlier discussions. In so far as the procedures by which we decide whether to accept or reject a scientific claim are logical procedures, we do not actually test our claims against 'reality', but only against other propositions. At every step of the evaluation process we are dealing with linguistic formulations and with relations between linguistic formulations, and are thus continually working within the framework of our language. Now this would generate no special problems if language were simply a vehicle for reporting what we found out there in the world – indeed, it would be enough if this were true only of that part of our language that we use to describe the observations that form the basis for empirical testing of scientific hypotheses. In this case we would not be testing complex scientific claims against reality directly, but we would be testing them against a universally available, theory-independent, touchstone. But there are reasons for doubting that language works in this way, and for maintaining instead that our recognition of even the most elementary 'facts' is colored by features of our language. On this view, the possession of a language is a central feature of all human cultures, different languages are structured in different ways, and to a large degree the structure of our language determines how we experience the world around us, how we report what we experience, and what we take to be 'the facts'. One of the early exponents of this view, Benjamin Whorf, puts it this way:

> The point of view of linguistic relativity changes Mr.
> Everyman's dictum: Instead of saying, 'Sentences are unlike
> because they tell about unlike facts,' he now reasons: 'Facts
> are unlike to speakers whose language background provides
> for unlike formulation of them.' (1956, p. 235)

Thus Whorf introduces

> a new principle of relativity, which holds that all observers are
> not led by the same physical evidence to the same picture of
> the universe, unless their linguistic backgrounds are similar,
> or can in some way be calibrated. (1956, p. 214)

I want to sketch some of the evidence that Whorf cites to support this claim.

As a first example consider the notion of 'time', one of the central concepts involved in our everyday dealings with the world and with each other, and a central scientific concept. One important characteristic of our familiar understanding of time is that we tend to think that definite quantities of time pass independently of us, and this is captured in such customs as the production of uniform clocks and calendars which allow us to count the time that has passed since our last pay day, or the number of days remaining until a birthday. Our ability to do this, Whorf argues, derives from certain features of the grammar of our language, in particular, our ability to speak of both

> perceptible spatial aggregates and metaphorical aggregates.

We say 'ten men' and also 'ten days.' Ten men either are or could be objectively perceived as ten, ten in one group perception – ten men on a street corner for instance. But 'ten days' cannot be objectively experienced. We experience only one day, today. . . . (1956, p. 139)

Whorf contends that we would not be able to think of groups of days and count days as individual units if we were speaking and thinking in the Hopi language, which does not permit the construction of such imaginary aggregates. This can be illustrated by noting that in Hopi the word for 'day' cannot be pluralized. We can see the significance of this by noting that in English, as well as in other Western languages, we cannot pluralize proper names such as 'Mary Smith'.[7] As a result, Whorf argues, we are *constrained by the grammar of our language* to think of two successive appearances of Mary Smith as the reappearance of a single individual, rather than as the appearance of two different individuals. We may be inclined to claim that we are just reporting facts, and that there is only one Mary Smith who reappears, but Whorf maintains that this is only because we are thoroughly enmeshed in the version of the 'facts' that is filtered through our language. In a similar way, we think of days as distinct individuals because we are able to pluralize 'day'. Since Hopi grammar does not permit 'day' to be pluralized, the Hopi think of successive 'days' in a way that is analogous to the way we think of Mary Smith, i.e., as if there were a single individual day that keeps returning.

Now just as our way of thinking about time is deeply implicated in many of our most characteristic customs – the way we divide up our lives into times to work, times to play and so forth – so the way the Hopi think of time is related to many aspects of their culture. For example, activities aimed at altering the course of future events are analogous in the Hopi perspective to our attempts to alter a person's future behavior:

Hopi 'preparing' activities . . . show a result of their linguistic thought background in an emphasis on persistence and insistent constant repetition. . . . As we have seen, it is as if the return of the day were felt as the return of the same person, a little older but with all the impresses of yesterday, not as 'another day,' i.e. like an entirely different person. This principle joined with that of thought-power and with

119

traits of general Pueblo culture is expressed in the theory of the Hopi ceremonial dance for furthering rain and crops, as well as in its short, piston-like tread, repeated thousands of times, hour after hour. (1956, pp. 151–2)

We have here a different vision of the world from the one we are familiar with, but it would be a mistake to claim that it is an inferior vision. Rather, Whorf maintains,

the Hopi language is capable of accounting for and describing correctly, in a pragmatic or operational sense, all observable phenomena of the universe. . . . Just as it is possible to have any number of geometries other than the Euclidean which give an equally perfect account of space configurations, so it is possible to have descriptions of the universe, all equally valid, that do not contain our familiar contrasts of time and space. (1956, p. 58)

It would be difficult to overstate how seriously this claim is intended. Whorf insists that 'various grand generalizations of the Western world, such as time, velocity, and matter, are not essential to the construction of a consistent picture of the universe' (1956, p. 216), and he proceeds to sketch parts of an alternative physics built in terms of the Hopi framework:

How would a physics constructed along these lines work, with no T (time) in its equations? Perfectly, as far as I can see, though of course it would require different ideology and perhaps different mathematics. Of course V (velocity) would have to go too. The Hopi language has no word really equivalent to our 'speed' or 'rapid.' (1956, p. 217)

The central concept of this alternative physics, Whorf suggests, would be a kind of 'relative intensity', and a wide variety of phenomena that we now tend to consider as fundamentally different would come to be grouped together as instances of this basic parameter – Whorf mentions acceleration, electric charge, rates of chemical reactions, and the difference between a good horse and a lazy horse (1956, pp. 217–18).

This last point brings us to another crucial respect in which our language affects our understanding of the world: our language determines which of the items we encounter are to be considered members of the same class – and thus, for cognitive purposes, identical – and which are different; but different languages make this division in different ways.[8] Again, Whorf is a rich source of illustrations. For example, we would consider the two sentences 'I pull the branch aside' and 'I have an extra toe on my foot', as well as the phenomena they describe, to have little in common. The Shawanee, however, would very likely see things differently. They would tend to focus on the forked shape of the two configurations and see them as virtually identical – and their linguistic descriptions of the two cases differ only in the final syllable, *ni-l'thawa-'ko-n-a* for the first case, and *ni-l'thawa-'ko-thite* for the second (Whorf, 1956, pp. 233–4, substituting 'th' for Whorf's theta). On the other hand,

> the English sentences, 'The boat is grounded on the beach' and 'The boat is manned by picked men' seem to us to be rather similar. Each is about a boat; each tells the relation of the boat to other objects – or that's OUR story. (1956, p. 235)

But in the 'Nootka language of Vancouver Island' the two linguistic expressions are quite different, agreeing in only a single syllable, and 'Neither sentence contains any unit of meaning akin to our word "boat" or even "canoe"' (1956, p. 236). Illustrations of this point can be derived from the history of science as well. In the language of medieval astronomy, for example, the earth was not a planet and the sun was not a star, although this changed after the acceptance of Copernican astronomy.

Still, we are tempted to ask, what about reality itself? Would it not be more accurate to say that reality is what it is, and that different ways of describing it are attempts, more or less successful, to capture that reality? The social relativist response is that this view has things backwards. To put the thesis in its sharpest form, the only 'reality' we know anything about is the reality that we encounter through the framework of our language. People with different languages thus live in terms of different realities, and can legitimately be described as knowing different truths in the sense in which a true statement must conform to reality. Modern science, in these terms, provides us with one more language, and thus one more reality, and one more set of truths – but the resultant scientific reality is real only for those who speak the language of science, and its truths are true only for the members of this linguistic community: 'Every society has its own particular view of reality, its own universe of thought indeed its own universe of truth' (W. Stark, *Sociology of Knowledge*, quoted in Tennekes, 1971, p. 175, n. 70). In a similar vein, David Silverman, discussing Carlos Castaneda's reports of his experiences with the Yaqui Shaman Don Juan, considers the question of whether Castaneda 'really' flew after taking a psychedelic drug, and concludes:

> To speak is to locate oneself within a way of knowledge. Hence we are able to recognize experiences, find out facts and check assertions because we know *already*, as members of some language community, what it is (properly) to do all these things. So to see as a Yaqui sees is to see men fly with the devil's weed. And there is no '*neutral*' way of testing this assertion. For not to see men fly with the devil's weed is simply not to see the Yaqui way. . . . (1975, p. 19)

Many proponents of this position maintain that it receives support from the views of language found in the later work of Ludwig Wittgenstein.[9] Wittgenstein's early work was an attempt to defend the view that there is one language that correctly mirrors the structure of reality, and that properly constructed claims about the world must be couched in that language. In his later work Wittgenstein rejected that thesis and developed a new approach to understanding language; the following sketch of Wittgenstein's new view relies heavily on the account in Peter Winch's *The Idea of a Social Science* (1958, pp. 24–33), one of the major attempts to apply Wittgenstein's ideas to the issues that concern us here.

Consider, first, referring terms, i.e., terms such as 'Mount Everest', which refer to some particular object: how does it come about that I can mean this particular object when I utter 'Mount Everest'? We can approach this question by considering how I might have learned the meaning of this term. The classic answer is that this is done by means of ostensive definition: I learned this meaning when someone pointed to the mountain, or some representation of it, and uttered the words 'Mount Everest'. And a similar analysis has been applied to generic terms, e.g., we presumably learned the meaning of the word 'red' when someone uttered this word while pointing to a variety of red objects. But

Wittgenstein suggests that this analysis cannot be correct because there are crucial ambiguities involved in the pointing process. In order to use a term correctly, the language learner must learn to apply it in cases other than the ones that were used to teach the term, i.e., she must learn the *rule* involved in recognizing new situations to which the word can be applied. But the suggestion that this rule can be abstracted from ostensive definitions is most implausible. How is the language learner *who has not yet mastered the conventions involved in the teacher's language* to know that the teacher is indicating this particular mountain, rather than the generic mountain, or the space between herself and the mountain, or perhaps the pointing finger? To put the point another way, to learn the meaning of a word I must learn the rule for determining which situations are to be considered *identical* for purposes of the use of this word, and the old story about ostensive definitions does not explain how this occurs even in the case of referring expressions. In addition, ostensive definition certainly does not account for our learning to use such terms as 'and', 'or', 'please' and 'thank you'. 'So the question: What is it for a word to have a meaning? leads on to the question: What is it for someone to follow a rule?' (Winch, 1958, p. 28).

In order to deal with this new question, consider someone who is carrying out a sequence of acts, and let us ask under what circumstances it would be legitimate to say that she is following a rule. One possible answer – that she is following a rule if we can find a rule that fits the sequence – must be rejected. As we saw earlier in our discussion of induction, it is always possible to find a rule that fits any finite sequence of events; if the rule leads to incorrect predictions about new members of the sequence, we can always start again and find a different rule that covers the available members of that sequence. Thus the fact that I can find a rule that fits all of the available cases does not imply that our subject is following this rule, or even that she is following any rule at all. Still, if all attempts to formulate the rule fail – if, no matter how hard we try, and no matter how many consultants we employ, every prediction that we make on the basis of a proposed rule is rejected as incorrect – then we would begin to have good reasons for doubting that any rule is in fact being followed (other than the trivial rule always to thwart the investigator).

All of this suggests a very important feature of the concept of following a rule. It suggests that one has to take account not only of the actions of the person whose behaviour is in question as a candidate for the category of rule-following, but also the *reactions of other people* to what he does. More specifically, it is only in a situation in which it makes sense to suppose that somebody else could in principle discover the rule which I am following that I can intelligibly be said to follow a rule at all. (Winch, 1958, p. 30)

Consider the same point from another direction. Suppose we observe someone who is generating a sequence of items. If we were to allow that this person is acting in accordance with a rule that cannot, in principle, be discovered, there would be no way in which she could be found to be mistaken about the next item in the sequence, since we lack a criterion for determining members of that sequence. But Winch maintains that this is unintelligible:

> the notion of following a rule is logically inseparable from the notion of *making a mistake*. If it is possible to say of someone that he is following a rule that means that one can ask whether he is doing what he does correctly or not. Otherwise there is no foothold in his behaviour in which the notion of a rule can take a grip. . . . (1958, p. 32)

In other words, rules function evaluatively: they provide not only a means of guiding behavior, but a standard for judging the correctness of behavior. It is because I have mastered the rules involved in using my language that I can teach this usage to another person, and point out that someone is misusing a term. But a standard cannot operate meaningfully unless we can refer to something independent of an individual's behavior in order to determine if that standard is indeed being followed. In the absence of such an independent check, we would have returned to the incoherent notion that someone might be following a rule even though it is in principle impossible for anyone to discover that this person had failed to follow the rule correctly.

This brings us to the next problem: where are we to find standards that transcend individual behavior? If there were a Platonic heaven that contained the meanings of words, and to which we could refer to determine if our linguistic behavior was correct, this problem would be solved. Unfortunately, no such realm exists, and Wittgenstein suggests that the required standard is provided by the body of people who use my language. In other words, linguistic rules are essentially social rules: such rules exist 'in' the members of the society that use those rules, and would cease to exist if that society went out of existence.

We can now tie this view of language up with our earlier discussion by noting that there is nothing in our physical environment that imposes one set of linguistic rules on us rather than another. In particular, we cannot appeal to some pre-linguistic awareness of the world in order to determine what kinds of entities it contains, and thus what sorts of things we should have words for. In order to do this, we must first have criteria for deciding what items are to be treated as 'the same', and we do not have these criteria until we have a language. Moreover, in the absence of such criteria we are not, properly speaking, dealing with a *world* at all, since this notion requires that there be some coherence, some order, in whatever we are dealing with, and no such order can appear until we have criteria for identity. Thus there is no world for us to experience and know independently of a language, and in this sense our language constitutes our world:

> Our idea of what belongs to the realm of reality is given for us in the language that we use. The concepts we have settle for us the form of the experience we have of the world. . . . The world *is* for us what is presented through those concepts. That is not to say that our concepts may not change; but when they do, that means that our concept of the world has changed too. (Winch, 1958, p. 15)

Finally, the view that our language constitutes our world, along with the thesis of the social nature of language, leads directly to the claim that reality is 'socially constructed'.

We can now see more clearly why social relativism provides a challenge that we must contend with here. According to this view, it makes perfectly good sense *within a society* to distinguish truth from falsity and reality from illusion; but when we attempt to evaluate the ways in which these distinctions are made in one social structure in terms of the framework of another social structure our attempt becomes incoherent. Thus Winch writes:

125

Magic, in a society in which it occurs, plays a peculiar role of its own and is conducted according to considerations of its own . . . to try to understand magic by reference to the aims and nature of scientific activity . . . will necessarily be to *mis*understand it. (1958, pp. 99–100)

And,

It follows that one cannot apply criteria of logic to modes of social life as such. For instance, science is one such mode and religion is another; and each has criteria of intelligibility peculiar to itself. So within science or religion actions can be logical or illogical: in science, for example, it would be illogical to refuse to be bound by the results of a properly carried out experiment; in religion it would be illogical to suppose that one could pit one's own strength against God's; and so on. But we cannot sensibly say that either the practice of science itself or that of religion is illogical or logical. . . . (1958, pp. 100–1)

This is the version of social relativism that concerns me, and we must now examine how well the arguments on its behalf stand up, and how powerful a threat they pose to the attempt to build a model of rationality that transcends my culture.

I want to begin by discussing what is probably the oldest and most commonly cited argument against social relativism. We can approach this argument by noting that while relativism is indeed widely approved among anthropologists and other social scientists, it is by no means universally accepted even in this field. (See Tennekes, 1971, for discussion and references.) This is not surprising since, if taken literally, the anthropological arguments on behalf of social relativism become self-defeating. (See Jarvie, 1984, Parts 2 and 3 for an extended discussion in the context of both cognitive and moral relativism.) These arguments are aimed at showing that the results of Western science have no validity beyond the culture in which they have emerged, but the arguments in question are themselves dependent on our accepting the results of one particular Western science – anthropology. This is not a quibble. Anthropology is a modern Western science, one which is not found in, say, ancient Greek or medieval cultures, nor in the societies that have provided the basis for much of the anthropological argument on behalf of relativism, and relativism is incompatible with the central beliefs of those societies. If we were to take social relativism literally, we would have to conclude that this view is true for a subculture of contemporary Western thinkers, period. Clearly, the intended scope of the doctrine is much greater than this. The thrust of the doctrine seems to be that we should, universally, recognize that people's modes of cognition are a feature of their culture, not just that this is true for anthropologists, yet it is extremely difficult to see why we have a basis for adopting *this* view as universally true, while withholding such status from, for example, the view that the earth is not flat, that the stars are much farther away than many people think they are, that many diseases are caused by micro-organisms, or that people who take psychedelic drugs do not fly. It seems that those who cite anthropological data in support of the doctrine of social relativism are, in effect, reserving a special cognitive position for their own particular science, and have done so without providing any grounds for making this exception. From a social relativist perspective, they would seem to be open to a charge of extreme ethnocentrism.

The same point can be made from another direction. Social relativism is itself a particularly striking example of a view that has not only emerged as a result of Western science, but that is only accepted by a small number of highly sophisticated individuals. As we have noted, tribal people are not relativists, they generally believe that the members of their own tribe occupy a privileged place in the universe, and that their beliefs are true, *simpliciter*. Nor is the doctrine of relativism accepted by all subcultures in the Western world. In the United States, for example, there has been vigorous opposition to the teaching of relativism in the schools, opposition at least as great as the opposition to the teaching of evolution. What are we to make of the beliefs of members of these cultures and subcultures? Again, if taken literally, social relativism would require that we conclude that these various anti-relativist views are true for the members of the groups that hold them, and that social relativism itself is simply one more view that characterizes one particular social group.

Many of those who write in defense of relativism have noted this problem. Consider, for example, the opening paragraph of Silverman's book on Castaneda:

Sociology rests on a happy irony. It seeks to study socially organized practices. Equally, it itself is inevitably a socially organized practice. Sociological descriptions, methods and claims to truth are brought off and recognized (like lay descriptions, methods and claims to truth) by and for members of a certain community. (1975, p. ix)

And somewhat later:

in describing the world, social scientists necessarily constitute its character (for them). In getting themselves 'closer' to 'the way things are', they commit themselves to the ways of speaking that their community makes available to them. Hence their descriptions are intelligible and their explanations testable only *within* the language-game which they (tacitly) propose; only *within* the mode of existence in which we recognize and could want to play such games. (1975, p. 23)

Silverman notes that this generates 'the threat of an infinite regress' (1975, p. x) and suggests that it leaves social scientists with the task of explaining how they can produce intelligible accounts of societies in spite of this, but he does not take up this task. Similarly, Berger and Luckmann write:

How can I be sure, say, of my sociological analysis of American middle-class mores in view of the fact that the categories I use for this analysis are conditioned by historically relative forms of thought, that I myself and everything I think is determined by my genes and by my ingrown hostility to my fellowmen, and that, to cap it all, I am myself a member of the American middle class? (1967, p. 13)

Their response is to insist that such epistemological issues cannot be included in a sociological analysis of knowledge:

To include epistemological questions concerning the validity of sociological knowledge in the sociology of knowledge is somewhat like trying to push a bus in which one is riding. . . . Far be it from us to brush aside such questions. All we would contend here is that these questions are not themselves part of the empirical discipline of sociology. They properly belong to the methodology of the social sciences, an enterprise that

belongs to philosophy and is by definition other than
sociology. . . . (1967, p. 13)

Yet Berger and Luckmann go on to argue that reality is 'socially
constructed' and they are prepared to interpret many forms of
cognition in these terms. It seems odd, then, that they evade the
analysis of their own discipline in this perspective, especially since
they attribute a generality to their results which is insupportable
if they are only examining a reality which is constructed by
sociologists.

There are two issues that present themselves at this point. One
has already been raised, but it is worth repeating: what are we to
make of the large number of social groups that do not accept the
thesis that their 'descriptions, methods and claims to truth' are
only true for members of their community, or that their views
'are conditioned by historically relative forms of thought'? Second,
if we take seriously Berger and Luckmann's attempt to evade the
epistemological problem that they raise, then we are surely justified in doing the same for other sciences, and in particular, we
are justified in accepting the view implicit in much work in, say,
physics and biology, that reality is not socially constructed at all,
and that results in these sciences can be considered trans-socially
valid.

Essentially the same points hold for the relativistic arguments
based on Wittgenstein's philosophy of language. This too is
treated as a correct theory of how language works, not just as the
view of a particular group of twentieth century Western thinkers.
Silverman argues for this view of language, and sums up his
conclusion thus: 'Words do not represent things. They are not
pictures of things, accurate or otherwise' (1975, p. 27). But there
are many social groups that reject this view of language, some
implicitly and some explicitly. For example, many forms of magic
depend on the belief that words do represent things. Yet we find
writers arguing that this piece of a magical world view is wrong,
and attempting to use the falsity of this view of language as a
basis for maintaining that a magical world view is wholly adequate
on its own terms. The appropriate conclusion seems to be that a
general social relativism seems plausible as long as we do not look
at it too closely, and that when pressed, it falls apart.

I am not maintaining that there is nothing of value in the social relativist doctrine, but only that a universal social relativism, one which allows no purchase for any trans-social mode of cognition, cannot be coherently defended. If we cannot consider claims whose import goes beyond the confines of our own culture, we cannot begin to explore the role that culture and language play in determining beliefs. And once we back off, and acknowledge that it is possible for social scientists to do research that is relevant to such matters, we certainly have no grounds for denying that physics and biology – sciences that are much better developed than any of the social sciences – provide a potential source of knowledge that transcends the culture in which these sciences first appeared. I will return to this topic in chapter V, after we have developed a new model of rationality, but we can get some further support for the project of constructing that new model by considering one more problem with the arguments offered on behalf of social relativism.

Many of those who defend social relativism seem to take it as obvious that we can infer directly from the fact that a doctrine was developed in a particular culture to the conclusion that that doctrine is valid only in that culture. Yet it is clear that this inference is invalid; we require a substantial set of additional premises before we have grounds for rejecting the possibility that an individual living in a particular society could discover a result – say, a medicine or a weapon or a set of techniques for surviving in a particular environment – that is quite as effective outside her culture as in it. Much of the apparent plausibility of the inference derives from the additional claim that we do not have any trans-socially valid rules for choosing between the ideas that derive from different cultures. Now the notion that we can only make a reasonable choice between two doctrines on the basis of some set of rules that is independent of those doctrines is, as we have seen, characteristic of the classical model of rationality. If we were working in terms of a different model of rationality, one which does not include this demand, then we might indeed be able to elaborate a basis for making such decisions without requiring trans-social rules.

Let me put this point another way. I have already argued that the classical model of rationality requires a foundationalist epistemology. I now want to suggest that social relativism is itself a response, *within the framework of the classical model*, to the failure of foundationalism. The classical model demands that rational decisions be made on the basis of rules, and the search for the foundations of knowledge arose, in part, out of the need to determine which rules should be used. If there are no foundations, there is no universal basis for selecting one set of rules in preference to another. If we acknowledge this point, but are not prepared to reject the classical model of rationality in its entirety, and do not want to give up the concept of rationality as unintelligible, a natural move is to maintain that different groups use different sets of rules, and that each set of rules specifies a different form of rationality. Consider some further remarks from Winch.

> Rationality is not *just* a concept *in* a language like any other; it is this too, for, like any other concept, it must be circumscribed by an established use: a use, that is, established in the language. But I think it is not a concept which a language may, as a matter of fact, have and equally well may not have, as is, for instance, the concept of politeness. It is a concept necessary to the existence of any language [!]: to say of a society that it has a language is also to say that it has a concept of rationality. There need not perhaps be any *word* functioning in its language as 'rational' does in ours, but at least there must be features of its members' use of languages analogous to those features of *our* use of language which are connected with our use of the word 'rational'. . . . This, however, is so far to say nothing about what in particular constitutes rational behaviour in that society; that would require more particular knowledge about the norms they appeal to in living their lives. In other words, it is not so much a matter of invoking 'our own norms of rationality' as of invoking our notion of rationality in speaking of their behaviour in terms of 'conformity to norms'. But how precisely this notion is to be applied to them will depend on our reading of their conformity to norms – what counts for them as conformity and what does not. (1970, pp. 99–100)

In many respects this is an odd passage. Aside from its explicit statement that we know of certain universal trans-social characteristics of language, we might also wonder what is going on when Winch insists on the rationality of any culture that has a language, even if that language includes no term corresponding to our term 'rational'. Why not say, for example, that rationality is a concept peculiar to some cultures, and absent from others? Why not treat this as just one more way in which cultures differ, and hold that any attempt to discuss the rationality of other cultures is ethnocentric?

No doubt Winch would respond by insisting that he is not a relativist at all, and he does maintain that there are other familiar universals, which he calls 'limiting notions'. Winch cites three, 'birth, death, sexual relations' (1970, p. 107), and he maintains that 'forms of these limiting concepts will necessarily be an important feature of any human society and that conceptions of good and evil in human life will necessarily be connected with such concepts' (1970, pp. 110–11). But, again, if we can know that these are universal features of human life, what basis do we have for denying that we know myriad other universals as well? Some of these, such as the need to eat and deal with wastes, are explicitly dealt with by societies, and others play an important role in human life, even though many people are unaware of them – the genetic transmission of certain diseases, the environmental damage done by some agricultural practices, and the fact that human beings cannot fly without sophisticated mechanical aids, for example. This much, however, is clear: Winch distinguishes between a general concept of rationality, and its particular elaborations in different cultures. The general concept is that rational behavior consists of rule-governed behavior, and this must occur in any culture that has a language because linguistic behavior is the paradigm case of rule-governed behavior. This, of course, is exactly what we would expect from the classical model of rationality, and in the absence of the long sought foundations of knowledge, we should not be surprised to find ourselves being led to the view that different systems of rules generate different forms of rationality. Note also that Winch provides us with a quasi-formal rule for recognizing rational behavior: it is behavior that follows a set of rules, the exact content of the rules being irrelevant.

This connection between social relativism and the classical model of rationality is extremely interesting, and I think that part of the plausibility of social relativism comes from its attempt to salvage what we can from the classical model. Moreover, the vacillation we have found between the pronouncement that there are no universal principles and the special exceptions made by social relativists on behalf of certain selected universal principles derives from the fact that they are indeed trying to offer *reasons* for accepting their doctrine, but that, in the classical framework, they cannot offer any reasons without some universal principles. Thus we have discovered one more path into the same morass that we have already encountered several times under the guidance of the classical model of rationality. If we are to avoid this morass altogether, we must construct an alternative model.

Part Two

CHAPTER IV

Judgement

> We have today no adequate reason for refusing to believe in our capacity for doing any of the things which we manifestly do. (Vickers, 1965, p. 75)

Judgement is the ability to evaluate a situation, assess evidence, and come to a reasonable decision without following rules.[1] This is an idea that makes many philosophers uncomfortable, and it has long stood as a paradigm of the sort of notion that has no place in an analysis of rationality. Nevertheless, a growing number of philosophers, including philosophers of science, have been slowly coming to the conclusion that we cannot make sense of human knowledge without recognizing the role that judgement plays at key epistemic junctures. (See, for example, Wartofsky, 1980; Newton-Smith, 1981, pp. 232–5; Putnam, 1981, ch. 8; Elster, 1983, pp. 16–17; Lugg, 1985.) I want to examine judgement in this chapter, and judgement will play a central role in the new model of rationality that I will propose in chapter V, although it will not be the entire story. In the first section I will discuss some characteristic features of judgement, and argue that the exercise of judgement is far from arbitrary, even though judgement is not rule-governed. In the second section I will attempt to clarify the notion of judgement further by comparing it with the closely related notions of 'deliberation' and of a 'skill'. Finally, I will argue that judgement is not a form of mysterious intuition, and that judgement can be included in a thoroughly naturalistic view of human cognition.

4.1 Judgement

We commonly invoke the notion of judgement in a wide variety of situations, e.g., when we describe an individual as exercising 'professional judgement' or 'scientific judgement' or when we describe an umpire in a baseball game as making a 'judgement call'. Wartofsky notes that:

> scientific judgement is analogous to . . . aesthetic judgement in the arts, clinical judgement in medicine, judicial judgement in law, technological judgement in engineering and applied science, and practical judgement in moral, social and personal contexts. (1980, p. 2)

This list is by no means exhaustive. What all of these cases have in common is that they involve decisions which are based on information, and which are not arbitrary, although they are not arrived at by following rules. I want to explore this idea.

Note, to begin with, that admitting a central role for judgement in decision-making is completely compatible with the goal of seeking algorithms for solving problems wherever possible. It would be foolish for someone who knows the appropriate algorithms to attempt to balance a checkbook or differentiate a function in any way other than by the application of that algorithm. But this still leaves two key points untouched. First, our discussions of rules and of foundationalism suggest that it is not possible to reduce *all* decisions to the application of algorithms. For example, the decision to use a particular algorithm is itself ultimately based on some nonalgorithmic decision process – although we will see that this is not always a judgement in the sense that concerns us here. Second, many decisions which might be handled by algorithmic procedures are *in fact* made on the basis of judgements; this can occur for a number of reasons. Sometimes the required algorithm has not yet been discovered; sometimes the algorithm has been discovered, but the individual who must decide is not aware of it; sometimes a known algorithm cannot be applied to a real world situation because of limitations of time, or other constraints. An umpire is guided by a set of rules that provide necessary and sufficient conditions for distinguishing balls from strikes, but must decide whether a particular pitch is a strike without stopping the ball in flight and taking the measurements that would be required to apply these rules in a rigorous manner. Similarly, truth-tables provide a decision procedure for assessing the validity of any argument in propositional logic, but truth-tables can rapidly become lengthy, and there are cases in which it is more efficient to seek a deductive proof of validity than to use a truth-table, even though we have no algorithm for generating proofs. Note also that we do not have an algorithm for deciding whether we should use truth-tables or attempt a proof. The above examples suggest that the exercise of judgement is sufficiently important to justify the attempt to understand more clearly what it involves. I want to proceed by considering three characteristics of judgements in greater detail: (A) judgements are not made by following rules, (B) judgements are fallible, (C) judgements must be made by individuals who are in command of an appropriate body of information that is relevant to the judgement in question. The last of these conditions will provide a crucial constraint that will further clarify the difference between judgements and random choices.

Let me begin with item (A). Our earlier discussion of cases in which we find ourselves at the end of the available hierarchy of rules and meta-rules provides good examples of situations that require judgement, but before pursuing such examples we should note that it would be a mistake to hold that these cases always require judgement. In many familiar situations we apply rules in an automatic manner, without the need either to invoke further rules or to judge which rules are applicable. Much of the training we receive as we grow up in a society or prepare for a particular kind of work is aimed at producing just this condition. We do not have to think twice about which algorithms to apply when balancing a checkbook or when differentiating a simple expression, and an experienced plumber will rarely if ever find herself considering whether a standard copper tubing joint should be soldered. These are cases in which we have been trained to act in a particular way, and as long as we do not get into trouble, questions of justifying our behavior do not arise. There are, however, also situations in which we run out of rules, but cannot act in this unreflective manner. I want to examine three such cases: cases in which we are attempting to develop new rules, cases in which we have to choose between a number of competing rules, and cases in which familiar rules fail us.

Computer programming provides a striking example of the first of these cases, since the programmer's job is to invent new algorithms. One thing about this task is clear: however the programmer proceeds, she does not follow an explicit set of rules for writing programs. There are rules that provide constraints on the program writing process, e.g., the rules of logic and the syntax of the programming language, but these rules do not generate new programs. To the extent that the process of writing a program can be captured in a set of rules, the job can be turned over to the computer, and the programmer becomes unnecessary. And while there are programs that write other programs, these programs were not themselves all generated by computer programs; at some point we reach programs which in fact some person wrote, and did so in a way that required her to operate beyond the range in which the outcome of her work could be determined by explicit rules.

In the course of her work a programmer will make many decisions as to how to proceed, and she will encounter cases in which more than one possibility will occur to her; these possibilities must be evaluated, and a decision made about which one to pursue. In some of these cases the correct procedure would be obvious to any experienced programmer, while in other cases different, equally experienced and capable programmers would proceed differently. This is a typical case that requires judgement, and note particularly that even though different programmers might proceed in different ways, it does not follow that their decisions are arbitrary. If their decisions were arbitrary we would have no good reason for preferring experienced programmers to novices, since we have no reason for expecting one person's arbitrary decisions to be any better than another's. Moreover, an experienced programmer can often give coherent reasons for preferring some option, although these reasons will not reduce to the description of a set of premises or a body of data, plus the invocation of an algorithm. The fact that such reasons can be given indicates, again, that the decisions involved are far from arbitrary.

It is worth noting that reasons of this sort are even found in formal logic. Natural deduction systems always begin with some arguments that are either accepted as clearly valid, or are justified by informal reasoning. For example, Quine makes use of the following two equivalences in *Methods of Logic*:

$$(x)(Fx \ . \ Gx) \equiv (x)Fx \ . \ (x)Gx$$
$$(\exists x)(Fx \lor Gx) \equiv (\exists x)Fx \lor (\exists x)Gx,$$

and he notes that the parallel expressions with the existential and universal quantifiers interchanged are not valid. Quine offers the following justification for these decisions:

> The statements:
>   *Maud* is a book and is boring
>   *Maud* is a book and *Maud* is boring
> are clearly interchangeable, as are:
>   *Maud* is in prose or in verse,
>   *Maud* is in prose or *Maud* is in verse;
> but the statements:
>   Something is square and round,
>   Something is square and something is round
> have opposite truth values, as do these:
>   Everything is visible or invisible,
>   Everything is visible or everything is invisible.
> (1982, pp. 138–9)

Quine's reasons for rejecting the two invalid expressions are impeccable, since he has provided clear counter-instances; the situation with respect to the two equivalences that Quine accepts is not so neat. His remark that they are 'clearly interchangeable' is an appeal to our logical and linguistic competence, and on a foundational approach it would have no place at all unless accompanied by an account of logical intuitions. Quine does seem to be appealing to some form of intuition here, but I prefer to avoid the term 'intuition' because it carries an aura of indubitability. Instead, I suggest that Quine is appealing to our logical judgement, and that we exercise such judgement in deciding whether to accept these equivalences. Note especially that the judgement of an experienced logician is to be preferred to that of a novice, and the judgement of a competent speaker of the language in which Quine is writing is to be preferred to that of a young child or a beginning student of the language. Note also that this is a case in which we exercise judgement in order to choose a set of logical rules that will then provide the basis for justifying other logical rules. If we are not prepared to acknowledge the epistemic legitimacy of this kind of judgement, we will have no basis for establishing any natural deduction system.

This kind of coherent but non-algorithmic decision-making is common and important. It can also be illustrated by the ability of a trained scientist to recognize reasonable and competent approaches to a problem – even if they are different from her own – and to distinguish them from approaches that are unreasonable, unfruitful, and perhaps even incompetent. Similarly, it includes the ability of a teacher or a journal referee to evaluate papers in a field such as philosophy, where we must separate those lines of argument that are worth pursuing, even though we reject them, from those that simply miss the boat. This last example underlines the fallibility of judgements, a point to which I will return, but the fallible judgements of professionals in a field carry weight that is not shared by the judgements of those who do not know the literature and techniques in that field. Moreover, even if we found individuals who could cite algorithms on the basis of which they made their decisions, we would rapidly find ourselves disagreeing on the appropriateness of these algorithms, and would lack a further acceptable algorithm for mediating this dispute.

Let us return to the programming example and note that in many cases there are clear, even algorithmic, techniques for evaluating the resulting program after the fact, and for choosing between two such programs, e.g., on the basis of such criteria as speed or compactness of the code. Thus the process of writing and then subsequently testing a program can sometimes be separated into one phase in the context of discovery and a second phase in the context of justification. This will lead proponents of that distinction to suggest that judgement occurs only in the former context, and that such judgements are irrelevant when we are considering the rational acceptability of the resulting program. For the moment I want to note that much (but not all) of the discussion of the present chapter will take place in the context of discovery and I will consider the significance of this for our new model of rationality in the next chapter. But it should be clear from the discussion thus far that, whatever else we might say about the context of discovery, the view that judgements of the sort we have been considering here amount to the random proposing of hypotheses with no coherent reasons behind them just will not stand up.

Consider next a simple case in which we have to choose between alternative, explicit rules, e.g., when we are attempting to deduce a conclusion from a set of premises in accordance with rules of a particular natural deduction technique. The challenge of such problems lies in the fact that we do not have an algorithm that tells us how to generate a proof – but we could easily take a number of standard deduction rules and turn them into algorithms. We might, for example, take the rule that allows us to conjoin any two existing lines, and generate a rule which instructs us continually to conjoin lines in some regimented manner; or we might begin at a specified point in the problem and, in a standard way, replace each simple expression by its double negation, and, when we have completed this task, go back to the beginning and repeat this procedure until we drop. Obviously, both of these procedures are quite mad, even though each is guided by an algorithm, and no law of logic is violated at any point. We expect the person doing a deduction to be able to choose among the available rules and to apply them in a sensible way, and the better one can do this, the better one is at solving deduction problems. Learning to solve such problems involves the development of intellectual skills that are, in many ways, analogous to physical skills: we expect such skills to improve with practice, and we recognize that some individuals will always be better than others no matter how much the latter practice. More importantly, exercising these skills does not reduce to the application of an algorithm – if it did we would teach the algorithm instead of putting students through the routine of studying examples and doing problems in the expectation that this will improve their performance. And again, the fact that we have good reasons for rejecting the silly rules described above indicates that there is more to the decision to choose a particular rule than a random choice.

Now look at cases in which long familiar rules break down. Much of what has already been said about creating new rules and deciding between competing rules will apply here, but there is an additional element worth considering. As noted above, we deal with much of the world around us in accordance with rules that we have been trained to apply in an automatic manner, and if this were not the case the burden of decision-making might soon overwhelm us. If we had to determine the best way to add a column of numbers each time we encountered one, or assess alternative ways of starting a car every morning, we would not get anywhere. Yet there are cases in which the familiar routines on which individuals depend become unreliable. The history of science is one rich source of examples. For many centuries research in astronomy was guided by the principle that all celestial motions are circular, but there came a time at which astronomers could no longer simply assume this. Similarly, there came a time at which physicists had to reflect on whether they should continue the search for causes behind every event, and at which physicians had to give up such long settled, unquestioned procedures as cupping and blood-letting. But science is not the only place in which such things occur. We can, for example, move to another country, or leave a small town to attend a cosmopolitan university (or *vice versa*), and encounter people who expect conformity to very different rules of elementary courtesy than those we had previously adhered to unreflectively. And entire societies can be faced with economic phenomena that do not fit any of their existing models, or can develop new weapons that are so destructive as to demand an entirely new look at the traditional role of military force in the pursuit of national goals. In such situations we can no longer confidently rely on familiar rules, and we lack rules that will generate new rules. Thus we must draw on cognitive resources other than those involved in applying algorithms.

Let us turn to point (B). Judgements are clearly fallible, but we must avoid the tendency, too common in the Western epistemological tradition, to jump from 'fallible' to 'baseless'. Indubitable knowledge would be wonderful if we could achieve it but, with the possible exception of some trivial cases, indubitability is not within our grasp. If we give up this demand, the concept of judgement provides the basis for a new look at the problem of foundations, for we do indeed stop epistemic regresses, even though we do not do so because we have reached a firm foundation. Rather, we stop either because we judge that we need go no further in the present context, or because we have reached the point at which we have been trained to stop – but the fact that we have been trained to stop at just this point usually rests on judgements made earlier in the history of the society or discipline in question. This leaves us with a starting point, but a tentative and fallible one that is open to reconsideration under appropriate circumstances. This point applies even in the case of deductive logic. Recall the example from Quine that we discussed above, and note that the decision to accept two equivalences is fallible. We can underline this fallibility by returning to the two cases that Quine rejects and noting that Quine's counter-instances may not have come instantly to mind. How much reflection is required before we decide that there are no counter-instances to the favored cases? There is no straightforward answer to this question. We cannot *prove* that there are no counter-instances as long as we are dealing with one of the initial principles of our deductive system, although we can prove this for other cases once we have adopted a starting point. Rather, we reflect long enough to come to a clear decision, and we check our results against those of other competent individuals. Still, as we saw in chapter II, such decisions can be mistaken. Similarly, we accept the conclusions of inductive arguments when we judge that enough evidence has been provided, and we should not be surprised to find that inductive inferences are fallible – which is not the same as being utterly unreliable.

One crucial consequence of our discussion, then, is that we must resist the impulse, which has become a philosophical reflex since Descartes, to jump directly from the recognition that our starting point can be reconsidered, to the conclusion that it must be reconsidered now. The bare logical possibility that we are wrong, even when this possibility is shored up by stories about brains in vats or malevolent demons, is not a sufficient ground for withholding belief. Such considerations did play a legitimate role as long as logically invulnerable knowledge seemed achievable, but they lose their significance once we have conceded that that is not an acceptable epistemic goal. The trouble with such arguments is that, whatever grounds they provide for doubting a claim, they provide equally good grounds for doubting its contradictory. We do not judge a starting point to be acceptable solely because it is logically possible, but as a result of considerations that are specifically relevant to the matter at hand, and once we have found a set of principles to be useful and fruitful, we need specific reasons for doubting them (cf. Shapere, 1984, pp. xxv-xxvi, 226, 243 n. 19). This is not a form of dogmatism. As our discussions of the history of science indicate, there is no incompatibility between accepting a set of fallible claims for substantial periods of time, and being prepared to reconsider them when we have relevant reasons for doing so. The decision that reconsideration is in order is, of course, a matter for professional judgement.

These remarks bring us to point (C), and to a constraint on judgement that has been implicit in our discussion thus far: judgements on a topic can only be made by those who have mastered the body of relevant information. This information will typically consist of two parts: a body of background knowledge (including techniques), and a body of information relevant to the case at hand. For example, in order to be in a position to make a medical decision, or design a bridge, we must master both the methods and knowledge of the applicable disciplines, and also the available information relevant to this particular situation. We should not wish to have our medical diagnoses done by individuals who have not studied medicine, but neither would we rely on the judgement of a thoroughly competent physician who had not bothered to study the facts of our particular case. Note also that expertise in a field is not acquired once and for all. As knowledge and techniques change, one must keep informed in order to maintain one's expertise. The key point here is that *not everyone can exercise judgement on every topic*. This, however, raises two particularly tricky matters, at least as viewed from the perspective of the classical model of rationality: what are we to make of cases in which experts disagree, and how are we to determine who has expertise? I will consider these in turn.

A major source of much contemporary disillusionment with rationality comes from the recognition that experts in a field do not always achieve unanimity. Students find instructors in different courses holding contrary views, physicians disagree on the interpretation of X-rays or the best treatment of a patient, judges at successively higher appeal courts overturn or reinstate a lower court's decisions, and perhaps most strikingly, even in science fundamental disagreements are common, and the best supported and most widely accepted views of one period are replaced by new views that were previously rejected, or that were never even considered. Given this situation, it becomes difficult to see why one should give any special weight to expert opinion – most of the disagreeing parties, maybe all of them, are wrong in any case, so why not stick to my own opinion, however uninformed and incorrect it may be, since the experts are not doing any better?

Note, however, that the path to this conclusion is a surprisingly easy one: it requires that we show that experts sometimes fail us, not that they are regularly and uniformly unreliable. Reflection on actual cases will rapidly lead us to reject the latter proposal. Not only are experts often right, but we regularly insist on expertise when important issues are involved. When we travel on a commercial airliner, for example, we are not prepared to have anyone at all act as pilot – or as mechanic, designer, welder, etc. We demand that only skilled people do these jobs, even though skilled people sometimes make mistakes. At the same time, we depend on the skills of other groups who train those who do the actual work, and certify their competence. We would be quite unhappy either to discover that the pilot of our plane was selected at random, without any regard to skills or training, or to be assured that the pilot was carefully selected by a specialized group of pilot certifiers, but that the members of this latter group were chosen without any consideration of their knowledge or skills. Myriad other examples are available: we expect competence and expertise whenever we rely on a machine, sit in a dentist's chair, take a course at a university, or consult a lawyer. The last example is particularly interesting since the practice of law might be offered as a paradigm case of the unreliability of specialists – after all, it is always possible to find a lawyer to argue any side of any issue, and in an adversary proceeding one of the lawyers must lose. But while this is true, it is not the entire story. We go to a lawyer because she knows the relevant laws and the way they have in fact been interpreted, and because she has experience in dealing with the courts. It is this knowledge and experience that makes it sensible to put ourselves in a lawyer's hands, and it is at best short-sighted to think, after losing a case, that the lawyer's work was worthless.

In other words, expertise does not guarantee success. Not only do lawyers lose cases, and sometimes lose them because of blunders that we could have made just as well without them, but airplanes crash, and do so because of errors on the part of pilots, mechanics, designers, welders, etc. Physicians misdiagnose, or make use of widely accepted techniques that later research will show to have been more harmful than helpful. Physicists accept theories that will later be rejected, logicians accept inferences whose validity will be called into question, and so on. But while such cases are sufficient to demonstrate that experts are fallible, the step from fallibility to generalized doubt about reliability requires an additional premise, and classical epistemology, along with the classical model of rationality, provides one that is by now familiar: only infallible methods are of any cognitive significance. Cite one case in which a method has failed us – or one logically possible situation in which it would fail us – and that method's cognitive credentials have been revoked. Yet once we step out of this familiar framework, we are in a position to begin taking seriously the point that in spite of human fallibility, we are capable of doing an enormous number of things, and solving an enormous number of problems, that were not within our competence, say, 100 years ago.[2] Once we free ourselves of the idea that only infallibility counts in epistemic matters, we can no longer reject the importance of expert judgement simply by citing some cases in which it has failed. And once we are out of that morass, we can accept a point that has always made sense in concrete situations: that the ability to judge what is to be done in a particular situation requires a body of information relevant to that situation – that pilots should be trained to fly, that book reviewers ought at least to read the books they write about, that surgeons should know both anatomy and the details of the case at hand, that lawyers should have read the law, and so forth. Moreover, we should not expect that somewhere there must be lurking a set of rules for determining just what information is relevant in each case.

This brings us to the second point, which can now be handled briefly: how do we determine who the experts in a field are, and how are those who choose the experts to be determined? My response should at least cause no surprise: the experts are recognized by the existing experts. Again, a number of traditional red flags begin to wave: What is to determine if these folk really are expert? What is to prevent a closed society from simply perpetuating itself? And so forth. But again, the best response seems to be to turn to cases. How are new physicists trained and certified? They are trained and certified by present physicists, and who else could we expect to be in a position to do the job? How are physicians trained and certified? By trained physicians. What about pilots, engineers, welders, mechanics, etc? Who else would we expect to train and evaluate these people other than those who already have the necessary expertise? Is the process fallible? Of course it is, but note that many of these fields involve continual interaction with the populace at large who are capable of recognizing when airplanes crash and bridges fail, even though they could not select a competent pilot or engineer on their own. Thus while it may be entertaining to imagine the abstract possibility that a secret cabal has taken over the certification of airline pilots, we have no reason for taking this possibility seriously in the absence of a significant breakdown of air safety. The reaction is so deeply ingrained that, at the risk of being tedious, I will repeat my point once more: we really can build bridges, fly airplanes, and safely remove an appendix, and there is something odd about the notion that all of this evidence pales, for purposes of epistemological analysis, as long as we can cite an occasional failure, or imagine logically consistent situations in which the entire structure falls apart.

In the context of the philosophy of science the idea of decision by judgement is clearly anathema to the long attempt to capture scientific decision-making in a set of formal algorithms. The point of a formal algorithm is that its application requires no knowledge of the *content* of any of the scientific claims at issue. Just as we can check the formal validity of any deductive argument without needing to know its subject matter, or verify a piece of arithmetic without having to know what entities, if any, are associated with the numerals before us, so philosophers have sought means of evaluating scientific theories against the data that did not require that the evaluator know anything about the content of those theories or that data. For reasons which we have already discussed, there are now strong grounds for doubting that scientific decisions can be either made or retrospectively assessed in terms of such formal structures, and in their absence we seem to have little choice but to acknowledge that the making of such decisions requires detailed knowledge of the scientific issues involved. In other words, such decisions rest on professional judgement, and judgement is always founded on a grasp of content.

4.2 *Judgement, deliberation and skills*

The proposal that judgement plays a central role in rational decision-making grates against many familiar epistemological reflexes. In order to clarify further what is involved here, I want to compare judgement with two related notions: first with the complex of ideas involved in Aristotle's discussions of 'deliberation', 'practical wisdom', and 'equity', and then with the notion of a 'skill'.

The concept of judgement has a number of analogies, as well as several disanalogies, with Aristotle's concept of 'deliberation'. (All citations from Aristotle in this chapter are from the *Nicomachean Ethics*.) According to Aristotle, deliberation is an intellectual ability that we draw on when we must make decisions in cases in which we cannot achieve certainty, but are not totally lacking in relevant information. Consider first two types of situations in which Aristotle holds that we do not deliberate:

> Now about eternal things no one deliberates, e.g. about the material universe or the incommensurability of the diagonal and the side of a square. But no more do we deliberate about the things that involve movement but always happen in the same way, whether of necessity or by nature or from any other cause, e.g. the solstices and the risings of the stars; nor about things that happen now in one way, now in another, e.g., droughts and rains; nor about chance events, like the finding of treasure. But we do not deliberate even about all human affairs; for instance, no Spartan deliberates about the best constitution for the Scythians. For none of these things can be brought about by our own efforts. (1112a; 1941, p. 969)

That is, deliberation does not occur, first, when certain knowledge is available. We do not deliberate about whether to accept a mathematical theorem; we prove it. Similarly, Aristotle believed that we had certain knowledge of the nature of the physical world, and this too is not a matter for deliberation. Now much has happened in physical science since Aristotle's day, including the recognition that science does not provide us with certain knowledge of necessary truths, and as a result, we do find scientists deliberating about whether to accept a particular result or to pursue a line of research. And deliberation also occurs in mathematics, not only when seeking a proof, but also in deciding how to deal with mathematical conjectures. For example, the Goldbach conjecture holds that every even number can be expressed as a sum of two primes. It is a conjecture in that there is neither a proof nor a disproof for the claim, but many competent mathematicians believe that it is likely to be true, and that the proof of this claim is worth pursuing. A mathematician who is attempting to decide whether it is likely that this claim is true, or whether it is worth working on, is engaging in deliberation.

Aristotle also maintains that we do not deliberate about things that are beyond our control, rather, 'We deliberate about things that are in our power and can be done . . .' (1112a; 1941, p. 969). Aristotle has several points in mind here. First, we do not deliberate about unpredictable events or about chance events, and one reason why we do not deliberate in these cases is that we lack any information relevant to determining whether the event in question will occur, or how to bring it about or prevent it, and any decisions we might make on the matter would be baseless. Deliberation, like judgement, can only occur in the context of relevant information.

But Aristotle's claim that we only deliberate about what is in our power goes beyond this limitation, since he holds quite literally that we only deliberate in cases in which we can act on the results of our deliberation. In this regard, the notion of judgement is rather more comprehensive than Aristotle's concept of deliberation: there is no reason why a Spartan could not come to an informed judgement about the best way of constituting Scythian society, independently of whether the Spartan could act on that judgement. Similarly, we make informed judgements about what the weather is likely to be, even though we cannot alter it. This difference between judgement and deliberation is closely related to another difference. According to Aristotle:

> We deliberate not about ends but about means. For a doctor does not deliberate whether he shall heal, nor an orator whether he shall persuade, nor a statesman whether he shall produce law and order, nor does anyone else deliberate about his end. They assume the end, and consider by what means it is to be attained. . . . (1112b; 1941, p. 970)

But ends are not always given with the clarity that Aristotle requires. It is not clear that doctors should always heal, nor is it clear that orators ought always to persuade – or in what direction they ought to exercise their persuasive powers. There are often situations in which we must consider what ends to pursue, and in which our decisions are made in the context of a substantial body of relevant information, and with some accepted principles to guide us, but without sufficient information or a sufficient body of principles to permit us to calculate a result. These are matters which require judgement. This, in turn, opens up the large and difficult question of the nature of 'value judgements', but I will not consider this matter here beyond noting one consequence of our discussion: the fact that such decisions require *judgement* is not a sufficient basis for considering them to be epistemically suspect.

Aristotle's discussion of deliberation is closely connected with a key concept of his ethics, 'practical wisdom'. In addition to professional expertise in specific fields, Aristotle believed that one can develop the ability to make decisions with regard to what constitutes a good life, and this is the domain of practical wisdom:

> Regarding *practical wisdom* we shall get at the truth by considering who are the persons we credit with it. Now it is thought to be the mark of a man of practical wisdom to be able to deliberate well about what is good and expedient for himself, not in some particular respect, e.g. about what sorts of thing conduce to health or strength, but about what sorts of thing conduce to the good life in general. This is shown by the fact that we credit men with practical wisdom in some particular respect when they have calculated well with a view to some good end which is one of those that are not the object of any art. It follows that in the general sense also the man who is capable of deliberation has practical wisdom. (1140a; 1941, p. 1026)

There are several points worth noting about this description.

To begin with, Aristotle's concern is with 'the man of practical wisdom', i.e., this is an ability which must be exercised by individuals and which cannot be captured in a set of rules. Aristotle sharply distinguishes practical wisdom from what he calls 'science', where the characteristic mark of science is that it provides demonstrations through syllogisms. Science offers certainty, and does so on the basis of explicit rules; practical wisdom does not proceed by rules, and we do not achieve certainty through the exercise of practical wisdom. Similarly, practical wisdom must be distinguished from what Aristotle calls 'intuition'. We saw in Chapter II that Aristotle's view of science requires that we be capable of grasping the first principles on which demonstrations must be based, and that this is the task of 'intuitive reason' (see, for example, 1140b–1141a; 1941, p. 1027). Intuitive reason provides us with universal, necessary, certain first principles, while practical wisdom can offer no such thing. But in spite of these limitations, when we exercise practical wisdom we are not making arbitrary choices; rather, we are making use of a 'reasoned state of capacity to act with regard to things that are good or bad for man' (1140b; 1941, p. 1026). The key difference between judgement and practical wisdom is that judgement is a wider concept, and practical wisdom is one example of the exercise of judgement. The abilities that Aristotle attributes to those who exercise practical wisdom are just those that are involved in any exercise of judgement, but judgement is required in a wide variety of fields that Aristotle exempts from the range of deliberation.

Aristotle provides us with one more striking example of the exercise of judgement when he discusses 'equity'. The context is Aristotle's discussion of justice, and although there is much here that is worth considering, my present concern is only to note that Aristotle argues that what we take to be just becomes expressed in laws which must be formulated universally, but that universal laws often fail to cover specific cases adequately. In such cases we must be prepared to go beyond the law, and this requires the exercise of equity, which is:

> a correction of legal justice. The reason is that all law is
> universal but about some things it is not possible to make a
> universal statement which shall be correct. In those cases,
> then, in which it is necessary to speak universally, but not
> possible to do so correctly, the law takes the usual case, though
> it is not ignorant of the possibility of error. And it is none
> the less correct; for the error is not in the law nor in the
> legislator but in the nature of the thing, since the matter of
> practical affairs is of this kind from the start. When the law
> speaks universally, then, and a case arises on it which is not

covered by the universal statement, then it is right, where the legislator fails us and has erred by over-simplicity, to correct the omission – to say what the legislator himself would have said had he been present, and would have put into his law if he had known. (1137b; 1941, p. 1020)

Aristotle speaks in this passage of cases which are not covered by a universal law, but he seems to intend that equity also applies in cases that are covered, but inappropriately. Two points support this interpretation. The first is that if a law simply did not apply at all to a given case, the need to exercise equity would not arise. There must be some sense in which a law is relevant to the case at hand if we are to correct that law in this case. Second, Aristotle does discuss one situation in which equity explicitly involves rejecting the literal statement of the law. This is when he describes an 'equitable man' as one who 'is no stickler for his rights in a bad sense but tends to take less than his share though he has the law on his side . . .' (1137b–1138a; 1941, p. 1020). One example of the exercise of equity, then, is the decision to suspend the law because we recognize that its strict application will do more harm than good in the case at hand. This is a clear case of judgement: it requires that one assess a situation knowing the relevant laws and the details of the particular case, and determine what is fair and reasonable even if it falls outside of the accepted rules, and do so without appeal to some higher-order rules.

It is interesting to compare Aristotle's views on equity with the contrasting views of Hume. Like Aristotle, Hume recognizes that there are situations in which the strict application of a law to a particular case is harmful, and that such cases are unavoidable; but unlike Aristotle, Hume maintains that we must never suspend the law in such cases. Hume believes that social life is not possible unless we can confidently rely on definite, inflexible rules. Violations of these rules on behalf of specific cases undermine this confidence, and do damage to society. Thus the decision to make an exception for a specific case, no matter how pressing, will always amount to choosing the greater of two evils. Hume writes:

General peace and order are the attendants of justice or a
general abstinence from the possessions of others; but a
particular regard to the particular right of one individual
citizen may frequently, considered in itself, be productive of

pernicious consequences. The result of the individual acts is here, in many instances, directly opposite to that of the whole system of actions; and the former may be extremely hurtful, while the latter is, to the highest degree, advantageous. Riches, inherited from a parent, are, in a bad man's hand, the instrument of mischief. The right of succession may, in one instance, be hurtful. Its benefit arises only from the observance of the general rule; and it is sufficient, if compensation be thereby made for all the ills and inconveniences which flow from particular characters and situations. (1975, p. 304)

Hume continues:

Public utility requires that property should be regulated by general inflexible rules; and though such rules are adopted as best serve the same end of public utility, it is impossible for them to prevent all particular hardships, or make beneficial consequences result from every individual case. It is sufficient, if the whole plan or scheme be necessary to the support of civil society, and if the balance of good, in the main, do thereby preponderate much above that of evil. (1975, p. 305)

Note that this particular disagreement has its roots in a deeper difference between Hume's philosophy and Aristotle's, a difference which concerns their views on the range of cognitive capacities available to human agents. On Hume's view – and on the view which has been characteristic of the empiricist tradition – these capacities are extremely limited: they go no further than what can be captured in sensation and deductive logic, and perhaps a careful extension into inductive logic (cf. Hooker, 1975, pp. 187–8). Beyond this range, human cognition ceases to be reliable. Thus it is not surprising to find Hume arguing that once we have a set of rules for organizing a society these must not be violated, since there is no room in Hume's epistemology or his philosophy of mind for any cognitive ability that could provide the basis for this violation. Yet, on reflection, something seems to be missing. What, for example, is the source of these rules that we must uniformly apply? Hume would certainly agree that they are human inventions, but in his attempt to discover the foundations of all human cognition, he has left no room for the ability to promulgate rules which are likely to generate more good than ill. We might grit our teeth and simply claim that the rules are chosen randomly, and that it does not matter what rules we choose, but that once in place, overall well-being requires that we stick to these rules. But then we must ask what basis we have for this claim about what is beneficial for society overall? The suggestion that it is based on judgement is tempting, but there are no grounds for any such proposal in Hume's philosophy, and it is difficult to see how *he* could justify his claims about the necessity of universal rules.

It is important that the thesis I am defending here not be overstated. I am not suggesting that sane societies can exist without rules, nor that the obvious duty of a judge to exercise judgement means that a judge should ignore the law and simply do whatever she thinks appropriate. Nor am I proposing any approach to legal or social philosophy. My only concern here is to emphasize that we do have an ability to think and reason beyond the range that is captured in our ability to follow rules. We exercise this ability when we are creating rules, when we modify existing rules, and when we recognize that we have an unusual case at hand, and decide how to deal with it. This does not preclude the possibility that a judge may assess a particular case and decide that no exception should be made, for this too is a possible outcome of judgement. Nor does it preclude the possibility that we may judge that we lack the necessary expertise, and decide to seek assistance. But even if we follow Hume's advice and accept the meta-rule that there shall be no exceptions to our rules, we do so because we judge that Hume is right in thinking that this is the best of the available options. If we did not have the ability to make such judgements, neither the rule-governed society that Hume describes, nor Hume's social philosophy, could exist.

Let us move on to a second comparison. I have argued that the ability to exercise judgement is a learned ability that is not explicitly rule-governed. This combination is characteristic of skills, and I am maintaining that when we develop the ability to exercise judgement in a particular field, we are developing a skill. I want to examine this idea, and we can begin by discussing a number of points due to Hilary Putnam. Putnam's remarks are set in the context of philosophy of language and philosophy of science, and his main concern is to reject the claim that all genuine knowledge consists of propositions that are explicitly formulable and testable by inductive methods. In addition to our explicit knowledge, Putnam argues, we also have a great deal of knowledge that is embodied in skills, and there is no basis for believing that this knowledge can be captured in explicit theories. Many of these skills, Putnam maintains, are 'too complex to describe by a theory' (1978, p. 71), while skills

> don't always depend on *theories* (as the example of *walking* already illustrates). And knowledge – even verbalized knowledge – can be embodied in a *skill* and not a theory. (1978, p. 71)

A key example here is our ability to translate from one language to another, a task that has proven surprisingly recalcitrant to computerization. Part of the reason for this is that our use of language in practical contexts draws on a large body of background knowledge that we would probably be unable to lay out in advance of having to make use of it. Putnam illustrates this by considering a small portion of what is involved in asking an Israeli gas station attendant, in Hebrew, to check the oil:

> I am assuming (1) the attendant wants to sell gas and oil; (2) it is not *obligatory* in Israel to say 'bevakasha' (*please*) when making a request; (3) if someone wants to sell oil, and a customer asks 'check the oil' in the language of the seller (and no obligatory politeness-rules have been violated) the seller will check the oil (or, perhaps, say 'I'm out of oil' in his language, or – rarely – 'I'm too busy', but *not* punch the customer in the nose); (4) someone driving up to the gas station will be treated as a customer. (1978, p. 69)

Obviously, Putnam *has* just articulated some of the assumptions involved in having one's oil checked, but the point is that we do not consciously attend to these assumptions in a familiar situation. If I were not comfortable in this situation, I might have to consider the proper words and the appropriate formulas required for a polite request. But this explicit checking of the rules is not a model of competent behavior – it is a model of unskillful behavior. Once I have mastered the relevant linguistic and social skills, I need no longer think about the rules.

In the case of a science such as physics, the trained practitioner relies on a large set of skills. While this is particularly clear in those laboratory situations that involve physical tasks, it also occurs when an experimenter immediately grasps the physical significance of a reading from an instrument or a track on a photograph; and it occurs in such intellectual tasks as deciding whether to apply a precise mathematical theory to a specific situation:

> What the theory actually describes is (typically) an idealized 'closed system'. The theory of this 'closed system' can be as precise as you want. And it is *within* this idealization that one gets the familiar examples of the 'scientific method'. But the *application* of physics depends on the fact that we can produce in the laboratory, or find in the world, *open* systems which approximate to the idealized system sufficiently well for the theory to yield very accurate predictions. The decision that conditions have been approximated well in a given case – that it is even *worthwhile* to apply the idealized model to *this* case – typically depends on unformalized practical knowledge. (Putnam, 1978, p. 72)

In the language of the present discussion, it requires professional judgement on the part of the physicist to decide whether a theory is applicable to a real situation. Putnam concludes this discussion by noting that he is in effect invoking Michael Polanyi's notion of 'tacit knowledge'; I want to consider Polanyi's views on the role of skills in knowledge.

The central thesis of Polanyi's epistemology is captured in his remark that *'we can know more than we can tell and we can tell nothing without relying on our awareness of things we may not be able to tell'* (1958, p. x; cf. 1967, p. 4). Polanyi is not always consistent about the exact force of 'can' in this remark, but his main point is that our cognitive abilities depend on a grasp of items that are not currently in the focus of our attention. We may, in another context, shift our attention in order to formulate and analyze those items, but in doing so we will be depending on an awareness of other items that are not now at the focus of our attention. Let us explore this idea, beginning with cases involving perception.

Polanyi begins his discussion of perceptual skills by distinguishing between 'focal awareness' and 'subsidiary awareness'; consider the following example:

> When we use a hammer to drive in a nail, we attend to both the nail and the hammer, *but in a different way*. We *watch* the effect of our strokes on the nail and try to wield the hammer so as to hit the nail most effectively. When we bring down the hammer we do not feel that its handle has struck our palm but that its head has struck the nail. Yet in a sense we are certainly alert to the feelings in our palm and the fingers that hold the hammer. They guide us in handling it effectively, and the degree of attention that we give to the nail is given to the same extent but in a different way to these feelings. The difference may be stated by saying that the latter are not, like the nail, objects of our attention, but instruments of it. They are not watched in themselves; we watch something else while keeping intensely aware of them. I have a *subsidiary awareness* of the feeling in the palm of my hand which is merged into my *focal awareness* of my driving in the nail. (1958, p. 55)

This subsidiary awareness of the feelings in my hand functions as tacit knowledge, and the crucial point here is not only that I depend on this tacit awareness in carrying out my task with the hammer, but that this awareness must remain tacit if the performance is to be carried out in a skillful way. If I were to shift my attention so that the effects of the hammer on my palm became the object of my focal awareness, my efficiency in driving in the nail would deteriorate. Moreover, if I do shift my attention in this way, so that I now pay explicit attention to the sensations in my hand, I must still keep hammering if I am to have any sensations to analyze. Thus my new focal awareness of the sensations in my hand will become dependent on a subsidiary awareness of the hammer and the nail.

This same dual structure is involved in our ability to recognize common situations. When we read a text in a familiar language, the object of our focal awareness is the meaning of the text, yet our ability to recognize this meaning is dependent on a subsidiary awareness of the printed page, and the objects of this subsidiary awareness need never enter full consciousness. Polanyi reports the following experience:

My correspondence arrives at my breakfast table in various languages, but my son understands only English. Having just finished reading a letter I may wish to pass it on to him, but must check myself and look again to see in what language it was written. I am vividly aware of the meaning conveyed by the letter, yet know nothing whatever of its words. I have attended to them closely but only for what they mean and not for what they are as objects. (1958, p. 57)

Experiences of this sort are not uncommon. A competent reader working in only a single language can usually report accurately the content of a text without being able even to approximate a literal recitation of that text. Similarly, we can often recognize a person, a scene or a melody, without explicitly attending to those features on which our recognition is based.

Let us pursue the example of reading a bit further. There are situations, such as proof-reading, in which it becomes desirable to pay attention to the words on paper, and we are generally capable of shifting our attention in this way. When we do so, the words enter our focal awareness, but there is still a substantial body of subsidiary information that this focal awareness depends on, and that could itself become an object of focal awareness if we shift our attention once again. For example, I might proof-read a text and never notice if it was printed with a dot matrix printer, or the condition of the ribbon, but if my interests changed, I could pay attention to the print quality, and in doing so I might lose sight of whether the text was printed in English letters or in Greek. In any actual case this process must stop: eventually I run out of questions which can lead me to shift my attention. More-over, subsidiary awareness is a form of genuine awareness, and perceptual recognition is not built on an actually infinite hierarchy of instances of subsidiary awareness. Still, this does not require that there be some absolute stopping point. Where I stop will be determined by my background beliefs and the present state of my interests and training. Five years ago it would never have occurred to me to ask if the text had been printed on a dot matrix printer, nor would I have been capable of identifying such a text had I been asked to – and five years from now I may be prepared to ask and answer questions that have not yet occurred to me. Thus there is a potential regress of ever deeper levels of subsidiary awareness that is analogous to the regresses we encountered earlier in our discussion of foundations, and this new regress is broken in a similar way: we simply end it when we have no basis for going any further, and we open it up again if we encounter a reason for doing so.

The distinction between focal and subsidiary awareness applies only in cases of perception, but an analogous dual structure would seem to be involved whenever we perform in a skillful manner. When we are learning a new skill, or trying to improve a skill that we have already learned, we may pay careful attention to each of the component activities that the performance requires. But paying attention in this way impedes the smooth flow of our performance, and that flow will not be achieved until we can carry out that activity without paying attention to each act that goes into it. So, in learning to play a musical instrument, we may initially have to pay careful attention to each placement of our fingers, and we will not begin to play well until we get beyond this need. In an analogous way, a baseball player in a batting slump may examine every aspect of her stance and swing, and work to eliminate some quirk in that swing. But she will not be able to use the modified swing efficiently in a game until she reaches the point at which she no longer has to think about its details while attempting to hit a ball.

Now essentially the same point holds for rule-governed activities: there is a considerable class of skills which are governed by rules that we know and that we could state, but these skills are not exercised by explicitly following those rules. For example, a competent writer may be able, on request, to formulate the grammatical rules of her native language, but she does not have to stop repeatedly and call to mind whether adjectives go before or after nouns, or how to conjugate a verb. These rules may guide her writing, but they do so tacitly, and thinking about these rules would likely interfere with her writing. Similarly, a beginning chess player may have to pause to remember how the knight moves, but a competent player need not ponder this. Polanyi puts this point rather strongly when he writes, '*the aim of a skilful performance is achieved by the observance of a set of rules which are not known as such to the person following them*' (1958, p. 49). In many cases this remark would be more accurate if we replaced 'known . . . to' with 'used . . . by': the performer knows the rules, and knows that they are the rules that govern this activity, but she is not attending to them in the way a beginner might. But there are also cases in which Polanyi's description is literally correct, i.e., cases in which we skillfully perform a presumably rule-governed activity without being able, even with a shift of perspective, to state the rules that we are following. We can even learn to engage in a rule-governed activity without ever having encountered an explicit formulation of the rules, and without any explicit knowledge of the rules on which our resulting competence is supposed to rest. This is especially common in the case of physical skills. Polanyi notes that most people cannot formulate the rules by which they maintain their balance on a bicycle (1958, pp. 49–50); when pressed, many will assert that they keep their balance by leaning in a direction opposite to the one in which they are about to fall. If this were correct, it should be just as easy to balance on a stationary bicycle as on a moving one. Yet this failure to know the rules, and even the possession of a set of mistaken beliefs about which rules are operative, need not prevent an individual from riding well or from teaching others to ride. An analogous point holds for intellectual skills. Language use is often taken as the paradigm of a rule-governed activity, but it is not at all uncommon for a competent speaker to be utterly unable to formulate many of the rules that she seems to follow every day. Moreover, we do not learn our native language by being taught to follow rules. Indeed, those from whom we learn to talk not only do not tell us what rules we should follow, but often could not state these rules if they were asked, and might state incorrect rules if we insisted on a response.

Let us consider another kind of case. Sometimes, we learn an activity by being taught explicit rules, but as our skill develops, we not only cease to make explicit appeal to those rules, but even forget them altogether. For example, much learning of a foreign language, after we have mastered our native language, does involve the explicit formulation and application of rules – rules for conjugation and declension, for where to put the adjective and verb, and so forth. Once the level of skillful performance is achieved, these rules cease to function explicitly, and are frequently forgotten. This need not leave the speaker any worse off than the individual who never encountered an explicit formulation of the rules for her native language.

Note that skills share the three features that concerned us in discussing judgement. Consider, again, the competent use of my native language: it is not explicitly rule-governed, it is fallible, and it can only take place in the framework of a body of knowledge, in this case knowledge of the language. Yet competent use of a language is far from a random activity. Similarly, a physician reading an X-ray, or a physicist assessing an experimental result in order to decide whether a line of work is worth pursuing further, draws on a rich background. Part of the background that provides the basis for such skills does consist of rules that the individual learned as such, and that she could formulate on request. But part of this background will consist of ways of seeing and thinking that were learned in the course of training, much as an individual learns her native language, without these ever having been presented as rules. Polanyi, who was originally trained as a physician, offers the following description of the process of learning to read X-rays.

Think of a medical student attending a course in the X-ray diagnosis of pulmonary diseases. He watches in a darkened room shadowy traces on a fluorescent screen placed against a patient's chest, and hears the radiologist commenting to his assistants, in technical language, on the significant features of these shadows. At first the student is completely puzzled. For he can see in the X-ray picture of a chest only the shadows of the heart and the ribs, with a few spidery blotches between them. The experts seem to be romancing about figments of their imagination; he can see nothing that they are talking about. Then as he goes on listening for a few weeks, looking carefully at ever new pictures of different cases, a tentative understanding will dawn on him; he will gradually forget about the ribs and begin to see the lungs. And eventually, if he perseveres intelligently, a rich panorama of significant details will be revealed to him: of physiological variations and pathological changes, of scars, of chronic infections and signs of acute disease. (1958, p. 101)

Is the instructor remiss, or perhaps sadistic, in making the student go through this process instead of just laying out the rules for reading X-rays? The issue is not just whether a complete set of explicit rules exists, because even if it did, the student would still have to go through this procedure to be able to apply them – just as a physicist who knows how we keep our balance on a bicycle must learn to ride by practice along with the rest of us. And again, the same point holds for purely intellectual skills. When we teach a natural deduction technique in symbolic logic we give our students a set of rules for doing deductions, but we know that this is not sufficient to allow them to solve deduction problems. Thus we also give them sample problems illustrating the use of these rules, we expect them to do problems on their own, we provide sets of progressively more difficult problems, and we expect that their ability to do such problems will improve with practice. Moreover, we expect that in doing such problems they will develop an ability for which we have not given them a sufficient set of rules: the ability to discover proofs. Yet logic instructors are no more sadistic than radiology instructors. We do not withhold the rules for generating proofs – we do not have a set of rules, and do not even know if such a set exists – yet we still teach students how to construct proofs, and help them to improve their skills.

Let me emphasize one aspect of the above examples. We have seen that conscious attention to rules interferes with a skillful performance, and even when we do not forget the rules that govern an activity, we must still cease paying attention to those rules if we are to carry out that activity in a skillful manner. In other words, if our behavior is to conform smoothly to a set of rules, we must not consciously follow those rules. This may sound paradoxical, but instead of a paradox, this point provides us with a new approach to one of the problems about rule-following that we discussed above: the potential regress of rules and rules for the application of these rules. This regress arises when we seek some basis for applying rules, and we cannot close the regress as long as we insist on further rules. But the discussion in this section suggests that there is another way to close this regress: when we learn to apply a specific set of rules we develop a skill. As a result, the transition from a tentative, fumbling attempt to follow rules to a smooth performance that conforms to those rules does not occur because we grasp a meta-rule, but because we reach the point at which we need no longer proceed by following those rules. The classical model of rationality takes rule-following to be a fundamental cognitive ability and attempts to capture skills in sets of rules, but this has things backwards since the ability to act in accordance with a set of rules is itself a skill.

There are two key points that I want to draw out of this discussion of skills. The first is that, in general, the exercise of judgement is analogous to skillful behavior. In both cases we behave in a coherent manner without consciously following rules, and in both cases our ability to do this requires a combination of prior training and attention to the case at hand. Second, there is more than just an analogy here. The ability to exercise judgement in a particular field is a skill. We have seen that we may depend on judgement for a number of different reasons, e.g., because no rules are available, or because available rules are inadequate given the details of the situation at hand. In other words, the ability to exercise judgement is a skill that we call on when we run out of rules.

4.3 Judgement naturalized

The above discussion raises two important difficulties. I have argued that we do not consciously follow rules when we exercise judgement, but this leaves open the possibility that we may be following rules in some other way. More importantly, it may seem that judgement is a mystical phenomenon that has no place in a naturalistic view of human cognition. My main concern in this section will be to respond to the second objection, and we will be able to deal with the first objection in the process. Before beginning this discussion, however, I want to consider two preliminary matters: what I mean by 'naturalism', and why it is important that judgement conform to the demands of naturalism.

The central thesis of naturalism is that human beings are complex physical systems that are part of the natural world, and that human cognition is a natural phenomenon. By way of contrast, there is a long tradition in Western philosophy which holds that our cognitive abilities exist in, and are exercised by, a mind or soul that is not part of the natural order. Plato, for example, considered the soul to be a denizen of the 'intelligible world' where the nonmaterial forms exist, and maintained that all of our knowledge ultimately derives from a vision of the forms that we achieved before our souls were connected with our bodies.

For Descartes, the knower is a conscious being that is not spatially extended, while the natural world is made up of nonconscious, spatially extended beings; thus mind is not part of nature. Similarly, Kant locates the genuine self in the noumenal world, outside of space and time. It is this noumenal self that wields the categories and generates an empirical world of which it is not itself a member. Items in that empirical world – including the temporal, but nonspatial empirical self – are studied by the sciences, including empirical psychology, but the noumenal self is not subject to scientific study.

A naturalistic approach requires that we attempt to understand human knowledge without introducing such nonnatural entities. To illustrate, consider briefly the role of sense perception in knowledge. None of the examples of non-naturalistic epistemologies noted above were taken from the empiricist tradition, and to a large degree empiricists have tended to be more sympathetic to naturalism than philosophers from other traditions. Still, many empiricists exclude perception from the realm of scientific study, holding that sensations provide the foundation on which all scientific knowledge is constructed, and are thus not themselves amenable to a scientific account (e.g., Price, 1964, pp. 2–4 and Chapter 10). From a naturalistic perspective our senses are physical objects that respond to physical features of the world around us: our eyes respond to a portion of the electromagnetic spectrum, our ears to certain pressure waves, and so forth. These senses provide a source of information about some features of the world we live in, information that, at least thus far, has been sufficient to permit us to survive, and maybe even thrive, on the surface of this planet. But the range of phenomena that our senses respond to is limited, and even within this range our senses are subject to a variety of defects that come along with their physical nature. For example, the lenses of our eyes behave in accordance with the same optical laws, and are subject to the same defects, as any other lens, and anyone who wears eye glasses knows we can sometimes correct these defects by the introduction of supplementary lenses. If we are to understand how far our senses are to be trusted, and where they must be used with care, we must understand the laws which govern their operation, laws which we learn in the same way as we learn the laws that govern any other physical entities or processes. (See Brown, 1985, 1987a, 1987b, for further discussion.)

Similarly, for the naturalist, thinking and reasoning do not take place outside the physical world, but in the nervous system (in which, for brevity, I will include the brain). Defects in that system, such as brain damage, can interfere with the ability to reason, and we have grounds for expecting that differences in reasoning ability among different individuals are based on physical differences in their nervous systems. Now this last remark must not be misunderstood: nothing is being said here about the relative significance of 'genetic' and 'environmental' factors in determining intellectual ability. Brain damage can interfere with intelligence irrespective of whether it occurs because of genes passed on from parents, chemical problems in the prenatal environment, inadequate early nutrition, inadequate early sensory experience, or a blow to the head. Moreover, our ability to reason well in a particular situation will also be at least partially a function of what we have experienced and learned – but if past experiences are to enter into my present thinking, it must be because they have had some physical effects on my nervous system. Thus however my nervous system got to be in its present state, the thought processes that I go through now depend on the present state of my nervous system, along with its present inputs, and the laws that govern its activity.

Here too a common misunderstanding should be noted and avoided: the notion of a 'natural law' must not be understood in an overly simplistic way. Not only may natural laws be exceedingly complex, but as science develops we learn about types of laws that were completely beyond our grasp at an earlier stage. Consider, for example, elementary Newtonian gravitational problems involving interactions of three bodies, such as the earth, sun and moon. The equations that we use to describe this system cannot in principle be solved exactly. For practical purposes this presents no problem, since these equations can be solved to any desired degree of approximation, yet it is striking that while we cannot derive an exact solution for the locations of these bodies at a specific time, the earth-sun-moon system itself presumably solves this problem exactly at each instant. Thus even in relatively elementary physics, the set of law-governed processes that we are now aware of is larger than the set of equations that we can currently formulate and solve. (I owe this example to Clifford

Hooker.) At some time in the future we may discover new ways to formulate and analyze the laws that govern these interactions. As a second example, recall that quantum theory makes use of natural laws that are *irreducibly statistical*, and thus that we must not identify the idea of a 'natural law' with the idea of a 'causal law'. Note also that even taking these cases into account, we have no grounds for assuming that we now know all of the major *kinds* of natural laws, and we may well encounter significant surprises as scientists work out the laws that govern cognitive processes in the nervous system. The actual discovery of the laws that govern cognition is a subject for scientific research, not for philosophical reflection, and my only reason for mentioning this topic at all is to reject the assumption that natural laws must be simple causal laws.

Consider next why compatibility with naturalism should be of special interest to us. Note, first, that throughout the course of this century developments in biology and psychology, as well as in philosophy, have provided progressively stronger grounds for taking naturalism very seriously. We have, for example, learned much more about the physical basis of human behavior than had previously been imagined, and we have learned that the cognitive gap between humans and other mammals is not nearly as great as many have wanted to believe (see, for example, Hooker, 1974, 1975; Churchland, 1979, ch. 5; Griffin, 1984), while the theory of evolution has provided a powerful framework for understanding ourselves as part of the natural world. Given these developments, the time has surely come to begin attempting to set reason in a naturalistic framework, i.e., a framework that will bring it into conformity with the growing body of science.

At the same time, the attempt to do this does not require that we be totally convinced that naturalism is the final word. One of the major lessons we should derive from the failure of foundationalism is that we need not wait for foundations to be firmly established before we begin to build. While debate on the ultimate adequacy of naturalism continues, we can begin exploring how far we can go in the attempt to understand reason in a naturalistic framework, and the attempt to do this has at least two virtues: if naturalism is correct, we will be advancing the development of a naturalistic theory of knowledge; and if naturalism is defective, the attempt to develop it may well be the best way of discovering its defects. In the remainder of this section I will consider how judgement might be understood in naturalistic terms. I will not attempt to give a naturalistic account of judgement – that is a task for science – but I will sketch some possibilities in order to show that there is no incompatibility between the notion of judgement and a naturalistic account of cognition.

I want to approach the discussion by considering a variety of related cases from the point of view of introspection. Let me begin with an example that does not involve judgement, although, as we will see, it shares certain interesting features with cases that do require judgement. When we learn to multiply numbers we typically first memorize a set of elementary multiplication facts, and we are then drilled in a technique for applying these facts to more complex cases. An adult who has properly learned her elementary multiplication facts will respond to a simple problem, such as multiplying six by seven, immediately, we might even say as a reflex; someone who has not learned her multiplication table properly might go through a routine such as adding up six sevens, while using her fingers to keep track of her progress. The second person is clearly following rules, but, at least in terms of what occurs in consciousness, the first person is not following rules. Rather, the first person simply has the answer pop into her mind; I want to explore this difference further.

I have acknowledged throughout our discussion that rule-following does occur, and that it is important, but we saw in the previous section that one aim of training is to free us from the need to follow rules. In the case now before us, a competent individual need not do the calculation; rather she somehow becomes aware of the result when she needs that information. Sometimes this occurs as a result of memorization, as in the case of the multiplication table, but this is not the only way it happens; a similar phenomenon occurs as a result of our having acquired a cognitive skill which we can apply in a variety of cases, including cases that we have not previously encountered. Let me illustrate this with two examples from formal logic, a discipline that, from a traditional point of view, brings us right to the heart of rationality.

Consider, first, a case in which someone who is reasonably adept is attempting to construct a proof in logic (or geometry, or any other deductive discipline). Suppose the proof is moderately difficult, and consider how we might proceed. We have already noted that we do not follow rules, at least because there are no known rules for generating proofs. Rather, we reflect on the problem, try a variety of approaches, and if we are sufficiently skillful, one of these approaches will eventually yield the desired proof. Now from an introspective point of view, what occurs when we decide to try a particular approach – where does the proposal come from? The question is an odd one, because typically the proposal just occurs to us, and we proceed from there; one characteristic of an individual who is skilled at doing proofs is that fruitful ideas will occur to her. Note, however, that the appearance of an idea to consciousness is, introspectively, similar to the appearance of the answer to a simple problem in arithmetic. In the logical case there may be a considerable time lag before some idea occurs to us, and many other ideas may precede it, but in both cases we become aware of an idea without being aware of its source.

The last example will have only limited interest for many proponents of the classical model of rationality because it occurs in the context of discovery; advocates of a sharp distinction between discovery and justification have long acknowledged that new ideas just occur to us with no discoverable rational basis. I want, then, to press the point by considering a related case that falls squarely in the context of justification: a case in which we are checking the validity of someone else's proposed proof, and doing so in terms of a specific set of rules of inference. Our task amounts to examining each step and determining whether it follows from some combination of premises and previous steps via one of the accepted rules of inference. What is striking here is the difference between the way this would be done by a novice and by a master. The novice might well have to keep the rules in mind and painstakingly check whether each step conforms to these rules, so the novice might indeed consciously follow rules when checking the proof; we would expect the skilled logician's approach to be rather different. She would not have to consult or consciously follow rules. Rather, the fact that a particular step did or did not conform to the rules would be obvious – it would leap to the mind, much in the way that a lesion will leap to the eye of a skilled radiologist examining an X-ray, while that same lesion would have to be painstakingly searched out by a beginner. There is no relevant literal sense in which the logician is engaged in a perceptual task; nevertheless, what the skilled logician experiences in simply recognizing whether a step in an argument is valid is more closely analogous to what the skilled radiologist experiences in looking at an X-ray, than it is to the case in which one continually consults and follows an explicit set of rules. Similarly, the way a skilled logician recognizes a valid step is more nearly analogous to the way the product of six and seven should occur to us than it is to the process of following rules that we must engage in if we have not learned arithmetic properly. In all of these cases, explicit following of rules is characteristic of an unskilled, rather than of a skilled, performance. This does not mean that no analysis or thought takes place when a master is at work, but it does suggest that these do not occur consciously, and that it is only the outcome of these processes that appears to consciousness.

Now let us turn to cases that require judgement, irrespective of whether these occur in the context of discovery or of justification. We can include here, among others, cases in which a logician or a mathematician is deciding how to proceed in attempting to construct a proof; cases in which a scientist is deciding whether to pursue a theory further, or how to test an hypothesis exper-imentally, or what to make of an apparent disconfirmation of a theory; and cases in which an individual is deciding whether to pursue a particular career or purchase a stock. One common experience in such cases – there is no need to insist that it is the only one – is that in which the individual consciously reflects on different options, examines data, considers pros and cons, perhaps sleeps on the matter, and then finds that she has arrived at a decision. There is nothing mysterious about such cases as long as we recognize that more is going on than appears to consciousness, and on a naturalistic approach, these additional processes do not involve a mysterious nonphysical realm, or the exercise of a mystical intuition. Rather, naturalism suggests that the work that leads to a judgement is done by our nervous system, and that it is the outcome of this work that appears to consciousness. The capacity of our nervous system to do a particular job is a result of both the general abilities that have resulted from its evolution, and a variety of factors specific to an individual – including the education and training that this person has undergone.[3]

Many philosophers and psychologists, including many with strong naturalistic leanings, prefer to hold off this appeal to physical processes as long as possible. One standard way of attempting to do this is by proposing that we follow rules 'unconsciously'. It is not always clear what is meant by this claim. One interpretation is that our behavior conforms to rules even where we are not conscious of following those rules; I will discuss this interpretation below. A second interpretation amounts to claiming that the cognitive work we are unaware of takes place in a second, unconscious, mind that exists alongside the conscious mind, and that wields the rules that we are not aware of wielding. But this proposal only pushes the issue back a step without providing any clear gain. For if our unconscious mind is exactly like our conscious mind, only hidden, all of the above discussion will have to be repeated, and we will have the unconscious mind receiving results from some other source that is hidden from it. Presumably we will want an unconscious mind that is sufficiently different from the conscious mind to eliminate these problems, but the introduction of this new entity generates further problems. One issue that naturalists must eventually face is the nature of the relation between consciousness and the nervous system. Fortunately, we need not attempt to solve this problem here, but it is worth noting that the introduction of an unconscious mind does nothing to resolve it, while introducing problems about the relation between the nervous system and a second mind, as well as problems about the relations between the two minds. Such problems need not deter us if we have strong reasons for introducing an unconscious mind, but a naturalistic approach suggests that this is quite unnecessary. At some point we must reach a physical foundation for cognitive processes in the nervous system, and naturalism suggests that we move to the nervous system as quickly as we can, rather than attempting to stave off this move as long as possible. On this view, those processes that lead to the appearance of an idea in consciousness take place in the nervous system, and the results of these processes are presented in completed form to consciousness, without being filtered through yet another mind. The details of these processes are a matter for scientific research, and outside the scope of the present discussion.

If we reject the notion of an unconscious mind, we must also reject a common analysis of the relation between a skilled performance and that of a novice. On this analysis, when we develop expertise in a field, we 'internalize' the rules, and we continue to follow them, in some sense. The obvious problem here is to specify this sense, and the natural response is to introduce, again, an unconscious mind that follows rules. A naturalistic approach suggests a different view of what occurs when we develop expertise: learning involves training the nervous system much as we train our muscles and reflexes when we learn to hit a baseball or play a musical instrument. In these cases too we consciously follow rules when we begin, but no longer need those rules once we have developed competence. In other words, I am suggesting that the development of cognitive skills is more closely analogous to the development of physical skills than has been traditionally held – and this is not surprising if we are in fact wholly physical systems.

I now want to consider an objection to the approach that I have sketched: whatever it is that nervous systems do, they do not judge. There are at least two ways in which this objection might be developed. First, it could be suggested that judgement is, perhaps by definition, mental, and thus must be located in a mind. But this type of argument is much less impressive than it sometimes seems to be. If the processes by which we arrive at a judgement do not take place in consciousness, then the claim that these processes must still occur in a 'mental' rather than a physical domain is an hypothesis that is subject to evaluation as the relevant science develops, not an *a priori* principle that constrains scientific development. Our common notion of judgement may include the demand that judgements be mental, but it also includes a number of paradigm examples of judgements, and once we focus on the paradigm instances – which is what I have done here – their genesis becomes an open question.

Alternatively, it might be argued that a nervous system operates in accordance with physical laws, and that although these laws may be exceedingly complex, their operation is ultimately mechanical, guaranteeing that we will always arrive at the same outcome for a given state and input. One of the central characteristics of judgement is that it is not mechanical: different, equally competent individuals who have access to the same body of information may arrive at different judgements. One way of responding here would be to insist that different judgements must result from differences either in the information used or in the way that it is processed, and that many judgmental situations are sufficiently complex for subtle differences in one of these to lead to significantly different judgements. But I want to note a more striking possibility. The objection we are considering draws on the familiar identification of physical laws with strict causal laws, but we have already seen that quantum theory has led to the introduction of irreducibly statistical laws. These laws yield a range of outputs for a given state and input. The set of permissible outputs may be large, perhaps even infinite, but this does not mean that all logically possible outcomes must be given equal weight. There are disjoint infinite sets (e.g., the sets of odd and of even integers), and even when there is an infinite variety of possible responses to an input, many infinite sets of possibilities may be excluded. At the same time, the statistical laws that govern a system typically impose definite probabilities on the permitted outcomes, and some of the possible outcomes will occur much more frequently than others. These features of statistical laws are striking because they match features that we have encountered in discussing judgement. (Recall that I am not identifying a rational decision with a judgement; I will consider additional constraints required for rationality in chapter V.) A judgement is not rigidly determined by the available information and rules, but this does not mean that judgements are constrained only by logical possibility, or that all genuinely possible outcomes are equally likely. I am not arguing here that judgements are in fact governed by statistical laws, but only that we no longer have any reason to assume that a constrained but variable phenomenon like judgement could not be governed by natural laws.

Let us consider a second line of objection: physical systems, it will be maintained, including nervous systems, operate in accordance with rules, even if these are statistical rules, and one aim of researchers studying nervous systems is to find those rules. Thus if judgement is a natural phenomenon, it will be a rule-governed phenomenon, and we will be on the road back to the classical model of rationality. In order to deal with this objection, we must note that the notion of behaving 'in accordance with a rule' is ambiguous: we must distinguish cases in which a rule is being *followed* from cases in which behavior *conforms to* a rule, but the agent is not following that rule (cf. Sellars, 1963, pp. 324–7; Bennett, 1964, pp. 8–21). In order to follow a rule we must be aware of it and consciously guide our behavior by it. Clear examples of this would include cases such as setting up a truth-table while attending at each step to the rules that determine the number of rows required and the initial layout of the truth-values; or differentiating an expression in accordance with one of the standard rules for differentiation; or following directions to a friend's new home in an unfamiliar town. By way of contrast, consider a falling stone that moves in accordance with the rule that its acceleration shall increase in inverse proportion with the square of its distance from the center of the earth. The stone does not follow this rule, even though the rule accurately describes the stone's behavior. In general, showing that an item's behavior can be accurately described by a rule shows only that its behavior conforms to that rule; considerably more is required to show that the rule is being followed.

Before proceeding we should note that we can now deal with the alternative interpretation of the view, mentioned above, that we follow rules unconsciously, along with the view that we 'implicitly follow' rules even when we are not aware of following any rules. Both of these proposals amount to the claim that it can be shown that our behavior conforms to rules, but this is not the same as showing that we follow those rules – again, the acceleration of a falling stone conforms to a rule, but the stone does not follow that rule. Finding a rule that covers some behavior is not sufficient to show that that rule is being followed.

Now the classical model of rationality requires not just that rational behavior conform to rules, but that these rules be followed. Contrast, for example, a person who carries out a valid deduction or computation in full consciousness of what she is doing, with someone who arrives at the same result through an arbitrary choice on encountering the premises. In both cases the relation between premises and conclusion conforms to the appropriate rules, but the first person has a rational basis for accepting the conclusion, while the second does not. Thus even if we find a set of rules that the nervous system conforms to when making judgements, it would be necessary to show that the nervous system follows those rules in order to return to the classical model of rationality.

The line between conforming to and following rules is not always clear, and it will be helpful to examine a case that is especially susceptible to confusion: the case of a computer operating in accordance with a program. A computer program is a set of rules, and when a programmer works through a program in order to test its logic, she follows those rules. We write programs in order to control the computer's behavior, and we get the computer to behave in the way that we want by entering the program into the machine. Still, it would be a mistake to conclude from all of this that the computer then *follows* the program in a sense that is at all analogous to the way in which we follow the program when we are analyzing it. For the sake of simplicity, consider a program which does not require any inputs once it has been initiated, e.g., a program that calculates ascending prime numbers. When we enter the program into the computer, say by typing it in on a keyboard, we are creating a particular electronic state in the machine, and once the program has been started, the computer runs through a sequence of further electronic states. Each state in this process is determined by the machine's circuitry and by the initial state created by the program. We enter the program into the machine in order to create a particular initial state, and the set of rules that constitute the program helps *us* create that state; the computer does not need these rules. If we could generate the desired initial state in the computer by direct manipulation of electric charges in the circuitry, the computer would proceed exactly as it had before.[4] We might follow rules in manipulating the electrical state of the machine, but that would still not show that the machine itself followed these rules. Indeed, we would follow different rules when manipulating charges than we do when writing and typing the program, but the machine behaves in exactly the same way in both cases once its initial state has been established.

Let me put the point a slightly different way. There is a set of rules that I follow when I calculate prime numbers; when I write a program I express these rules in a programming language and I then enter the resulting program into the computer. But it would be a mistake to assume that once the program is started in the computer, the machine 'calculates prime numbers' in a sense that is at all analogous to what occurs when I calculate prime numbers. A parallel example will help to underline my point. Given that the distance a stone falls when dropped from rest is proportional to the square of the time of fall, we could determine square roots by dropping stones through measured distances and reading the time of fall off properly calibrated clocks, but stones do not calculate squares of times as they fall, and clocks do not compute square roots. In a similar way, many physical systems whose behavior can be described as conforming to rules are unaware of, and do not follow, those rules. But once this is recognized, we are no longer compelled to admit that if judgement is a function of neural processes, and if these processes are controlled by natural laws, then judgement is a rule-following activity after all.[5]

Note particularly that I have not proposed any view of how nervous systems operate – that is a scientific question. My only concern in this section has been to argue against the view that if we allow the notion of judgement into our epistemology, we have condemned ourselves to a non-naturalistic view of knowledge. Rather, it may well be that when we arrive at a judgement we become aware of the outcome of neural processes that are not present to our consciousness. We do not consciously control these processes, but we lay the groundwork for them when we develop expertise in a subject, and when we immerse ourselves in the information relevant to the decision at hand. On this view, the development of cognitive skills is closely analogous to the development of physical skills, and the conscious, explicit, rule-following that has long been taken as the paradigm of intelligent mental life captures only a small portion of our cognitive resources.

CHAPTER V

Rationality

In this chapter I will explain what I mean by a *model*, propose an alternative to the classical model of rationality, and discuss some consequences of this new model.

5.1 *Concepts and models*

There is one more preliminary matter that must be dealt with before I propose a new model of rationality: I must explain what is involved in offering a new model of a familiar concept. Let me first note some of the things that I am *not* going to do. I am not going to claim that the classical model of rationality is based on an incorrect account of what we normally mean by 'rationality'; in many respects it is, I think, based on a correct analysis. Nor will I argue that there exists an essence or form of rationality that is not adequately captured by our ordinary talk of rationality. Nor am I going to introduce a new concept and then appropriate the word 'rationality' for this concept – that would be singularly useless and confusing. I want to approach what I am after by reflecting a bit on concepts.

It is difficult to explain with precision what a concept is, but it will not be necessary for us to have a complete account; for present purposes the following points will suffice.[1] First, although a concept is not the same thing as a word, our concepts are reflected in the way we use words, and an exploration of the way a word is used often provides the best way to get at the associated concept. The dictionary definition of a term is a convenient compendium of information about the related concept, and there are usually two parts to a dictionary definition. One part is '*intra-*

linguistic': it describes the way the term functions within the language, including its grammatical role and its relations to other terms. The second part is '*extra*linguistic': it indicates how the term in question relates to items in the world. In some instances this second job is done by providing a picture, but more commonly it is done linguistically by describing or referring to items that are presumably familiar to the reader. This will be of little help to those who do not have some mastery of the language being used, but I am not concerned with novice language users here; I am only concerned with how we specify the meaning of a term to those who have sufficient linguistic competence to be discussing such matters. For some terms one of these components will be more important than the other, and the meanings of some terms may involve only one component. For example, definitions of logical constants have no extralinguistic component; we define these terms completely when we describe their role in the language. Simple color terms, on the other hand, have few intralinguistic connections; dictionaries define them by directing the reader to circumstances in which she can see that color. Thus my *Random House Dictionary* tells me that red is 'any of various colors resembling the color of blood; a color at the extreme end of the visible spectrum'. The meanings of most terms, however, involve both an intralinguistic and an extralinguistic component.

Now in considering the extralinguistic component of meaning we must not make the classical empiricist assumption that this is always some set of sensory qualia. Rather, the extralinguistic aspect of a definition picks out typical items to which the term applies, and we should not place any *a priori* restrictions on what may be appropriate. These may be sensory qualia in the case of quality terms, but they can be material objects for terms such as 'table' or 'book'; complex systems of material objects and social structures for a term such as 'nation', and so forth. Sellars also divides the extralinguistic component into 'language entry transitions' and 'language exit transitions'. The former are the familiar moves from the experience of some item into the language; these occur when we subsume an item under a concept. The latter are moves from the language to the world, e.g., taking an action as a result of a set of inferences carried out within the language. In other words, there are different kinds of terms that are connected with extralinguistic items in different ways, and some terms are fully meaningful even though they have no extralinguistic component. Note especially that for terms that are connected to the world by language entry transitions, paradigm instances play a role in specifying the meaning of the term. We recognize this when we turn to paradigm cases in the course of developing and criticizing an analysis of some concept, but many philosophers seek to express their analyses in a set of necessary and sufficient conditions, and leave the paradigm cases out of the final summary of their results.

Let us move on to a second point: the concepts that we use are not, somehow, built into reality, and given to us. Rather, concepts are human inventions, introduced to do specific cognitive jobs. Consider, for example, why we make use not only of the notions of a chair and of a table, but also the notion of a piece of furniture. We wield the first two concepts because there are situations in which we find it useful to distinguish objects on which we normally sit from those that we normally use as a support for other objects; although these uses can be interchanged, there are also characteristic shapes and sizes that, by and large, go with one use or the other. There are, however, also situations in which it is convenient for purposes of communication and thought to group chairs and tables, along with other objects, under a single rubric, so we have produced the concept of furniture. Given various interests, we often shift items from class to class, and the fact that two items are considered part of a single class for one purpose tells us little about what will happen in another case. Items of furniture are grouped with different items when our concerns turn to items made of wood, or to four-legged items, and we may create new concepts and abandon old ones as new concerns develop. We have a great deal of freedom in generating concepts. People in different cultures have generated different conceptual systems, and organized the items they encounter differently, but this freedom is not unlimited. Concepts can be so narrow or so diffuse as to be of no cognitive or practical value, and while new conceptual structures can give us new ways of looking at previously familiar items, we cannot make nuclear wastes or cancer disappear by dropping a concept from our repertoire. Features of the world we live in exercise a considerable constraint on the range of concepts we can successfully employ, and individuals or social groups may fail to cope with the world they live in because the groupings and distinctions that are embodied in their concepts are, or become, inappropriate for guiding them among the situations they encounter.

Many of our concepts are developed in the course of everyday, practical concerns, and for everyday purposes these concepts need not have the clarity and precision that we typically seek when we carry out a philosophical analysis. We do not have clear definitions of 'table', 'chair', or 'furniture', and these concepts are not of sufficient intellectual interest for philosophers to have spent much effort analyzing them. We do not need philosophical precision in the everyday contexts in which we use these notions, and we should not expect all of our concepts to have the clarity and precision that we sometimes find in some of them. Moreover, there is no guarantee that an everyday concept is consistent. Many common concepts have a variety of different notions packed into them, and as long as we do not get into trouble, we do not worry about consistency. Indeed, it is worth recalling that even a fully explicit mathematical concept, such as the concept of a set, can be inconsistent, and that we may use such a concept for many years without becoming aware of this inconsistency. In addition, many common concepts are vague. Reflection on intralinguistic connections will often show that certain ties to other concepts are necessary, but leave some ties uncertain and subject to dispute. Similarly, consideration of extralinguistic connections will usually show that some items must be included under a concept, and that others must be excluded, but still leave cases about which there is no clear answer. As long as we are concerned with practical matters, we usually need not worry about these borderline cases. But sometimes one of these cases does become important, and there need not be a preordained answer to the question of whether this item shall be included under the concept in question. Here we do not require further analysis, but a conceptual *decision*.[2]

The considerations of the previous two paragraphs are not limited to everyday practical concepts; examples from science and philosophy abound. The early mathematical concept of a set was inconsistent, and the history of science is full of examples of abandoned concepts such as 'phlogiston' and 'natural place', as well as concepts such as 'matter', 'energy', 'atom' and 'time' that have undergone complex transformations in response to new discoveries. As an example from philosophy, consider the notion of a 'concept'. I have been attempting to sketch some features of this concept, and it is a concept that has been central to the history of philosophy, and especially central to the work of those who engage in conceptual analysis. Yet we are far from having a clear, precise definition of what a concept is. A rough sketch seems to be sufficient for many purposes, although some key transformations in the history of philosophy have involved reconsideration of the nature of concepts.

Clearly there is much more to be said about concepts, but the above remarks will suffice for present purposes. On the view that I have sketched, attempts at philosophical analysis of a concept often turn out *not* to be attempts to formulate a set of preexisting necessary and sufficient conditions, but rather attempts to *generate* such a set. There are many reasons why this attempt has often seemed desirable. If our conceptual boundaries were precise many verbal disputes and miscommunications might disappear, and after all, in logic and mathematics, which have so often provided our paradigm of knowledge, concepts usually do have complete, explicit sets of necessary and sufficient conditions. Attempts to generate a clear concept begin from reflection on the existing concept, and when successful they result in a concept that is more precise than our everyday concept, and more likely to be consistent. In attempting to construct a precise, consistent concept, some features of our preanalytic concept may be taken as fundamental, while others are considered less important, and are perhaps left out of the final analysis completely. Moreover, the decision as to which aspects of a preanalytic concept are to be taken as fundamental will often be guided by other philosophical concerns, and one reason why philosophers may find it so hard to agree on the 'analysis' of a familiar concept is that they approach the concept with different philosophical programs.

The outcome of an attempt to build a clear and distinct concept out of a relatively inchoate concept is what I have been referring to as a *model*.[3] I will illustrate this thesis for the case of rationality in the next section, where I will argue that the classical model of rationality selects certain features of our preanalytic concept of rationality and leaves out others, and that the motivation for these choices lies in foundationalism. The failure of foundationalism, and the problems that this failure generates for the classical model of rationality, suggest that we should turn to those aspects of our common concept of rationality that have been left in limbo in order to find the basis for an alternative model.

5.2 *Rationality*

Let us consider some aspects of our everyday concept of rationality; I will focus first on rational beliefs. Perhaps the central idea included in our preanalytic concept of rationality is that we have reasons for our rational beliefs and can provide those reasons on request. Thus rational beliefs can be distinguished from those beliefs that are not properly grounded in reasons, and from those that conflict with what we have reason to believe. If we are to be rational, we must believe on the basis of relevant evidence, and be prepared to alter our beliefs if the weight of evidence changes. We also expect rational beliefs to be, on balance, more reliable than nonrational or irrational beliefs exactly because our rational beliefs are based on appropriate evidence.

At the same time, we also have the notion of a 'rational person', i.e., a person who can exercise good sense and good judgement in difficult cases, particularly cases in which we lack clear guiding principles. We expect a rational person to be amenable to new ideas, and even to be capable of making new proposals in a sticky situation. We also think of a rational person as one who is prepared to compromise, and who fits Aristotle's description of the equitable man who 'is no stickler for his rights in a bad sense but tends to take less than his share though he has the law on his side . . .' (*Nicomachean Ethics*, 1137b–1138a, 1941, p. 1020). Note particularly that we expect a rational person to be capable of functioning well in the context of discovery; the distinction between discovery and justification, along with the limitation of rationality to the latter, is not an idea that commonly leaps to the mind when we think of a rational human being. Instead, I think that most of us, at first blush, take the scientist or the physician who is struggling to solve a problem without benefit of clear rules as paradigms of a person involved in a task that requires rationality. Similarly, newspaper editorials do not issue calls for rationality in balancing checkbooks or differentiating algebraic functions, but they do call for rationality in moral and political situations, and in doing so they are not urging people to follow well known rules. When appropriate rules are available we expect a rational person to follow those rules. But we also expect a rational person to be capable of acting sensibly without rules, and we expect a rational person to provide reasons for whatever conclusion she eventually arrives at even when no rules are available. This is not the entire story, but it will suffice to get us started.

The classical model of rationality is considerably more precise than this everyday concept, and I submit that we arrive at the classical model if we make two key moves. First, we take the notion of a rational belief as fundamental, and the notion of a rational person as derivative (cf. Bartley, 1984, pp. 233–4). Philosophical attention then turns to the question of what constitutes adequate reasons for believing a claim, and a rational person is one whose beliefs meet these standards. Second, we attempt to explicate the notion of 'reasons for a belief' in foundationalist terms. This leads us to focus on the proposition believed, and on the relations between that proposition and other propositions. Many of the vagaries of philosophical discussions of rationality have resulted from changes in our understanding of the range of activities in which acceptable reasons could be supplied, and from changes in what we are willing to accept as a legitimate foundation. As an example of the former note that the elimination of rationality from the context of discovery is a relatively recent development, one that resulted from the recognition that there are no methods for generating new discoveries in the way we generate truth-tables or the products of numbers. The latter can be illustrated by the myriad developments that have seemed to threaten irrationality at every turn by opening up regresses that had once seemed to be permanently blocked. These developments include new doubts about whether there is a cause for every physical event, doubts about the consistency of arithmetic and the power of axiomatic systems, the development of alternative logics, and so forth. In other words, the classical model of rationality is not an analysis of the concept of rationality, it is a model that has been guided by a philosophical programme. This suggests that one way of responding to these doubts about rationality is to return to our preanalytic concept of rationality and take features of that concept that were relegated to a secondary status or neglected altogether by the classical model as the basis for an alternative model. I want to propose an alternative in three steps.

The first step is to take the notion of a rational agent as fundamental, and such notions as 'rational belief' as derivative in the sense that a rational belief will be one that is arrived at by a rational agent. The remaining steps in the construction of our new model will impose constraints on rational agents, but there are two points I want to note before proceeding. First, we must distinguish between a rational *agent* and a rational *person*, for we will see that a single person may be capable of acting as a rational agent in some circumstances, but not in others. Second, this initial step provides a good illustration of the relation between a concept and a model. Our everyday concept of rationality includes the idea that a belief's rationality is connected with the way we arrive at that belief: a belief that we arrive at on the basis of an adequate body of appropriate evidence is a rational belief, while a belief that we arrive at without evidence, or against the evidence, or on the basis of irrelevant evidence, is not rational. This aspect of the concept of rationality is included in the classical model of rationality and will be included in our new model, but it is developed differently in each of these models. In the classical model the central emphasis is placed on the logical relations between the evidence and the belief, while the role of the agent is minimized, or left out. Our alternative model will take the agent to be basic, and the way in which an agent deals with evidence in arriving at a belief to be determinative of the rationality of that belief for her. We will see that this involves considerable relativization of rational belief to individuals, but that this is not the same as a relativization of the notion of rationality.

As a second step I will take the ability to make judgements in those situations in which we lack sufficient rules to determine our decision as a characteristic feature of a rational agent. This makes the notion of judgement central to our new model of rationality, and entails that our ability to act as rational agents is limited by our expertise. This does not quite mean that only experts can be rational, but it does mean that in cases in which I lack expertise, there may only be one rational decision open to me: to seek expert advice. For example, given the limits of my medical knowledge, it would be irrational for me to attempt to diagnose and treat an illness in the overwhelming majority of situations, but it would be rational for me to seek competent medical advice. We depend on our ability to be rational when we lack clear rules. When rules are available, an informed agent will recognize that this is the case, and will apply those rules; it is when rules are not available that we require rational assessment. Thus one reason why it is desirable to discover algorithms for the solution of as many problems as possible is that this leaves our rational abilities free to operate in other situations – those in which no algorithm is available. On our new model, explanatory and justificatory regresses do not block the exercise of rationality. Rather, the situation is turned on its head: when a regress threatens, rational decision-making is required, and those who have the necessary expertise must exercise judgement in order to terminate the regress – for the time being. Note also that the result of a judgement is sometimes best described as a 'decision', sometimes as a 'belief', and that the points that follow will apply to both. I will thus talk about either decisions or beliefs as the context demands.

This proposal is, I think, consistent with aspects of our preanalytic concept of rationality that were noted above and that have been rejected by the classical model, but it is not enough. Our common concept of rationality also requires that rational decisions and beliefs should be considerably more reliable than nonrational ones, and while we expect those with expertise in a subject to be more reliable than those who lack this expertise, human judgement is still notoriously fallible. While there are cases in which we have no recourse but to rely on judgement, we also recognize that it would be foolish for an individual to place total confidence in her own judgement. The classical model of rationality attempted to circumscribe judgement with rules, and one attraction of that model was undoubtedly its promise that rationality would bring along an increase in reliability that would transcend the cognitive limitations of individuals. This suggests that we need another element in our model, one which will place a further constraint on rational agents, and reduce our dependence on individual judgement. In effect, we are seeking something that will replace rules as a check on individual judgement, and we can get some guidance in this task by returning to two topics that were discussed above. First, we saw that Wittgenstein's reflections on linguistic rules led to the conclusion that if rules are to do the epistemic job that has traditionally been required of them, these rules must be irreducibly social. Second, we discussed Kuhn's analyses of normal and revolutionary science, but said little about how decisions are made during revolutionary periods, when the rules of normal science break down. In fact, Kuhn argues that decision-making in such periods must be understood as a socially mediated process rather than a rule-guided process. I will discuss both of these lines of argument below, but I want to note the conclusion that I am after. The third step required for our new model of rationality is the introduction of a social element: for a belief based on judgement to be a rational one, it must be submitted to the community of those who share the relevant expertise for evaluation against their own judgements. This demand that rational beliefs be subject to evaluation and criticism is in conformity with our normal understanding of rationality, but I shall argue that we can develop this proposal without a fouundationalist framework by taking rationality to be a social phenomenon. In these terms, Robinson Crusoe alone on his island could exercise judgement, but he would not be able to achieve rationality. This is not because of some failing in his faculties, but rather for a reason akin to the reason why he could not play baseball, even though he could throw balls in the air, hit them with a bat, and run bases. On the model I am proposing, ration-ality requires other people – and not just any people, but other people who have the skills needed to exercise judgement in the case at hand. We have already considered judgement at some length, and I now want to discuss this new element of our model.[4]

To begin with, this proposal seems to conflict with one feature of our everyday concept of rationality: I do not think we would consider it obvious that Robinson Crusoe could not arrive at rational beliefs, or that the last scientist left in the world could not practice science in a rational manner. But the fact that we are not in complete conformity with the preanalytic concept need not be overly troublesome, we are not trying to analyze that concept, but to construct a model based on it. Some departures from the common concept are to be expected, and in constructing a model we aim to do the job that the everyday concept is supposed to do, and do it better. The classical model of rationality is also at odds with features of our everyday concept of rationality, but if foundationalism had worked, the classical model would have provided a worthy replacement for that everyday concept. Still, we should be able to offer a motivation for any departures we make from the concept we are working with, and this is now the main task before us. I want to approach this task by discussing the two cases noted above in which philosophers have introduced social elements into areas in which such elements had previously been assumed to be irrelevant: Wittgenstein on rule-following and Kuhn on decision-making in revolutionary science.

In chapter III we discussed the line of argument that led Wittgenstein (1953) to hold that there is no sense to the claim that I am following a rule unless there is some public means of determining whether I have in fact obeyed that rule, and from there to the conclusion that rules are essentially social.[5] This involves an important departure from earlier views of rule-following, and the contrast will be clearer if we look briefly at the way rules function on a more traditional approach. The point I wish to make is particularly striking in philosophy of science, where it was long assumed that the special cognitive power of science lay in its application of a set of rules for deciding which claims are to be accepted and which rejected. These rules must be formulated by individuals, and once formulated, they are taught to members of new generations by those who have mastered them; but this does not make these rules social in the sense that concerns us here. On the traditional view, once these rules are available, no one else need exist either for me to possess them or for me to apply them appropriately. Whether we view these rules as having been invented or discovered, they function as quasi-Platonic entities that exist independently of us and that can be consulted as the need arises, much as we consult a table of logarithms. In other words, given a competent scientist, an hypothesis, and a body of evidence, we need some check on the scientist's decision as to how well the evidence supports the hypothesis, and this check must be independent of the scientist's preferences or inclinations. If the rules of scientific method exist independently of any individual scientist, and are available to all, they can provide this check. Thus the quasi-Platonic view of rules, and the view of science as essentially individualistic, go hand in hand. A single individual who was sufficiently intelligent and sufficiently long-lived could, in principle, create all of science, and the fact that the development of scientific knowledge has required the cooperation of numerous individuals derives from contingent features of human intelligence and the human life span. But if Wittgenstein's view of rules is correct – i.e., if there are no rules in the absence of an appropriate social structure – then science as a rule-governed activity could not exist without a community of scientists.

My only aim in returning to Wittgenstein here has been to offer one illustration of a case in which a philosopher has introduced a social aspect into the analysis of a cognitive phenomenon that had long been considered an individualistic matter. I want to turn now to an example that is more directly relevant to our present concerns: Kuhn's discussion of scientific choice in revolutionary situations. Let me begin by noting that, for Kuhn, normal science is also a social phenomenon – an achievement does not become a paradigm until it has been accepted as a basis for continued research by a community of researchers (1970c, p. 10). I argued in chapter III that Kuhnian normal science approaches a fully rule-governed endeavor, but I also noted that Kuhn maintains that the key rules are derivative from the paradigm; I want to consider this latter claim. Kuhn chose the term 'paradigm' to describe what it is that the members of a community of scientists hold in common because he wanted to emphasize that such a community is *not formed by accepting a set of rules*. Rather, a research community comes into existence when a group of researchers adopts a successful piece of problem-solving as a model for its own research, and trains new scientists to work in terms of that model. Scientists learn their trade by working through standard problems, both in the laboratory and on paper, and in doing so they acquire a body of cognitive and manipulative skills. We saw in chapter IV that such skills involve a richer body of knowledge than can be captured in a set of rules, and it is these skills that provide the basis for the professional scientist's attempts to apply the paradigm to the solution of new problems.[6] On reflection, much of what is involved in normal practice can be captured in explicit rules, and normal scientists can be seen as conforming to these rules, but such explicit rules are of little importance to the normal scientist who is practicing science, not reflecting on it.

During periods of revolutionary science this situation changes. Now previous practice is in question, and it is often useful to attempt to capture that practice in a set of rules – although any rules that have been abstracted from previous practice are now in doubt. Kuhn sometimes writes as if there is no longer any shared cognitive basis for decision-making among scientists, but I will argue in section 5 of this chapter that this is not correct. For the moment, however, my concern is to note that even in this extreme condition, Kuhn does not conclude that the decisions that terminate a period of revolutionary science are baseless or arbitrary. Rather, Kuhn invokes the central role of the scientific community in a new way, maintaining that, whatever may be in question, the community still exists, and that the responsibility for resolving the revolution rests in that community. Moreover, Kuhn maintains that the fact that such decisions are made by the scientific community is sufficient to prevent them from being arbitrary decisions. The following is Kuhn's clearest statement of this thesis:

> confronted with the problem of theory-choice, the structure of my response runs roughly as follows: take a *group* of the ablest available people with the most appropriate motivation; train them in some science and in the specialties relevant to the choice at hand; imbue them with the value system, the ideology, current in their discipline (and to a great extent in other scientific fields as well); and, finally, *let them make the choice*. If that technique does not account for scientific development as we know it, then no other will. There can be no set of rules of choice adequate to dictate desired *individual* behaviour in the concrete cases that scientists will meet in the course of their careers. Whatever scientific progress may be, we must account for it by examining the nature of the scientific group, discovering what it values, what it tolerates, and what it disdains. (1970c, pp. 237–8)

In a revolutionary situation different individuals will offer different proposals for a new research consensus. Each of these is offered on the basis of that person's professional judgement, but once a proposal has been made, it becomes a subject for discussion and debate among the members of the professional community. Note particularly that only those with the relevant expertise and information are in a position to make and evaluate proposals, and Kuhn is maintaining that it is the process of community evaluation that distinguishes a rational choice from one which lacks rational warrant. As one commentator has put it, for Kuhn, 'science's authority ultimately resides not in a rule-governed method of inquiry whereby scientific results are obtained but in the scientific community that obtains the results' (Gutting, 1980, p. 1).

It is worth emphasizing that Kuhn does consider the outcome of this process to be a rational decision. This view may be seriously at odds with the classical model of rationality, but Kuhn consistently maintains that the choice of science as a paradigmatically rational activity is more reliable than any views we may have as to what it is that makes science rational. If our model of rationality is at odds with the way science proceeds, then it is this model that will have to go. Thus Kuhn writes, 'No process essential to scientific development can be labelled "irrational" without vast violence to the term' (1970b, p. 235), and Kuhn describes his project as:

> an attempt to show that existing theories of rationality are not quite right and that we must readjust or change them to explain why science works as it does. To suppose, instead, that we possess criteria of rationality which are independent of our understanding of the essentials of the scientific process is to open the door to cloud-cuckoo land. (1970b, p. 264)

This is a strong statement of the methodology that I have followed in this book.

Note that there is a crucial difference between the way that a social element appears in Wittgenstein and in Kuhn. For Wittgenstein rules are social and any rule-governed activity must therefore be a social activity; for Kuhn the social aspect of science replaces rules as the basis for scientific research and decision-making. During periods of normal science a communally accepted paradigm is more fundamental than any rules that scientists may be conforming to, and in revolutionary science, where previously accepted practices and rules are in question, it is the scientific community that evaluates proposals and eventually arrives at a new consensus for normal science. Thus Kuhn proposes a consensual model of scientific rationality: rational decisions are those made by the scientific community, and in normal science these decisions become embodied in communally approved and transmitted practices. Note also that, for Kuhn, if an algorithm for making such choices were available, this communal element would not be needed, and Kuhn would prefer an algorithm. As we saw in Chapter III, Kuhn suggests that if we had an algorithm we would be able to avoid the 'arbitrary element' in theory choice, and Kuhn holds that it is this arbitrary element that is largely responsible for the eventual failure of every paradigm. Kuhn has often insisted that his views are more nearly traditional than his critics have acknowledged (e.g., 1977, pp. 321–5), yet Kuhn departs from tradition in holding that the absence of an algorithm does not automatically block rational decision-making. Instead, Kuhn holds that when the relevant scientific community reaches agreement, we have a rational decision.[7] At this point, the most competent available evaluation has indicated that the strengths of a proposal sufficiently outweigh the weaknesses to provide a basis for moving forward. This does not guarantee that the result is true, or wise, or even the best one that could have possibly been arrived at under ideal conditions. Unfortunately, there are no such guarantees, and it is a mistake, although a common one, to insist that only the best is good enough.[8] I will return to the relation between rationality and truth in section 5.3.

Now I am in agreement with most of what Kuhn has to say on this topic, but there are two key points at which we disagree. First, as should by now be clear, I do not think that there is any meaningful sense in which either individual judgements or communally mediated judgements can be described as 'arbitrary'. More importantly, Kuhn holds that once the community arrives at a conclusion, that conclusion is the only one that can be rationally accepted, and those who refuse to go along with it cease to be members of that community. But the model of rationality that I am proposing only requires that individuals submit their judgements for evaluation by their peers, and that they take this evaluation seriously. The model does not require that each member of the community agree with the majority, and indeed, agreement with the majority view is neither necessary nor sufficient for rationality. That it is not necessary should be clear from the discussion thus far: I have taken scientific practice as the key test case for my model, and rational disagreement is a pervasive feature of science. At the same time, agreement with the majority does not automatically make a belief rational. Our model requires that rational beliefs be based on judgement, and judgement requires assessment of evidence and arguments. If an individual does not exercise judgement in arriving at a belief, that belief is not rational no matter who agrees with it.

In other words, on the model I am proposing, the predicate 'rational' characterizes an individual's decisions and beliefs, it does not characterize propositions and it does not characterize communities. A community of individuals with the appropriate expertise is, on this model, necessary for an individual to arrive at a rational belief, but it is the individual's belief that is rational, not the community. A contrast may help to clarify my point. Morton Schagrin (1973) distinguishes between being 'rational' and being 'reasonable'. According to Schagrin, 'rationality' applies to individual's beliefs, but rationality is a weak notion (see also Schagrin, 1982, pp. 123–4) that involves few constraints. Individuals, however, cannot be reasonable, only a community can be reasonable – just as only a community can be democratic (1973, pp. 7–8) – and only decisions arrived at by a community can be reasonable. Now I agree with Schagrin that the term 'rationality' is best applied to an individual's beliefs, and I also think that the notion of rationality is considerably weaker than it was traditionally taken to be. But I think it is a stronger notion than Schagrin does, and I have been proposing constraints on rational belief. One of these constraints is that rational beliefs are arrived at through interaction with a community of individuals who share the appropriate expertise, and I have not offered any characterization of the community beyond its members' possession of that expertise.

Let me take a second comparison. Our new model of rationality is consistent with the spirit of critical rationalism, particularly its demand that acceptable claims must be subjected to critical evaluation, but the reasons why this evaluation is required, and the way it is carried out, are different on the two views. For Popper, critical evaluation is all there is to rationality, and such evaluation is a matter of logic in the strictest sense of the term: it is concerned with relations between propositions and does not involve human knowers in any significant sense. One of Popper's main goals, a goal which has become progressively more central as his philosophy has developed, is to minimize the epistemic role of cognitive agents (cf. Popper, 1972, chs. 3 and 4). Thus Popper has come to argue that knowledge consists of propositions that exist in a nonphysical, nonmental 'third world' (the first world is made up of all physical entities, the second of all mental entities), and that propositions are evaluated by testing them against other propositions in accordance with logical rules, all of which are members of this third world. Moreover, Popper's emphasis on criticism derives from the view that only criticism can be captured in the framework of deductive logic. By way of contrast, our alternative model of rationality makes the human agents who exercise judgement central to rational procedures, and it is the fallibility of judgement that leads to the requirement of critical evaluation.

We have also seen that, according to Popper, epistemic regresses are broken by convention when we accept basic statements and methodological rules; on my view these regresses are broken by communally mediated judgements. The difference between Popperian conventions and these judgements may seem slight, but recall that, for Popper, conventions are outside the realm of rationality. Popper continually maintains that we can provide no rational grounds for accepting one convention rather than another, and that it is only after conventions have been established that the notion of rationality comes into play at all. But on the view developed here, we can have rational grounds for discussing methodological proposals, and such considerations as the possible consequences of accepting a proposal, and the role that analogous proposals have played in previous science and in other fields, are all relevant to this discussion. (See Laudan, 1984, for a similar position on this point.) At the same time, perceptual experience enters into the processes that lead to a judgement even if we cannot completely capture this experience in propositions.

There is one consequence of our new model of rationality that some will find especially objectionable. If rationality involves nothing more than judgement and critical evaluation by the members of an appropriate community, there is a great deal more rationality in the world than has often been thought, and we may find rational belief and rational decision-making in communities that many would wish to characterize as irrational. Abandoned scientific views such as earth-centered astronomy and the phlogiston theory of combustion will typically turn out to have once been held on rational grounds. Similarly, various groups of theologians who belong to different religions may all be engaged in a fully rational endeavor, and the same may hold for, say, Azande witch doctors. But while this possibility does follow from our model of rationality, it does not have quite the pernicious significance that some will see there. In order to indicate why, I must refer to two points that I will discuss in greater detail in the next sections: to claim that a belief is rational is not the same as claiming that it is true, and while rational acceptance of a claim depends on assessing evidence, some forms of evidence provide a stronger warrant for belief than other forms of evidence. Thus while questions of denominational theology may be capable of a rational resolution, it does not follow that we have no basis at all for choosing between, say, a scientific and a theological worldview at those points at which the two views conflict. In other words, I will argue below that rationality is indeed a weaker notion on my model than on the classical model, but that rationality is not the only thing involved in the cognitive assessment of claims.

Note also that I have not returned to the relativist position, criticized in chapter III, according to which every social group is automatically rational. On that view, rational behavior is rule-following behavior and any group following socially accepted rules is *ipso facto* rational according to their own standards. Our new model involves tighter constraints on rationality than simply following rules, and while many different sets of beliefs may all be rational on this model, the question of whether any particular beliefs are in fact rational must be decided by examining the way in which those beliefs were arrived at. For example, on investigation we might discover grounds for doubting that the Azande poison oracle leads to rational beliefs. And this failure of rationality could occur for either (or both) of two reasons: because witch doctors refuse to submit their results for evaluation; or because there just is no relevant expertise. In other words, we must not confuse the thesis that what it is rational to believe or do is relative to a particular situation, with the thesis that rationality is relative. Nicholas Wolterstorff slides between these in the following passage:

> It must be clearly noted that rationality . . . is in good measure person specific and situation specific. When I was young, there were things which it was rational for me to believe. And for a person reared in a traditional tribal society who never comes into contact with another society or culture, there will

be things rational to believe which for me, a member of the
modern Western intelligentsia, would not be rational to
believe. Rationality of belief can only be determined in
context. . . . Rationality is always *situated* rationality. (1983,
p. 155)

I would be in full agreement with these remarks if we replaced
'rationality' with 'rational belief' in the first and last sentences.

There is another potential misunderstanding that should also
be avoided. A number of sociologists of knowledge move from
considerations similar to those which have led us to include a
social element in rationality to the conclusion that this is the only
significant element of rationality. (See, for example, Bloor 1976;
Barnes, 1982; Barnes and Bloor, 1982.) It should be clear that
this is not the position I am defending here. The social element
is one element in rational decision-making, and the demands of
expertise must be met before the social element comes into play.
Thus a consensus that is imposed on the members of a community
by external political authority, or by force, or by manipulation of
data, or by any of a number of other familiar, unsavory techniques, will not generate rational beliefs on this model.[9] Moreover, the point of requiring expertise is that individuals must
actually make decisions on the basis of that expertise. If, to take
a wild example, all of the physicists in the world were to agree
that, beginning today, data would be communally fudged, and
results announced would be those they had agreed to announce,
we would have communal decisions by the relevant experts, and
no qualified dissenters, but these decisions would not result from
the exercise of expertise, and would not be rational.

To sum up, on our new model a rational belief or decision is
one that an individual has arrived at through a two-step process
(these steps need not be chronologically distinct). The belief is
based on judgement – where possession of the relevant information and expertise is a necessary condition for a judgement –
and this judgement has been tested against the judgements of
those who are also capable of exercising judgement in this case.
Judgement remains fundamental, for each individual must still
arrive at her own judgement of the significance of her colleagues'
objections and proposals, but there is still a crucial difference
between the judgement of an isolated individual and judgements

that are results of critical debate. Both are judgements, but only the latter issues in a rational outcome. Finally, recall that one does not acquire the ability to exercise judgement in a field once and for all, but that in order to maintain this ability one must 'keep up' with new information and techniques. In a similar fashion, submission of one's judgements to community evaluation need not be a once-and-for-all event: rational beliefs are subject to re-evaluation as relevant new information becomes available, and new arguments are developed.

5.3   *Rationality and truth*

On the classical model of rationality there is a close tie between rationality and truth, and it was often taken as obvious that false propositions could not be rationally accepted. In this section I want to examine the relation between truth and rationality in the framework of our new model of rationality. There is, however, one topic that we should consider first: in recent decades the significance of the notion of truth has been subject to much criticism, and for many it is no longer clear why we should be concerned with truth. Relativists have emphasized that people from different societies accept radically different sets of claims as true, and have maintained that there is no way in which we can choose between those 'truths'. And even if we do not accept relativism, we must still acknowledge that there are cases in which it is extremely difficult to determine whether a claim is true or false, and cases in which long-held beliefs about the truth-value of some proposition have had to be revised. There are also numerous cases in which people function successfully in the world on the basis of beliefs that they later reject as false, and we have seen that there may be propositions which are neither true nor false. Indeed, most of these points can be made by reflection on the history of science, and some have argued that the notion of truth has no significant role to play in a philosophy of science. (See, for example, Kuhn, 1970c, ch. 13; Laudan, 1977.) Yet it is extremely difficult to dispense with the notion of truth completely. One common and important response to attacks on truth is that the attackers are making claims that they take to be true, and that if not, it is difficult to see their point. What are we to make, for example, of such claims as 'Different societies have radically different views about the nature of the world', or 'Claims that were taken as established truths at one stage in the history of science cannot be formulated in a new paradigm', if it is not being asserted that these claims are true? It is certainly possible to show that the notion of truth is not relevant in some domain in which it was previously thought to be important, but that is not the same as showing that we can do without this notion altogether. Presumably the point of such arguments is to establish a truth about the domain in question, and in doing so we are assuming that the concept of truth is relevant in some other domain. It seems that the notion of truth is so deeply embedded in our thinking about cognitive matters that we cannot get along without it, and while there remains the radical alternative of constructing a new framework in which this notion does not occur, no such framework is available to us now. Thus we have little choice but to work in terms of a framework that is available.

Several questions arise at this point. First, what exactly do we mean by 'truth', i.e., what is the proper analysis of this concept? This is much too large a topic to be tackled here, but a rough correspondence approach will do for our purposes. On this analysis, when we make a claim about some domain, we are asserting that there is a feature of that domain that holds independently of this claim. If I assert that there are three chairs in my study I am making a claim about my study that is correct or incorrect independently of what anyone may believe. Similarly, that the Hopi word for 'day' cannot be pluralized is a feature of the Hopi language that existed before non-Hopi linguists discovered it; and the connection between smoking and lung cancer was discovered, not created, by medical researchers. Nothing has been said here about how we decide whether a claim is true or false. This is a different question from the question of what we mean by 'true', and the detailed answer to this new question may be different in different domains. I will have something to say about this question at the end of the present section and in the next section, but I want to approach this topic by first considering why truth is important.

Consider, first, cases in which we use a set of claims as premises for a valid deductive argument. Such arguments guarantee that if we begin with true premises we will end up with a true conclusion, while if our premises are not true, we receive no guarantee at all as to the truth-value of our conclusion. Now apply this point to a practical situation, e.g., one in which we design bridges by carrying out deductions from premises consisting of a set of design principles and a body of information relevant to the particular bridge under design. If all of these premises are true, we have a guarantee that any conclusions we validly deduce from them will also be true, and that our bridge will behave in the intended manner; if one or more of our premises is false, we have no such guarantee. Note particularly that the falsity of one of our design principles is compatible with the fact that every bridge we have designed so far using this principle has stood, because it is possible to deduce true conclusions, as well as conclusions that are sufficiently close to the truth for practical purposes, from false premises. But if one of our design principles is false, we have no basis for deciding whether the next bridge we design using this principle will stand or fall. Now there are actually two different points involved in these remarks: first, if our premises are in fact true, then they will yield true conclusions independently of whether we have adequate grounds for believing that those premises are true. But, second, we have no basis for accepting the conclusions as true unless we have reasons for believing that the premises are true. For the moment I want to concentrate on the first point; the second will become important shortly.

An analogous result obtains when we use inductive arguments. Here we never achieve the guarantee that our results are true that we get from deduction, but inductive reasoning still attempts to use an available body of information as evidence for some conclusion, and the reliability of the conclusion depends on the accuracy of our evidence. Whatever other problems we may have about induction, it is at least clear that an inductive argument must begin from true premises if it is to be relevant to the truth-value of its conclusion. Similarly, one way of attacking a conclusion that was arrived at by a judgement is by questioning the accuracy of the information on which that judgement was based.

Now consider a case in which we knowingly make use of false principles, e.g., when we use Newtonian physics even though we take it to be false. The typical cases in which this occurs are those in which we believe that the principles we are using are false because they conflict with other claims that we take to be true, or closer to the truth. Newtonian physics has been superseded by relativity and quantum theory, but we still find it useful to apply Newtonian techniques in a restricted range of cases. These cases must meet two conditions: first, we must be dealing with a problem in which it is known that the results of the Newtonian calculation are sufficiently close to the results of the relativistic or quantum theoretical calculation that it makes no difference which we use, given our present purposes. Second, the Newtonian calculation must be easier to carry out than the relativistic or quantum theoretical calculation, else there would be no point to the approximation. But note that we appeal to relativity and quantum theory to determine whether we can get away with a simpler Newtonian calculation, and we do not reverse this procedure, i.e., we never appeal to Newtonian mechanics to decide if a relativistic or quantum theoretical calculation is acceptable. It would be hard to find a clearer indication of the fact that we have much greater confidence in the truth of relativity and quantum theory than we do in Newtonian mechanics, and that we only use the latter when it provides a convenient approximation.

Part of the above discussion turns on the claim that valid deductions from true premises guarantee true conclusions, but earlier I raised questions about the adequacy of our knowledge of logic: what happens if we lack a set of valid logical rules? Does this make our concerns about true premises pointless? Recall here that my doubts about logic were strictly epistemological: I did not argue that there is no set of truth-hereditary principles of logic, but only that there are reasons for asking whether we are currently in possession of those principles. An analogous situation arises in physical science where we can question whether we now have the correct description of an aspect of the physical world, without questioning whether there is any such description to be found. In the case of logic this suggests that we not only have a vital interest in the truth of our premises, but also have a vital interest in the truth of the claim that the logical rules we currently use are valid. Of course, deeper doubts are possible, e.g., we can ask whether there are indeed physical objects for which there is a correct description, and whether there is a set of valid logical principles that we should seek. But here too we are asking whether a particular claim is true. If, for example, it is true that there are no valid rules of logic, then this is important and requires adjustments in the ways we deal with a wide variety of situations.

Now let us consider explicitly a point that has been lurking in the above discussion. Beginning, again, with cases involving deductive reasoning, note that the possession of true premises and valid rules of inference will assure that we arrive at true conclusions, but this will be of only limited value unless we also have grounds for believing that our premises are true and our principles of reasoning are valid. In other words, we must distinguish between possessing truth, and being able to recognize that we possess the truth. A voice in a dream may announce that the stock of Juggernaut Industries is going up, and this may be true, but this provides no basis for deciding to buy the stock unless I have reasons for believing that the dictates of the dream are true. Without such reasons I might buy and benefit because in fact the dream told me the truth, but this would be a coincidence, no better than a random choice that I might abandon tomorrow just as easily as I accepted it today. A similar point holds for induction and judgement as well: true premises do us little good unless we have reasons for believing that they are true. This is where rationality enters the picture, since rationality is concerned with assessing reasons for believing one claim or another.

Here we can again see the great attraction of the classical model of rationality and the search for foundations. We only want to accept those claims that we have reasons to accept, and if the foundationalist project had been successful, we would know that rationally founded claims are true. The failure of this project leaves us in a genuine quandary. We are still in a position in which the only basis we have for accepting a claim is that we have reasons for it, but on our new model of rationality, having reasons does not assure us of achieving truth. Our reasons rest on the best available judgement, but those judgements are tied to the evidence available at a particular time. The significance of this evidence is never beyond question, and further evidence may show any judgement to be wrong. Again, this is not just a bare possibility, and a bit of historical reflection will serve to underline this somewhat melancholy conclusion. There are many cases in which those who possessed the relevant expertise came to what seemed the best supported conclusions after assessing the best available evidence, but were eventually seen to be mistaken. In the ancient and medieval periods the thesis that the earth is stationary at the center of the universe had powerful observational and theoretical support. The people who held this view were mistaken, but they were neither foolish nor irrational, and it may well have been irrational, at that time, to believe that the earth moves. Similarly, there were once powerful rational grounds for believing that every event must have a cause, that the geometry of space must be Euclidean, that space and time are distinct, and many other claims. We now have more powerful evidence that these claims are false, but it does not follow that those who believed them must have done so irrationally, or that those who doubted these views in the past must have done so rationally.

My point, then, is that the notions of rationality and truth are distinct in the sense that achieving one of them in no way entails that the other has also been achieved. Nevertheless, there is a weaker but vital tie between rationality and truth. We proceed rationally in attempting to discover truth, and we take those conclusions that are rationally acceptable as our best estimate of the truth.[10] In other words, while a rationally supported claim need not be true, and a claim chosen at random need not be false, it does not follow that either choice is as good as the other. We need not only truth, but reasons for believing that we have the truth, and it is through the process of assessing evidence and submitting our views to criticism that we develop those reasons. In many cases the search for truth is a long-term process – a point that was not generally recognized in the early days of foundation-alism – and we need organized, coherent procedures for carrying out this pursuit. This is the function of rationality.

5.4 Rationality and objectivity

Our new model of rationality preserves the idea that rational beliefs are based on evidence (cf. Siegel, 1985, for a recent state-ment of this thesis), but there are different sources of evidence for different claims. I want to consider one type of evidence here, and in doing so it will be convenient to distinguish between 'rationality' and 'objectivity', even though these terms are often used interchangeably. A full discussion of objectivity would easily double the length of this book, but I have explored this notion elsewhere, and I want to sketch the outcome of that discussion (see Brown, 1979a, 1987a for details).

To begin with, we must disassociate ourselves from the view that objectivity requires that we approach our subject without any preconceptions. As has regularly been pointed out by philosophers, sociologists, linguists, anthropologists, historians, and others, we cannot approach any subject matter in this state, and if we could, we would not know what questions to ask, and what answers to accept. But this model of objectivity involves an exaggeration of a considerably less dramatic claim: that the evidence supporting an objective belief must derive from a source that is independent of that belief. I want to develop this point, and I will begin with physical science, a discipline that has traditionally been considered one of the most 'objective'.

It is a central assumption of much research in physical science that scientists are attempting to understand items that exist and have properties independently of the researcher's beliefs (I have attempted to defend this assumption in Brown, 1987a). Thus, when a physicist maintains that all matter is constructed of electrons, neutrons and protons, or that every bit of matter in the universe exerts a gravitational attraction on every other piece of matter in the universe, she is claiming, correctly or incorrectly, that these are features of the physical world. To be sure, such claims are made by individuals who live in a certain historical epoch and culture, and are made in a language that is characteristic of that epoch and culture, but these are not claims *about* that epoch, culture or language. One of the things that language permits us to do is to make claims about items that exist apart from us and our language, claims that are either true or false, and for which we can have evidence.

While this point is particularly clear in the case of physical science, it also holds in other fields. It holds, for example, when a biologist maintains that genetic information is encoded in DNA, when an historian asserts that the first edition of Newton's *Principia* was published in 1687, when an anthropologist describes the role of the poison oracle in Azande culture, and when someone claims that there are three chairs in her living room, or that the universe was created out of nothing at a definite point in time. In many of these cases there are difficulties about how we assess the truth or falsity of the claim, and there are cultural and linguistic prerequisites that must be met before we can understand the claim. In addition, a given claim may have a function in a social setting that is quite independent of its truth or falsity. But once all of this has been acknowledged, the point remains that many claims make assertions about some state of affairs that is independent of those claims.

Consider now the kind of evidence that is required if we are to arrive at a rational assessment of these claims. Scientists seek this evidence by carrying out observations and experiments, and one feature of these procedures is particularly important: scientists attempt to gather information about an item by interacting with that item. Thus physicists study electrons by experimenting on electrons, biologists study DNA by observing DNA, and so forth. Similarly, an anthropologist who wishes to study a particular culture begins by travelling to the place where the people in question are to be found, and discussions of that culture must be based on evidence that was derived by interacting with that culture. And, to take one more example, a literary scholar is expected to justify her interpretation of a text on the basis of that text. Interpretations offered without reference to the text, or by people who have never bothered to read that text, will not be taken seriously.

Let us focus for a moment on the last example, and contrast the case in which a scholar appeals to a text in order to justify a reading of that text, with the case in which someone appeals to a text (say the works of a revered philosopher or a religious text) to justify a claim about the nature of the physical world. One crucial difference here is that in the first case we undertake to evaluate a claim about some item by examining that item, while in the second case we examine some other item whose relationship to the item of study is a bit more tenuous. Scientists use procedures of the first sort: they base their claims about items in the physical world on an examination of those items. In modern science this examination may be highly indirect (cf. Shapere, 1982; Brown, 1987a, ch. 3), but the complex observational procedures that modern scientists construct are designed to bring them into contact with the items that concern them. Similarly, anthropologists travel to other cultures and learn the local language in order to study that culture. I will take cases of this sort to be paradigm examples of the pursuit of objectivity, and I submit that we accept a claim about some item on an objective basis when we do so as a result of assessing evidence derived from a study of that item. There are a number of points here that need further elaboration.

First, it is an open question whether all subject matters can be studied objectively; some subjects may not deal with items that have the required ontological status. For example, there may be no objective basis for evaluating ethical claims, or rules of etiquette, or marriage customs – although there is an objective basis for deciding which of these exist in particular cultures. This does not, by itself, block the exercise of rationality in these fields, for there may be other considerations that can provide the basis for rational evaluation. One might, for example, have reasons for believing that an ethical system ought to have a certain degree of coherence, and this could provide grounds for rational analysis. Similarly, it is an open question whether pure mathematics is an objective discipline, i.e., whether mathematicians study entities which exist apart from their conception of them. The view of objectivity I am sketching does not require that we study material entities, but only that we study items that are independent of the claims we make about them. There are, however, grounds for evaluating mathematical claims that do not depend on the existence of a special class of entities.

Second, there are cases in which the contents of a text can be a source of information about something other than itself. Textbooks provide one example, as do historical documents, and such claims are often made on behalf of religious texts. I do not want to pursue these examples in detail here, but I do want to emphasize one key point: examining an item is clearly a legitimate means of obtaining information about that item, while we need an account of why it is legitimate to get this information by examining some other item. In many cases, including the case in which we are examining a text, this justification will consist of tracing out a set of relations between the item before us and the item that ultimately interests us.

Third, sometimes objective evaluation of a claim leads to the conclusion that the entities we were supposedly examining all along do not exist. The history of physical science is full of such cases. To understand this possibility we need only note that interesting claims do not just assert the existence of some item, they also make a set of assertions about how that item will interact with other items. When we test these assertions and do not get the expected results a number of options become available, including the possibility of reconsidering whether a postulated entity actually exists.

Finally, there may be cases in which it is rational to follow a non-objective procedure, even though an objective procedure is available. For example, one might build a social structure in which certain kinds of objective evidence are systematically ignored out of a conviction that attention to such evidence might lead to the destruction of the set of beliefs on which social well-being depends. Cases of this sort are tricky. It would seem that any group that wishes to survive ignores such evidence only at its peril, yet there may be social groups that do not take survival as their highest goal. My point here is only that these cases are complex, and that we should not automatically write off such groups as irrational even though they eschew objectivity.

Objective procedures provide us with an especially powerful source of evidence. Such procedures attempt to bring us into contact with the items we would study and, we might say, give them an opportunity to speak for themselves. But objectivity does not supplant rationality – given the evidence provided by objective procedures we must still decide what to make of this evidence. Is the available evidence sufficient to justify accepting a claim, or do we need more evidence? Does a negative result disprove a claim, or is the problem somewhere else? Should we seek a completely different hypothesis that is in conformity with the available evidence? These questions, and others, fall within the realm of rational decision-making, on which we must rely once the evidence that can be gleaned from the application of objective procedures is available. Thus rationality and objectivity should be distinguished. Rationality is often possible in the absence of objectivity, and objectivity alone, without rational assessment, leads us nowhere. Still, objectivity is epistemically important because it provides us with an especially powerful body of evidence to be used in the rational assessment of claims. Note that nothing in this discussion suggests that the pursuit of objectivity is easy or quick. Gathering objective evidence can be extremely difficult and time-consuming, but objective procedures provide evidence that may well offer the best path to substantive truth.

We should expect to have a better chance of actually being right about items in the world when our beliefs are based on a study of those items than in cases in which no such study is available.

We can now return to the question of why science provides an especially important test case for a model of rationality. Rationality requires the assessment of evidence, and we should be able to get our best examples of rationality by looking at cases in which the most varied and reliable evidence is systematically gathered and deployed. If we were to look at fields in which decisions must be made on the basis of minimal evidence, or dubious evidence, and in which decisions could not be checked by gathering further evidence, we would likely get a very distorted view of the significance of evidence in arriving at beliefs. Objective procedures provide the richest and most reliable evidence, and one of the characteristic features of science is its systematic pursuit of objective evidence. This is sufficient to justify the selection of science as a prime instance of a field in which we should expect to find rationality at work. Science is not the only field in which rationality is possible, but the special cognitive power of science, including its claim to be the best approach to truth in its domains, derives from the way in which objectivity and rationality interact – i.e., on the way in which rational assessment is applied to a particularly powerful body of evidence.

5.5   Rational disagreement

One striking feature of the development of scientific knowledge is the occurrence of wide-ranging disputes in which any principle that was previously accepted as established can be brought into question. For many thinkers these disputes raise problems about the rationality of science, and indeed, the classical model of rationality leaves little scope for disagreements in which we do not have to conclude that at least one of the parties to the dispute is irrational. On that model, all disagreements are analogous to those that occur when two individuals disagree on the outcome of an arithmetic calculation. The rules for doing the calculation are known, and there is no disputing these. Thus disagreement must occur either because someone has made a computational error, or, if the dispute concerns a substantive subject, because

207

they disagree on what numbers should go into the calculation. In either case the resolution of the disagreement is straightforward: rechecking the calculation should turn up any arithmetic errors, and rechecking the facts should resolve any disagreements over the data. The latter task may involve practical difficulties, e.g., comets and solar eclipses do not appear at our convenience, and some data collection procedures are expensive and time-consuming, but it is clear where the disagreement lies, and how it is to be resolved. Ideally, all disagreements would be amenable to this sort of resolution (recall Leibniz's proposal for a 'universal characteristic' that we discussed in chapter I).

The attempt to achieve this goal is particularly clear in logical empiricist philosophy of science. On this view, there are two features of science that provide the basis on which any dispute could ultimately be resolved: the rules of scientific method (analogous to the rules of arithmetic), and the data provided by sense perception (the inputs). Logical empiricists believed that rules of methodology were logical rules and were thus knowable *a priori*, while the data provided by our senses were taken to be independent of anything we might believe. The rational assessment of any hypothesis was thus a matter of applying methodological rules in order to assess how well the hypothesis was supported by the available data. Note especially that both the rules of methodology and the sensory data we have accumulated were considered to be independent of the actual content of science. As a result, they remain unchanged as science develops (although the stock of data may be increased), and they provide permanent standards against which scientific claims can be assessed. Philosophers working in this tradition have vigorously opposed the thesis that principles of scientific method could be challenged by developments in science on the grounds that this would leave no rational basis for choosing between competing scientific theories. At the same time, while empiricists regularly note that all scientific results are tentative and subject to reconsideration, many have resisted the claim that new developments have in fact required rejection of older theories in mature sciences (see Brown, 1979b, pp. 60–66 for further discussion).

From a naturalistic point of view the occurrence of radical transformations should not be surprising. We have no *a priori* insight into the nature of the world we live in, and no *a priori* grasp of the best means of learning about that world (cf. Hooker, 1974; Shapere, 1984, chs. 10 and 11 for extended discussion of this point). Thus there is no reason for expecting those views of the nature of the universe that appeared earlier in the development of science to prevail, and no reason for expecting views on scientific method to remain unchallenged as science develops. The thesis that radical change does occur in the mature sciences was introduced into the philosophical literature by Feyerabend and Kuhn, who described radically different competing theories as 'incommensurable', and they have generally been interpreted as holding that there is no rational basis for deciding between such theories. I have argued elsewhere that this is an incorrect interpretation of the incommensurability thesis (Brown, 1983a), and I now want to consider radical disagreements from the point of view of our new model of rationality.

Let me begin by noting that there is an important idea embedded in the classical view: if two individuals disagree on some subject matter, a necessary condition for rational debate is that they agree on something that is relevant to the dispute: some principles or some body of information that they can appeal to as a basis for discussion. Logical empiricists exaggerated this requirement and sought a set of genuinely universal principles, and a body of universally acceptable data, to which appeal could be made to settle *any* scientific dispute. But this is an excessive demand, and it can be abandoned and replaced by the thesis that rational disagreement requires some touchstone that is held in common by the parties to that dispute. Different individuals engaged in different disputes may agree on different things, and these points of agreement will provide the basis for rational discussion, and often for the rational resolution of the dispute. On our new model of rationality, rational decisions require the existence of an intellectual community, and any such community will be characterized by a substantial body of shared ideas and beliefs. Moreover, a science is a multi-leveled structure, which may include a body of observations, forms of instrumentation, low level empirical generalizations, theories of different degrees of generality, preferred mathematical techniques, a variety of methodological and even metaphysical principles, and much more. At the same time, the scientists who are actually engaged in a dispute will share many views that they derive from the wider culture in which they live. In any given dispute these shared scientific and extra-scientific views can provide a basis for rational discussion of the points at issue. Even in cases of radical scientific change, local agreements can provide a sufficient basis for rational debate. Different local agreements will play this role in different cases, and there is no need to postulate eternal, trans-scientific principles to account for the rationality of scientific disputes (cf. Brown 1977, 1986a; Laudan, 1984). This view can best be defended in terms of examples, and I want to discuss two examples, one at considerable length, and one more briefly.

My extended example will concern several aspects of the dispute between Galileo and his Aristotelian contemporaries. Although the central subject of the dispute was the new Copernican astronomy, this became one of the most wide-ranging debates in the history of science, and included disagreements on fundamental questions of both the content of science and scientific method-ology. Galileo entered into this discussion approximately 60 years after the publication of Copernicus' central book advocating the motion of the earth, and remained a key figure in the debate for close to 30 years. Initially the Copernican view faced many theoretical and observational problems, and Galileo made major contributions to the solution of both types of problems. I want to begin on the theoretical side, where one of the most pressing problems for the Copernican view was that the moving earth was radically inconsistent with the only existing system of physics. Galileo undertook the construction of a new system of physics which would be consistent with Copernicanism, as well as being independently defensible. In the next three paragraphs I will sketch the medieval view of the physical world that raised prob-lems for Copernicans; those who are familiar with this background can skip ahead. (See Kuhn, 1959, for a more detailed discussion.)

According to the medieval view, the physical world consists of two distinct realms, each obeying different physical laws. If we imagine a spherical surface surrounding the earth, located at the distance of the moon, everything from the earth out to this surface was considered the 'terrestrial' realm, while everything from the surface 'up', including the moon, constituted the 'celestial' realm; the earth was held to be at the center of the entire structure. Each item in the terrestrial realm was thought to be made up of some combination of four elementary substances: earth, water, air and fire. For present purposes the important distinction between these elements lies in their dynamical properties, i.e., the way they behave in motion. With each element there is associated a 'natural place', i.e., a location in the terrestrial realm to which any bit of that element moves unless it is forcibly prevented from doing so. The extreme natural places are the center of the universe for earth, and the sphere of the moon (i.e., our imaginary surface) for fire. The natural place of water is above earth, but below air, and the natural place of air is between water and fire. When a pure sample of one of these elements is forcibly removed from its natural place and then released, it will return to its natural place, and the motion involved is the 'natural motion' for that substance. Note that on this view there is no *force* involved in starting or sustaining natural motion, a force is required only in cases of non-natural or, as it was called, 'violent motion'. This includes motion that removes some item from its natural place, and any continued motion other than the natural motion for that item, e.g., the motion of an earthy object such as an arrow parallel to the earth. On this view, the downward motion of a falling stone and the upward motion of fire are two manifestations of the same phenomenon: the movement of an element to its natural place.

This framework provided explanations for a number of presumably familiar physical phenomena: why unrestrained stones fall and unrestrained fire rises; the overall structure of the terrestrial realm with water on top of earth, and air above water; the location of our planet at the center of the universe – for this planet is made of earth, and thus if it were removed from the center it would return there; and the long accepted view that the earth is spherical. None of this, however, applies in the celestial realm. This realm was taken to be composed of a fifth element that is not found in the terrestrial world, and that has one crucial dynamical property that distinguishes it from the terrestrial elements: natural motion is linear for the terrestrial elements, but circular for the celestial element. Moreover, there are no natural places in the celestial realm, and each bit of celestial material is eternally engaged in circular motion.

In both the celestial and the terrestrial realms we encounter examples of moving items that seem not to be engaged in their natural motion. Each of these is susceptible to a scientific account, but the Aristotelian view required the application of a different methodology in each realm. In the terrestrial realm we account for non-natural motion by locating the responsible force; in the celestial realm we do not acknowledge the possibility of non-natural motion, and we treat departures from circular motions as apparent departures – the annual motions of the planets provided the most important case. Explanation here consists of finding a system of circular motions that will account for the apparently non-circular motions that we see from our observational position on the earth. The attempt to carry out the latter project led to the existence of two systems of astronomy, the Aristotelian and the Ptolemaic. The latter is a completely mathematical astronomy that makes use of a number of geometrical devices in order to compute the locations of the planets, but on the Aristotelian view, mathematics is *not* an appropriate tool for understanding the physical world: mathematics deals with idealizations that are not actually found among physical objects – dimensionless points, one-dimensional lines, true spheres, tangent planes that touch a sphere at only one point, and such. There is nothing wrong with using mathematics as a tool for making predictions, and Ptolemaic astronomy was generally viewed as such a tool. But the fact that a mathematical device provides accurate predictions tells us nothing about the nature of the physical objects to which it is applied. The nature of the physical objects in the celestial realm was generally believed to be captured in Aristotle's picture of the heavens as made up of a number of eternally turning spherical shells, with the planets as denser areas on those shells.

Copernicus agreed that all celestial motions are circular, but, in effect, put the earth into the heavens, and this was incompatible with the Aristotelian picture of the physical universe. It destroyed the distinction between the celestial and terrestrial realms, and completely disrupted the natural places of the terrestrial realm. For example, if the fall of a heavy object is a return to the center of the universe, and the earth is no longer located at that center, but moving rapidly around the sun, an arrow shot high enough might miss the earth altogether on its return. Copernicus offered no alternative account of the physical universe, and Galileo took up this task. (See Brown, 1976, for further discussion and documentation of the following interpretation of Galileo's physics.)

Galileo saw that the division of the physical world into two distinct realms had to be abandoned. This required that there be only one kind of natural motion, and Galileo maintained that all natural motion was circular. For the motions of celestial objects, Galileo thus continued to hold a view that was, to a large degree, traditional, and did so even after he became aware of Kepler's arguments against the circular motions of the planets. To see what Galileo had in mind in the case of terrestrial motion, consider a ship moving on the sea. Force is required to maintain its motion against friction, but if we imagine the friction being reduced, less force will be required until, when the friction is completely eliminated, the ship will continue moving, Galileo maintained, around the earth at a constant distance from the center of the earth, forever (1967, pp. 145–8). On the other hand, any motion that involved an increase in the moving object's distance from the center of the earth would be vertical motion. In particular, motion tangent to the earth involves a continual increase in distance from the center of the earth and could not take place without the application of a force (1967, pp. 193–5).

If all natural motion is circular, one problem for the Copernican view – the need to explain what keeps the earth in motion – vanishes. Galileo argued that the earth has two natural circular motions: its daily rotation on its axis, and its annual motion about the sun; since these are natural motions, nothing is required to sustain them. Moreover, these natural motions are characteristic of all 'earthy objects', and this provided the basis for Galileo's response to a number of arguments against the motion of the earth. Focus, for a moment, on the daily rotation of the earth, and consider a stone dropped along the west side of a high tower. If, Aristotelians argued, the earth is rotating from west to east, then as the stone moves toward the center of the earth, the tower will rotate away from the stone, and the stone will not land at the base of the tower. Since the stone does in fact land at the base of the tower, we have an observational refutation of the daily motion of the earth. Similarly, on the Aristotelian view, an arrow that is shot vertically will first move directly away from the center of the earth, and then towards the center of the earth. If the earth is rotating while all this is going on, we would expect the arrow to land a considerable distance west of the point from which it was shot, which does not occur.

According to Galileo, these arguments fail to take into account the fact that the stone and arrow are themselves earthy objects, and thus share in the natural motion of the earth. On Galileo's view, the falling object is simultaneously engaged in two motions: a vertical motion towards the center of the earth, and a circular motion along with the earth. Thus the Copernican view, properly developed, is in conformity with the agreed-upon facts that the stone falls at the base of the tower, and that the arrow returns to the place from which it was shot. Galileo's response does not provide a positive argument for the motion of the earth, but it does show that many arguments that were commonly cited against the motion of the earth in fact prove nothing one way or the other.

Galileo's use of a notion of an 'earthy object' in the above example is more than coincidentally reminiscent of the Aristotelian doctrine of four elements. Galileo accepts the view that there are elements that are distinguished by their dynamical properties, as well as most of the elements from the traditional list, but he rethinks their dynamical properties in the context of his new physics. Earth is now characterized by two dynamical features: it has the pair of natural circular motions needed to account for the daily and annual motions of the earth, and it will sustain an additional circular motion that is impressed upon it. As our earlier ship example illustrated, if an earthy object is started in a non-natural circular motion by a force, it will continue that motion unless impeded by another force. Water, the second element, does not share in the natural motions of the earth, but it will sustain an impressed circular motion; air neither shares the natural motion of the earth nor sustains an impressed motion. Galileo did not include fire in this picture, and he expressed doubt about the existence of any such element.

There are some surprising consequences of this doctrine of elements that Galileo took quite seriously. Galileo's major positive argument for the motion of the earth was a theory of the tides which, though wrong, was based on the dynamical properties of water. Essentially, Galileo held that the tides are caused by the oceans sloshing around in their basins as the earth moves in its double (annual plus daily) motion. Since water does not share in the natural motion of the earth, it will not automatically follow the earth the way a falling stone does. But water will sustain an *impressed* motion, and each of the earth's motions has the effect of impressing such a motion on the water in the ocean basins. If there were only one such motion the water would be carried along with the earth, but the double motion results in each point on the earth's surface moving in a rather complex pattern, and this, Galileo maintained, generates the tides.

The failure of air to share the natural motion of the earth, along with its inability to sustain the motions impressed on it by the earth, raises two problems: we would expect the air to be left behind by the earth's annual motion, and we would expect the earth's daily rotation through the air to generate a powerful wind. In response to the first objection Galileo argued that the air follows the earth in its annual journey because it is carried along by the roughness of the earth, and because 'earthy vapors', which share the earth's natural motion, become mixed with the air. For the same reason, we do not experience any wind caused by the daily motion of the earth as long as we are on land. But these two conditions only hold over land, and we would thus expect the daily motion to generate a wind over long stretches of water where there is no roughness and no earthy vapors. Galileo thought that the trade winds are generated in just this way, and that this provided evidence for his new physics.

In addition to the general picture of motion outlined above, Galileo also discovered the quantitative law that all bodies fall with the same constant acceleration, and two key consequences of this law: that the velocity of a falling body increases proportionally with the time, and that the distance fallen increases as the square of the time. These discoveries resulted from an experimental study of falling bodies under highly artificial conditions,[11] and they provide particularly clear examples of Galileo's conviction that mathematics and experiment are the proper tools for the study of nature. We have already seen that Aristotelians denied that mathematics should play a central role in natural science, and while Aristotelian scientists made extensive observations of the natural world, this did not include the kind of intervention that is involved in experimentation. They believed that such intervention would result in *distorting* the properties of the objects studied, rather than in revealing them. Thus Galileo's entire methodology was viewed as inappropriate by his opponents.

Galileo's study of falling bodies provided us with one of the first modern quantitative physical laws, but Galileo had no notion of fall being caused by a gravitational force, and in an often quoted passage Galileo suggests that the attempt to discover the cause of fall (as opposed to describing it properly) is not an appropriate aim of physical science (1974, pp. 158–9). This was another fundamental departure from Aristotelian views on methodology, where the search for causes was taken as central to science. Galileo did not always maintain that we should not seek causes, and attempted, somewhat tentatively, to address the question of why bodies fall (but not why they fall with constant acceleration). This was in response to the problem of why a falling object that is seeking the center of the universe need return to the earth at all, if the earth is not located at the center of the universe. Here Galileo followed Copernicus in suggesting that we shift the definition of 'natural place', taking the natural place of an earthy object to be the earth itself, not the center of the universe. Thus an object still falls because it moves to its natural place, but in doing so, it seeks the earth, wherever the earth may be, rather than an abstract point in space. This involves a modification of a traditional concept, and we have already encountered this strategy in Galileo's handling of the elements.

Thus far I have been primarily concerned with Galileo's contributions to mechanics, but his observational work with the telescope was equally important. Even a brief summary of these contributions would add much to an already long story, but there is one aspect of Galileo's telescopic results that is especially significant for present purposes. There were several known astronomical observations that were inconsistent with Copernican astronomy. To take one key example, the Copernican view required that Venus show phases analogous to those of the moon, but to the naked eye there are no phases. Galileo saw the phases through his telescope, but this is turn raised a new problem: telescopic and naked eye observations were now in conflict, and why should one accept the telescopic observations as being more accurate than those made with the naked eye?[12] Galileo responded by attempting to show that, in those cases that were crucial for Copernican astronomy, telescopic observations were more trustworthy than those made with the unaided eye because there are inherent defects in the eye that are corrected by the telescope (Brown, 1985). In taking this position Galileo rejected a fundamental tenet of Aristotelian epistemology: that our senses are properly tailored to reveal the physical world to us as it is. This must be added to his wide-ranging rejection of central Aristotelian views on physics, astronomy and scientific methodology.

I have told this long story because it provides an excellent basis for illustrating how fundamental debates can proceed on a rational basis. The disagreements between Galileo and the Aristotelians occurred on a number of different levels. There were disagreements on such general methodological questions as the role of causality, experimentation and mathematics in physical science; there was disagreement on the overall structure of the physical world; there was disagreement on such relatively specific claims as whether a falling body is engaged in a single motion or in two; and, in the case of observations with the telescope, there was disagreement on what could be observed in the heavens. At the same time, there were large areas of agreement, and these, I suggest, provided the basis for rational debate. There was, to begin with, a great deal of agreement on relatively simple observations: everyone agreed that a stone dropped from a tower falls at the base of the tower, that an arrow shot straight up returns to the point from which it was shot, and that there is no constant wind from east to west over land. Moreover, it was agreed that all of these observations were relevant to the debate, and that a theory which leads to conclusions that are inconsistent with observation is in trouble. There was also substantial agreement on matters of logic. From Galileo's point of view, if Aristotelians inferred false conclusions from Copernican principles, there must have been a logical error in their reasoning, and Galileo attempted to show exactly where these errors occurred (see, for example, Galileo, 1967, pp. 130–1, 140, 174). Further, the parties to the dispute recognized that there were observable situations for which the two theories gave contrary predictions. Galileo's physical theory entailed that a stone dropped from the mast of a moving ship would land at the foot of the mast, while the Aristotelian view required that it would land toward the rear of the ship;[13] in astronomy it had long been recognized that a moving earth required stellar parallax, which had never been observed, while a stationary earth did not require stellar parallax. Not surprisingly, Galileo described a new way to search for stellar parallax using the telescope (1967, pp. 388–9).

Other aspects of the debate were a bit more subtle. Galileo's physics introduced a different system of concepts for thinking about the natural world from those required in Aristotelian physics, but there were several points of commonalty that provided a bridgehead from one conceptual system to the other. Galileo's claim that all natural motion is circular was surely understandable to Aristotelians, if surprising; things would have been much more difficult if he had rejected the notion of natural motion altogether or denied that planetary motions follow any simple geometric curve, conclusions at which Newton eventually arrived. We have also seen that Galileo sometimes introduced new concepts by modifying older ones, not by stipulation *ex nihilo*. Thus Galileo agreed with the Aristotelians that physical objects had natural motions that required no sustaining force, and that the fall of a heavy object was an instance of motion to a natural place – but Galileo associated the natural place of an earthy object with the planet earth, wherever it was, rather than with a point in space that was eternally occupied by a stationary earth. Similarly, Galileo accepted the view that a number of fundamental features of the physical world were to be explained by appeal to a small set of elements which could be distinguished by their dynamical properties, and he took his elements from the traditional list; but he made significant changes in the relevant dynamical properties, and dispensed with one of the traditional elements, fire. Much of this was rejected out of hand by Aristotelians, and may even have struck them as absurd, but Galileo's views were presented in a language that was sufficiently intelligible to his contemporaries for them to offer counter-arguments to which Galileo could respond.

I have been arguing that there was enough in common between Galileo and his Aristotelian opponents to provide the basis for intelligible debate, but this debate differed in many ways from the kinds of debates that take place in twentieth-century physics. For example, one of the first questions to be addressed in comparing two theories today would be the relative accuracy of their quantitative consequences; this could not have played a comparable role in the seventeenth-century debate because quantification was not yet accepted as a methodological condition for physics – this was one of the points at issue. Even in astronomy, where quantitative accuracy had long been a desideratum, it was not assumed that there was any particular tie between quantitative accuracy and adequacy as a description of the physical world. Moreover, Galileo offered no new quantitative arguments on behalf of Copernican astronomy. On the other hand, conformity with scripture was a mutually acceptable criterion for the adequacy of any physical theory, and Galileo attempted to show that the Copernican view did not conflict with scripture (1957, pp. 175–216); no such argument would be considered scientifically relevant today.

Let me summarize the key points that I want to draw out of this discussion. First, we are dealing here with a case of radical scientific innovation. Galileo challenged existing views on just about every level of the structure of science, from questions about what counts as an acceptable observation to sweeping issues of scientific methodology; but we are also dealing with individuals who were concerned with a common set of problems, and who shared many ideas about how such problems were to be approached. Their frameworks were sufficiently different that failures of complete communication undoubtedly occurred, but there were also enough points of commonalty to allow substantial discussion, and to permit the individuals involved to work toward further common understanding, even if this did not always bring total agreement.

Second, many features that would be fundamental to a contemporary scientific debate were missing in the debate we have examined, and several features that were central to that debate would have no place in a current scientific disagreement. This, however, is irrelevant to the question of whether this debate was rational. Rational disagreement requires a sufficient body of shared beliefs to provide grounds for discussion; these beliefs need not be true, nor need they be our beliefs.

Third, there was one feature of this debate that would be found in any current scientific debate; the demand for conformity with observation. I do not want to understate the significance of this point; it has in fact been a constant feature of scientific discussion, and we have every reason for believing that it will continue to play this role. Still, we must not overstate the significance of this point. One consequence of Galileo's use of the telescope was to change the existing notion of what counted as a scientifically relevant observation, and we saw in chapter III that theoretical developments can also change our understanding of the nature of observation. Moreover, while agreement with observation is a central feature for rational acceptance of a claim within science, it can hardly be elevated to a requirement for rationality in every subject, and even within science, agreement with observation is not the only criterion for rational acceptance of a claim.

Finally, we are dealing here with a case in which informed individuals were debating with other informed individuals. This meets the conditions of our model of rationality, and even though they disagreed, individuals on both sides of this debate continued to hold their views rationally.

The issue before us is sufficiently important to justify adding a more contemporary illustration, although a briefer one; I will discuss part of the debate over quantum theory that took place between Albert Einstein and Niels Bohr from 1925 to 1931. (See Bohr 1949; Jammer 1975, ch. 5; Pais, 1982, ch. 25.) Beginning in 1905, Einstein was one of the most important and prolific contributors to the development of quantum theory, but with the advent of the probabilistic interpretation of the theory (1925–6) he became one of its most vocal critics. Einstein's attack on quantum theory went through two main stages: first he attempted to show that the theory was inconsistent, then that it was incomplete; I will discuss only the first stage here. Einstein's attack focused largely on Heisenberg's uncertainty relations, which were derived from the fundamental assumptions of quantum theory. According to these relations, there are limits on how precisely we can simultaneously determine the values of certain pairs of physical parameters, e.g., the position and momentum of a particle, or the energy involved in a process and the time during which the process occurs. In any of these pairs, one parameter can be determined as precisely as we wish, but the more precisely this determination is made, the less precisely the other parameter can be determined; the uncertainty relations state the maximum simultaneous precision that is allowable. This result conflicted with Einstein's own ideas about the nature of the physical world, and about the aims of physics. According to Einstein, physical objects are characterized by definite properties, physics aims to discover those properties, and there can be no reason of principle which prevents us from determining all of these properties with any degree of precision. (The fact that there may be practical difficulties is irrelevant.) The notion that we are barred in principle from precisely measuring both the position and momentum of a particle, while we are capable of measuring any one of these as precisely as we like, suggests either that the particle has properties that we cannot discover, or that it does not have specific properties at all until a measurement takes place, or possibly both; Einstein found these results completely unacceptable. Moreover, the uncertainty relations are intimately connected with the noncausal nature of quantum theory, and Einstein remained convinced that the physical world is characterized by strict causality, and that physics aims to understand nature in causal terms.

Einstein attacked quantum theory by proposing a series of thought experiments aimed at constructing an example in which both of the parameters between which an uncertainty relation held could be determined to an arbitrary degree of precision. Since Einstein's arguments were developed in the context of quantum theory, while Heisenberg's uncertainty relations had been deduced from that theory, Einstein was in effect arguing that quantum theory is inconsistent. In each case Bohr responded with a detailed analysis of Einstein's example, and was able to show that the supposed violation of the uncertainty relations did not occur. I want to describe the last thought experiment in this series, which focused on the uncertainty relation between energy and time.

Einstein imagined a closed box full of radiation with a shutter at one end. The shutter was controlled by a clock inside the box which would permit the shutter to be opened long enough to allow one photon of energy to escape from the box; the amount of time that the shutter had been open provided the uncertainty in the time at which the energy had been released. According to special relativity, energy is equivalent to mass; the release of energy from the box would result in a definite decrease in the box's mass, and thus in its weight. If we weighed the box before opening the shutter, we could weigh the box again sometime after the shutter had been opened, and from the weight loss, we could determine the amount of energy that had been released. Moreover, we could weigh the box with sufficient accuracy that the resulting uncertainty in the energy, along with the time determination already available, violated the uncertainty relations.

Einstein proposed this example at a conference, and Bohr supposedly stayed up all night wrestling with it. Eventually Bohr realized that Einstein had neglected an additional effect that was involved in the experiment, one deriving from considerations of general relativity. According to that theory, the rate at which a clock runs in a gravitational field will be altered if the strength of the field changes. The release of mass from the box changes the strength of the gravitational field in which the clock is located, and thus introduces a variation in the rate at which that clock runs. Bohr was able to show that this effect generated an uncertainty in the time that the shutter was open that was sufficient to restore the limits imposed by Heisenberg's uncertainty relations. Einstein conceded defeat, acknowledged that quantum theory is consistent, and abandoned this line of attack on the theory (cf. Jammer, 1975, p. 136; Pais, 1982, pp. 448).

This example illustrates a number of the points that concern me. First, we are dealing here with a dispute over fundamentals, a dispute that included questions about the most basic features of the physical world, and about the aims of physics; yet we are also dealing with a paradigm instance of a debate that was carried out in a rational manner. This could occur because, as deep as the disagreements were, the debate took place in the context of a large number of other views on which there was agreement. There was no doubt that the uncertainty relations had been correctly deduced from the principles of quantum theory, and that these relations required a rethinking of both the aims of physical science and the nature of the physical world. It was also clear that Einstein's thought experiments were an appropriate means of attacking the new theory, and that Bohr's objections were relevant responses to these attacks. Finally, it was clear that other accepted physical theories, such as special and general relativity, were part of the background that could be invoked in developing and in criticizing thought experiments. Thus even though the dispute involved matters of fundamental principle, Einstein recognized when he had been defeated. There was no rule which dictated that Einstein must concede at this point, and we could invent logically possible responses on Einstein's behalf, and make up stories in which the debate continued indefinitely. To do so, however, would be to ignore the point that in scientific debates we are not concerned to achieve logical invulnerability, and that those best able to judge had reached consensus that this line of argument was finished. Einstein changed the focus of his attack, and it would take something considerably more striking than a mere logical possibility to reopen this debate.

Let me approach my second point by noting that there is a long philosophical tradition which holds that the structure of science consists of a number of hierarchically organized levels. In a recent study Laudan (1984) discusses this tradition and distinguishes three levels: on the lowest level is the content of science, including observations, theories and laws; next comes scientific methodology; and on the highest level we find the aims of science. On this view, disputes that cannot be settled on one level are mediated by appeal to a higher level: intractable disputes concerning matters of content can be discussed by appeal to methodology, and disputes about methodology can be discussed by appeal to the aims of science. But this view only permits appeals that go up the hierarchy, and leaves no basis for rational discussion once we reach disagreements over the aims of science; we have already encountered this view in our discussions of Popper. In response, Laudan argues that appeals can go down the hierarchy, as well as up, e.g., one can appeal to methodologies and scientific results in disputes about the aims of science, and to successful scientific theories in order to evaluate methodologies; thus the resources for rational debate are considerably greater than this particular philosophical tradition will allow. The present discussion provides support for Laudan's thesis.[14] We have just examined a fully rational debate concerning, among other matters, the aims of physics, and have seen that this debate took place in terms of several considerations, including the results of specific scientific theories. Consider, for example, the way Einstein introduced special relativity into the debate, and the way Bohr used general relativity to undermine Einstein's position.

Third, it is impossible to understand the issues in this dispute, and the judgements which led to its resolution, without paying attention to the content of science at the time the debate took place. The questions at issue and the matters invoked in debating these questions would have made no sense at all to Galileo or to Newton, and they might play no role at some future stage in the development of physics. But the fact that we are dealing with a local issue mediated by local concerns is irrelevant to the question of whether the dispute was a rational one.

Finally, let me note that Einstein's opposition to quantum theory was, on the model I have proposed, wholly rational and pursued in a rational manner. Einstein was certainly in a position to make informed judgements on the questions at issue, and he submitted his judgements, and the reasons for them, to the relevant community. Einstein would have been behaving in a non-rational manner if, having come to his own decision, he refused to discuss it with other physicists, or confined himself to making pronouncements in newspapers and magazines aimed at lay people who did not have the expertise required to evaluate his claims.

5.6   Rationality and language

A long tradition maintains that language is a necessary condition for rationality, and the exact relation between rationality and language has often been a topic for extended discussion. No central role for language has been explicitly built into our new model of rationality, and one consequence of this model is that the exact relation between rationality and language is an open question subject to empirical investigation. Thus my remarks on this topic can be mercifully brief.

Clearly language will be deeply implicated in the social aspect of human rational behavior since we carry on the necessary discussions linguistically. Whether there are species on this or other planets that engage in communal evaluation of proposals without linguistic mediation is not the sort of question that can be decided *a priori*. I have built the demand for social checks into our model of rationality, but I see no good reason for adding the demand that these checks only contribute to the rationality of a decision or belief if they are carried out through linguistic means. The fact that this turns out to be an empirical question is, I take it, a virtue of the model.

The situation is a bit more complex when we turn to the relation between judgement and language, although the outcome is the same. Judgement, as we have analyzed it, is not itself a linguistic phenomenon, but this does not settle any questions about the relation between the ability to exercise judgement and the possession of a language. Certainly the clearest available examples of individuals who can exercise judgement are also examples of individuals who have mastered some linguistic skills, and the mastery of such skills may be a necessary condition for the exercise of judgement. Given that the ability to judge is a function of the brain and nervous system, it may turn out that the neural structures involved in judgement overlap with those required for mastering a language, or perhaps that only those who have actually mastered a language can exercise judgement, but we will not be able to answer these questions until we know a great deal more about neural structures and functioning.

There is a related question that should also be considered briefly. Rationality is frequently considered the single characteristic that distinguishes human beings from other species, and thus the claim that only humans are rational is often considered to be true by definition. For example, Jonathan Bennett writes:

> I use 'rationality' to mean 'whatever it is that humans possess which marks them off, in respect of intellectual capacity, sharply and importantly from all other known species'. . . . It follows from my definition of 'rational' that humans are the only rational creatures we know of, though it does not follow from that definition that it is useful or interesting to describe humans as 'rational'. (1964, p. 5)

I have taken a different tack in this book. For although the entire discussion has taken place in terms of typically human behaviors, the resulting model leaves it an empirical question whether other species are rational. It may be that we can rapidly arrive at a negative answer for most known species, but that answer will derive from our familiarity with members of those species, not from reflection on a concept.[15] Further studies of animal behavior may generate surprises, and our model of rationality supplies some guidance as to what we should be looking for in attempting to decide if other species are capable of rational behavior, but does not prejudge the issue.

5.7   The value of rationality

We ended our discussion of the classical model of rationality in chapter I by discussing the value of rationality according to that model; it is appropriate that we conclude our discussion of the new model of rationality in a similar fashion. Thus we return to the question 'Why be rational'? It is striking that despite the differences between the two models, the answer to this question is the same in both cases: rationality provides *reasons* for accepting claims, i.e., it provides grounds for considering propositions to be worthy of belief and for acting on decisions. The main goal of inquiry is truth, but the possession of truth is of relatively little value if we cannot distinguish which of the propositions before us are true, and which actions are likely to achieve their goals. In some cases we have clear criteria for making these decisions, and we apply those criteria. But in many cases we have no such criteria, and it is in these cases that the two models differ. On the classical model, we are no longer in a position to proceed in a rational manner; on our new model this is the paradigm case in which rationality is called for. If the subject is one in which we have the necessary expertise, we gather information, apply whatever rules are available, weigh alternatives, and arrive at a judgement; then we discuss our judgement and the reasons for it with our peers, and re-evaluate that judgement on the basis of their recommendations and critiques. The outcome of this process is a rational decision or belief.

Let me emphasize, again, that this process does not guarantee consensus, and that it does not guarantee that the decisions we arrive at are right, or that the propositions we believe are true. The classical model of rationality provided strong grounds for maintaining that rationality would yield truth, and do so fairly rapidly. The relation between rationality and truth is considerably weaker on our new model of rationality. In many areas there seems to be no guarantee that we are more likely to achieve or approach truth by proceeding rationally than by, for example, simply picking views at random – although this result is mitigated in those fields where rational assessment is based on objective evidence. Moreover, there is a certain conservatism built into our model of rationality, for rationality requires peer evaluation, and this requires that even if we wish to introduce new ideas, they must be sufficiently similar to those of our contemporaries for them to understand these ideas and evaluate them. Some will find this problematic. After all, our contemporaries may be wrong! Why, then, must we submit to evaluation by their standards? Isn't this just a glorification of whatever standards the dwellers in the cave currently use for assessing each other's ability to distinguish shadows?

In response, note first that one of the vital lessons of the twentieth-century revolutions in science is that the search for truth is a long-term process that may still be in its early stages. Moreover, at each stage the rational evaluation of hypotheses takes time. There is, to borrow Lakatos' phrase, no 'instant rationality', and even when we have arrived at a conclusion rationally, this does not yield instant truth. If we are to proceed in a coherent manner we need some way of distinguishing propositions that are worthy of belief, hypotheses that are worth pursuing, actions that are worth taking, and so forth, from those that are not, and it is rationality that provides us with a coherent basis for making these distinctions. In the course of our search for truth we will rationally accept claims that will later be rejected, and rationally reject claims that will later be accepted, but a surer and more efficient method does not seem to be available.

Thus rationality is a weaker notion on our new model than on the classical model. At the same time, the scope of rationality is considerably greater on our new model and many of the traditional distinctions between the rational and the nonrational fade from this new perspective. For example, the sharp distinction between reason and experience no longer has a point. On our model, reason is not confined to grasping necessary connections, and in many situations the only rational thing to do is to act or believe on the basis of experience. Note especially that we are capable of forming judgements on the basis of experience and submitting those judgements for critical evaluation. Similarly, the fact that I accept a result on the basis of authority does not automatically make my acceptance nonrational. I am often capable of judging which authorities to accept, and I can seek advice and evaluations of my judgements by others. A scientist who proceeds on the basis of scientific results that she has not tested for herself is still accepting results that have been evaluated by members of the scientific community, and she is in a position to seek out those she judges to be best capable of advising her in areas beyond her competence, and of learning more if she judges that that is desirable. This is rational decision-making, and it would be quite irrational to believe that she could fully assess every wire, every transistor, every law of nature and every fundamental constant on her own. Similarly, in our everyday lives, when we choose a physician or an automobile mechanic on the basis of a judgement that takes account of socially established licensing procedures, our own experience, and experiences that have been reported to us, we are making a rational decision. It is important to keep in mind here that there is a difference between coming to a rational decision in a particular discipline, which is often beyond our capacity, and coming to the rational decision that we are beyond the limits of our own competence, and need advice. But those who demand that we accept authority without exercising judgement and without critical evaluation are demanding that we cease functioning as rational agents.

Throughout this book I have resisted any identification of rationality with logic, but there is an analogy between the value of rationality and the value of deduction that will help me summarize the key point of this final section. Recall that for a deductive argument to guarantee the truth of its conclusion two conditions must be met: the argument must be valid and its premises must be true. Now it is considerably easier to achieve deductive validity than to achieve true premises, but the knowledge that a deduction is valid provides us with no information about the truth-value of its conclusion unless we also know that all our premises are true. Thus the deployment of valid deductive arguments, and only valid deductive arguments, leaves open the possibility that all of our conclusions may be false. But the fact that valid deduction alone cannot guarantee truth in no way detracts from the value of deduction as a central tool in the search for truth. In a similar way, rationality is a tool for attempting to understand the world we live in and for deciding how we ought to act, and the fact that this tool is far from ideal does not undercut the point that it is the main tool that we have. To put the point another way: we seek truth, and it would be most valuable if we had it, but the demand that we only believe true claims is a demand that we are not capable of fulfilling. To require that we only accept those claims which are rationally grounded is to demand something that is within our grasp.

Notes

Chapter I A Classical Model of Rationality

1 Sometimes Plato writes as if there is a form for every conceivable property, but he seems to back off from this position in *The Parmenides*, 130a–130e.

2 It is not completely clear how much of the detail of a specific situation Plato and Kant will permit us to take into account when we assess the morality of an act, but it is clear that utilitarianism requires much greater attention to detail than the other two views.

3 I will consider this view in some detail in section 3.3.

4 Kant maintained that universality and necessity are inseparable (1963, pp. 43–4).

5 Throughout this book I will use 'reliable' in the everyday sense in which it is roughly equivalent to 'trustworthy'. A reliable result is one that we are prepared to believe, and on which we are prepared to act.

6 Algorithms are procedures that yield solutions to problems, thus it is not quite right to say that all computer programs are algorithms. A program which does not succeed in solving a problem, or a frivolous program that continually generates output, are still computer programs, but not algorithms.

7 Artificial intelligence researchers who work on automatic theorem proving seek such procedures, and it is an open question when and where they will be found. Obviously we can produce proofs without following such procedures.

8 A second line of research has sought rules that would confer a definite probability on the conclusion. I will discuss this attempt in section 3.1.

Chapter II Foundations

1 I will focus on beliefs in this chapter and the next, but it should be clear that analogous results will hold for decisions, choices, etc.

2 The phrase 'the classical model' should be read as referring to the model discussed in chapter I; I am not attempting to slip in the suggestion that there is one universally accepted classical model of rationality.

3 See Pollock (1979, pp. 93–6) and Haack (1983, pp. 144–5) for further discussion of the distinction between 'self-evidence' and 'self-justification', although in a different terminology. Haack also distinguishes between propositions that are 'certain' in the sense that they cannot be mistakenly believed, and propositions that are 'self-manifesting', that is, propositions that we cannot fail to believe if they are true. My use of 'self-evidence' includes the former of these two notions, but not the latter. 'Self-evidence' is closely related to 'indubitability' and 'incorrigibility'. The three terms are often used interchangeably, but the latter two are sometimes used to cover self-justifying propositions, and self-manifesting propositions.

4 Kant has obviously been omitted from the following discussion; I will remedy that omission in chapter III.

5 Strictly speaking, for Plato, grasping a concept is not yet sufficient for knowledge, since we do not yet understand why that concept is structured as it is, and we cannot understand this until we grasp The Good, the most fundamental concept of all. The points that follow apply in the case of The Good, as well as for other concepts.

6 There is some dispute as to the authenticity of this portion of the seventh letter (see Ross, 1963, p. 139), but it is difficult to see what other answer Plato could give to this question.

7 Spinoza provides the clearest example of a rationalist who attempts to proceed by deduction from intuitively established first principles.

8 See, especially, Descartes's 'Rules for the Direction of the Mind'.

9 I will return to this point in section 2.5.

10 The *cogito* is an important exception since it is a singular proposition that we must each establish for ourselves.

11 Wilfrid Sellars argues (1963, pp. 127–32) that standard versions of empiricism are based on three mutually inconsistent claims: that through perception we learn the truth of certain propositions without inference; that inference is not involved exactly because perceptual abilities are not acquired through learning; but that the ability to know the truth of any proposition requires previous learning. The argument that I am about to develop is an elaboration of Sellars' argument.

12 Cf. Pastin (1975). Audi (1983) extends modest foundationalism to include both weaker foundational propositions and weaker forms of justification than are demanded by classical versions of foundationalism. I will only discuss foundational propositions here.

13 In the following discussion 'incorrigible' and 'incorrigibly justified' are respectively equivalent to my 'self-evident' and 'self-justifying'.

14 The move that Alston makes has been developed further by proponents of externalist epistemologies. See BonJour (1985,

pp. 8–10, 30–33 and ch. 3) for discussion and a detailed critique along the same lines as the above argument.

15 This discussion would be much neater if an observation statement could be deduced from a single hypothesis. Unfortunately, this does not occur; I will discuss the significance of this complication below.

16 This should not be confused with the positivist thesis that these nonscientific disciplines are nonsense. Popper's claim is only that they are different from the sciences.

17 There was no mention of truth in the first edition of Popper's *Logic of Scientific Discovery*. See Popper (1965, ch. 10) for discussion.

18 I have been writing as if it is easy to quantify the empirical content of a proposition on Popper's analysis, but this turns out to be extremely difficult. I will not pursue these difficulties here because there are other problems with Popper's scheme that are more interesting in the context of a discussion of rationality.

19 Kuhn remarks that Popper has, 'despite explicit disclaimers, consistently sought evaluation procedures which can be applied to theories with the apodictic assurance characteristic of the techniques by which one identifies mistakes in arithmetic, logic, or measurement' (1970a, p. 13).

20 This is a familiar objection to Popper's view on scientific methodology. It was pointed out by Pierre Duhem in 1914 (1962, ch. 6), before Popper came on the scene.

21 Strictly speaking the principle of excluded middle is not a rule, but it does provide a rule which permits us to write down '*p* or not-*p*' for any sentence '*p*' at any point in a proof. Common linguistic practice will result in my speaking of the 'principle' or 'law' of excluded middle, but it should be clear that it is the rule that will concern me. An analogous point holds for other 'laws of logic' that I will discuss.

22 I will return to this topic in section 5.1.

23 Bartley (1984, pp. 251–3) argues that in certain situations abandoning the law of excluded middle can increase our ability to criticize claims, and thus that it is desirable that we abandon this law on methodological grounds.

Chapter III   Rationality and Science

1 Pure mathematics provides another important paradigm of a rational endeavor – indeed, we have seen that it provides a standard against which the rationality of other fields has been measured. To a large degree, the classical model of rationality results from reflection on mathematics, but this makes mathematics less interesting as a test case than empirical science.

2 There are many philosophers who doubt that we can actually get the required convergence in scientifically interesting cases. See, for

example, Hesse, 1974, pp. 117–19; Glymour, 1980, pp. 72–3; Putnam, 1981, pp. 189–92.

3 According to the currently accepted account, the blob is moving almost directly towards us at more than 99% the speed of light, and the 25-light-year lateral displacement is actually the relatively small lateral component of the motion of the blob. On this analysis, the light from the blob that reached the observers in 1980 was actually emitted almost 300 years after the light that was observed in 1977, rather than 3 years later. Thus the 25-light-year lateral motion of the blob took close to 300 years.

4 Kuhn is confusing, and perhaps confused, on the role of a world that is independent of the paradigm in scientific research. He does maintain that scientists working in different paradigms live and work in different worlds, and he talks of worlds as constituted by paradigms (see, especially, 1970c, chapter 10). Yet his discussion of the way the puzzles of normal science are generated makes no sense unless there is some object of scientific study that exists apart from our beliefs. Moreover, even when Kuhn is explicitly talking about the role of paradigms in constituting the scientist's world, he claims that this world is jointly constituted by the paradigm and what he now refers to as an 'environment' that is independent of the paradigm (1970c, pp. 112–13; see also Brown, 1983b, pp. 96–8). I will proceed on the assumption that physical scientists are attempting to understand a world that exists apart from them and their beliefs on the grounds that neither Kuhn's analysis of the sources of anomalies, nor science itself, makes any sense if we do not make this assumption.

5 Anomalies are not the only source of research problems, cf. Kuhn, 1970c, pp. 25–34.

6 Some writers distinguish between cultural and social relativism, but this distinction will not concern us here. See Tennekes, 1971, pp. 46–8 for discussion.

7 We can pluralize these names when we refer to a group, such as 'The three Mary Smiths that I have known', but this is not the case that concerns Whorf.

8 In addition to Whorf, see, for example, Winch, 1958, pp. 26–8; Berger and Luckmann, 1967, pp. 67ff; Silverman, 1975, 20–22; Barnes, 1982, pp. 22–7.

9 There is considerable controversy over the interpretation of Wittgenstein's writings, including controversy over whether Wittgenstein was a social relativist. I am not concerned here to defend any particular interpretation of Wittgenstein's writings, but only to discuss one interpretation that has been propounded on behalf of relativism.

Chapter IV   Judgement

1 In the first two sections of this chapter I will consider cases in which an individual is not consciously following rules when making a decision. I

will discuss the relation between following a rule and acting in conformity with a rule, as well as the possibility that one is following rules unconsciously or implicitly, in the final section.

2 We have also generated new problems that we did not face in the past, and the question of whether we are, on balance, better off than in the past, may be subject to dispute, but this does not cancel out the point that we have learned to do much that we could not do before.

3 Kathleen Wilkes (1984) has argued that much of what occurs in our everyday perceptual adjustment to the world also takes place outside of consciousness, e.g., when we drive a car while carrying on a conversation, or walk down the street while thinking of a problem unrelated to our walking. The fact that we can later call to consciousness some feature of our environment that we had not attended to does not entail that we must have originally been conscious of it. The fact that we 'took it into account' indicates that it had some impact on our nervous system, and this may be sufficient for later recall. See also Roberta Klatzky (1984, chs. 3 and 4) for examples of cases in which perceptual interactions that we are not aware of affect our cognitive behavior, and for discussion of cases in which 'awareness is debilitating to skilled performance' (p. 40).

4 Presumably we do something like this when we read the program in from tape or disk.

5 I am not, of course, maintaining that a failure to follow rules is sufficient for judgement. Nor am I maintaining that no computer will ever exercise judgement, only that currently available computers do not do so.

Chapter V   Rationality

1 The sketch which follows is based on the work of Wilfrid Sellars. For detailed discussion see Sellars, 1948, 1953, 1963, 1968, 1974, 1975; and Brown, 1986b.

2 In Brown, 1987b, I discuss cases in which we encounter conflicts between explicit definitions and paradigm cases, and in which we must reconstruct our definitions.

3 This is a convenient label; no connection with scientific models is intended. A scientific model seeks to capture features of a natural situation, often in a simplified or idealized fashion. The models I am concerned with are attempts to *replace* a concept with a more coherent concept.

4 See Popper, 1971, vol. 2, pp. 217–20, for a similar position, although in different terminology. Unfortunately, Popper has not developed this side of his views on scientific method.

5 I am not now concerned with whether this view entails some form of relativism.

6 Kuhn notes the relation between this view and Polanyi's analysis of tacit knowledge, 1970c, pp. 187–8.

7 Kuhn is not always consistent here. He seems to be holding that this decision is not arbitrary, although it contains an arbitrary element.

8 Cf. Stove, 1982, p. 83. In Herbert Simon's terminology, rational decisions are arrived at by 'satisficing'.

9 Cf. 'One of the strongest, if still unwritten rules, of scientific life is the prohibition of appeals to heads of state or to the populace at large in matters scientific' (Kuhn, 1970c, p. 168).

10 I take it that this is Putnam's point in maintaining 'that there is an extremely close connection between the notions of *truth* and *rationality*; that, to put it even more crudely, the only criterion for what is a fact is what it is rational to accept. . . . But the relation between rational acceptability and truth is a relation between two distinct notions. A statement can be rationally acceptable *at a time* but not *true* . . .' (1981, p. x).

11 Galileo measured acceleration by rolling steel balls down inclined planes. The balls traveled in grooves that Galileo had cut in the planes and then smoothed and lined with vellum in order to minimize friction. The grooves restrained what Aristotelians would have considered the 'free fall' of the balls, but they also eliminated the complicating effects of side sway. See Galileo, 1974, pp. 169–70.

12 There were, at least initially, a number of reasons for doubting the accuracy of telescopic observations of the heavens, e.g., the existing lenses were of poor quality and observers saw many strange things when looking through a telescope that all agreed did not actually exist in the heavens. See van Helden, 1974; Brown, 1985.

13 For an Aristotelian, once the stone is dropped it falls to the center of the universe, and its previous dynamical history is irrelevant. Note, however, that Galileo tried to hedge his bets so that when the experiment was tried, if the stone fell at the foot of the mast it would support his physics and Copernican astronomy, but if it fell towards the rear of the ship, it would not count against Copernicanism. In Galileo's terms, only impressed motions were involved in this experiment, and the crucial features of the Copernican view depended on natural motions. An outcome that undercut Galileo's views on impressed motion would say nothing about the more fundamental natural motions. But even here it was clear to all that if the experiment were tried and the stone fell at the rear of the ship, Galileo's physics would be in trouble.

14 I disagree with Laudan in that I think there are more levels involved in science than he acknowledges, and that these levels cannot be separated as neatly as he seems to think they can (cf. Brown, 1986a), but these are matters of detail that are unimportant in the present context.

15 But we should not jump too quickly even here, see Griffin, 1984.

Bibliography

Alston, W. (1976), 'Two types of foundationalism', *Journal of Philosophy*, vol. 73, pp. 165–85.

Amerine, M. and Roessler, E. (1983), *Wines: Their Sensory Evaluation*, revised edition, San Francisco, W. H. Freeman.

Aristotle (1941), *The Basic Works of Aristotle*, R. McKeon (ed.), New York, Random House.

Audi, R. (1983), 'Foundationalism, epistemic dependence, and defeasibility', *Synthese*, vol. 55, pp. 119–39.

Ayer, A. J. (1974), 'Truth verification and verisimilitude', in P. Schilpp (ed.), *The Philosophy of Karl Popper*, La Salle, Open Court, pp. 684–92.

Barnes, B. (1982), *T. S. Kuhn and Social Science*, New York, Columbia University Press.

Barnes, B. and Bloor, D. (1982), 'Relativism, rationalism and the sociology of science', in M. Hollis and S. Lukes (eds), *Rationality and Relativism*, Cambridge, MIT Press, pp. 21–47.

Bartley, W. (1984), *The Retreat to Commitment*, second edition, La Salle, Open Court.

Bennett, J. (1964), *Rationality*, London, Routledge & Kegan Paul.

Berger, P. and Luckmann, T. (1967), *The Social Construction of Reality*, New York, Anchor Books.

Bloor, D. (1976), *Knowledge and Social Imagery*, London, Routledge & Kegan Paul.

Bohr, N. (1949), 'Discussion with Einstein on epistemological problems in atomic physics', in P. Schilpp (ed.), *Albert Einstein: Philosopher-Scientist*, La Salle, Open Court, pp. 199–241.

BonJour, L. (1985), *The Structure of Empirical Knowledge*, Cambridge, Harvard University Press.

Brandt, R. (1967), 'Ethical relativism', in P. Edwards (ed.), *The Encyclopedia of Philosophy*, vol. 3, New York, Macmillan, pp. 75–8.

Brown, H. (1975), 'Paradigmatic propositions', *American Philosophical Quarterly*, vol. 12, pp. 85–90.

Brown, H. (1976), 'Galileo, the elements, and the tides', *Studies in History and Philosophy of Science*, vol. 7, pp. 337–51.

Rationality

Brown, H. (1977), 'For a modest historicism', *The Monist*, vol. 60, pp. 540–55.

Brown, H. (1979a), 'Observation and the foundations of objectivity', *The Monist*, vol. 62, pp. 470–81.

Brown, H. (1979b), *Perception, Theory and Commitment*, Chicago, University of Chicago Press.

Brown, H. (1983a), 'Incommensurability', *Inquiry*, vol. 26, pp. 3–29.

Brown, H. (1983b), 'Response to Siegel', *Synthese*, vol. 56, pp. 91–105.

Brown, H. (1985), 'Galileo on the telescope and the eye', *Journal of the History of Ideas*, vol. 46, pp. 487–501.

Brown, H. (1986a), 'Review of Laudan's *Science and Values*', *Philosophical Review*, vol. 95, pp. 439–41.

Brown, H. (1986b), 'Sellars, concepts and conceptual change', *Synthese*, vol. 68, pp. 275–307.

Brown, H. (1987a), *Observation and Objectivity*, New York, Oxford University Press.

Brown, H. (1987b), 'Naturalizing observation', in N. Nersessian (ed.), *The Process of Science*, The Hague, Nijhoff, pp. 179–93.

Burchfield, J. (1975), *Lord Kelvin and the Age of the Earth*, New York, Science History Publications.

Carroll, L. (1955), 'Symbolic Logic', in *Symbolic Logic and the Game of Logic*, New York, Dover Books.

Chisholm, R. (1977), *Theory of Knowledge*, second edition, Englewood Cliffs, Prentice-Hall.

Churchland, P. M. (1979), *Scientific Realism and the Plasticity of Mind*, Cambridge, Cambridge University Press.

Davies, P. (1979), *The Forces of Nature*, Cambridge, Cambridge University Press.

Descartes, R. (1985), *The Philosophical Writings of Descartes*, J. Cottingham, R. Stoothhoff, and D. Murdoch (trans.), Cambridge, Cambridge University Press.

Duhem, P. (1962), *The Aim and Structure of Physical Theory*, P. Wiener (trans.), New York, Atheneum.

Dummett, M. (1977), *Elements of Intuitionism*, Oxford, Oxford University Press.

Elster, J. (1983), *Sour Grapes*, Cambridge, Cambridge University Press.

Feuer, L. (1982), *Einstein and the Generations of Science*, second edition, New York, Basic Books.

Feyerabend, P. (1975), *Against Method*, London, New Left Books.

Feyerabend, P. (1981), *Philosophical Papers*, Cambridge, Cambridge University Press.

Finkelstein, D. (1972), 'The physics of logic', in R. Colodny (ed.), *Paradigms and Paradoxes*, Pittsburgh, University of Pittsburgh Press, pp. 47–66.

Fitch, F. (1946), 'Self-reference in philosophy', *Mind*, vol. 65, pp. 64–73.

Fitch, F. (1952), *Symbolic Logic*, New York, The Ronald Press.

Galileo (1957), 'Letter to the Grand Duchess Christina', in S. Drake,

Discoveries and Opinions of Galileo, Garden City, Anchor Books, pp. 175–216.

Galileo (1967), *Dialogue Concerning the Two Chief World Systems*, S. Drake (trans.), Berkeley, University of California Press.

Galileo (1974), *Two New Sciences*, S. Drake (trans.), Madison, University of Wisconsin Press.

Glymour, C. (1980), *Theory and Evidence*, Princeton, Princeton University Press.

Goodman, N. (1965), *Fact, Fiction, and Forecast*, second edition, Indianapolis, Bobbs-Merrill.

Greene, J. (1980), 'The Kuhnian paradigm and the Darwinian revolution in natural history', in G. Gutting (ed.), *Paradigms and Revolutions*, Notre Dame, University of Notre Dame Press, pp. 297–320.

Griffin, D. (1984), *Animal Thinking*, Cambridge, Harvard University Press.

Gutting, G. (1980), 'Introduction', in *Paradigms and Revolutions*, G. Gutting (ed.), Notre Dame, University of Notre Dame Press, pp. 1–21.

Haack, S. (1983), 'Theories of knowledge: an analytic framework', *Proceedings of the Aristotelian Society*, vol. 83, pp. 143–57.

Hardy, G. H. (1927), 'Srinivasa Ramanujan (1887–1920)' in *Collected Papers of Srinivasa Ramanujan*, G. H. Hardy, P. V. Seshu Aiyar, and B. M. Wilson (eds), New York, Chelsea, pp. xxi–xxxvi.

Hardy, G. H. (1959), *Ramanujan*, New York, Chelsea.

Hempel, C. G. (1966), *Philosophy of Natural Science*, Englewood Cliffs, Prentice-Hall.

Henbest, N. and Marten, M. (1983), *The New Astronomy*, Cambridge, Cambridge University Press.

Hesse, M. (1974), *The Structure of Scientific Inference*, Berkeley, University of California Press.

Hofstadter, D. (1983), 'Metamagical themas', *Scientific American*, vol. 248, no. 6, pp. 14–28.

Hooker, C. (1974), 'Systematic realism', *Synthese*, vol. 26, pp. 409–97.

Hooker, C. (1975), 'Philosophy and meta-philosophy of science: empiricism, Popperianism and realism', *Synthese*, vol. 32, pp. 177–231.

Hume, D. (1975), *Enquiries Concerning Human Understanding and Concerning the Principles of Morals*, third edition, L. A. Selby-Bigge (ed.), revised by P. Nidditch, Oxford, Oxford University Press.

Hume, D. (1978), *A Treatise of Human Nature*, second edition, L. Selby-Bigge (ed.), revised by P. Nidditch, Oxford, Oxford University Press.

Jammer, M. (1974), *The Philosophy of Quantum Mechanics*, New York, Wiley.

Jarvie, I. (1984), *Rationality and Relativism*, London, Routledge & Kegan Paul.

Kant, I. (1956), *Groundwork of the Metaphysic of Morals*, H. J. Paton (trans.), New York, Harper and Row.

Kant, I. (1963), *Critique of Pure Reason*, N. Smith (trans.), New York, Macmillan.

Klatzky, R. (1984), *Memory and Awareness*, San Francisco, Freeman.

Kornblith, H. (1980), 'Beyond foundationalism and the coherence theory', *Journal of Philosophy*, vol. 77, pp. 597–612.

Kuhn, T. (1959), *The Copernican Revolution*, New York, Vintage Books.

Kuhn, T. (1970a), 'Logic of discovery or psychology of research', in *Criticism and the Growth of Knowledge*, I. Lakatos and A. Musgrave (eds), Cambridge, Cambridge University Press, pp. 1–23.

Kuhn, T. (1970b), 'Reflections on my critics', in *Criticism and the Growth of Knowledge*, I. Lakatos and A. Musgrave (eds), Cambridge, Cambridge University Press, pp. 231–78.

Kuhn, T. (1970c), *The Structure of Scientific Revolutions*, second edition, Chicago, University of Chicago Press.

Kuhn, T. (1977), *The Essential Tension*, Chicago, University of Chicago Press.

Kuhn, T. (1978), *Black-Body Theory and the Quantum Discontinuity, 1894–1912*, Oxford, Oxford University Press.

Lakatos, I. (1970), 'Falsification and the methodology of scientific research programmes', in I. Lakatos and A. Musgrave (eds), *Criticism and the Growth of Knowledge*, Cambridge, Cambridge University Press, pp. 91–195.

Laudan, L. (1977), *Progress and Its Problems*, Berkeley, University of California Press.

Laudan, L. (1984), *Science and Values*, Berkeley, University of California Press.

Leibniz, G. (1951), 'Towards a universal characteristic', in *Leibniz Selections*, P. Wiener (ed.), New York, Scribner, pp. 17–25.

Locke, J. (1984), *An Essay Concerning Human Understanding*, P. Nidditch (ed.), Oxford, Oxford University Press.

Lugg, A. (1985), 'The process of discovery', *Philosophy of Science*, vol. 52, pp. 207–20.

Mill, J. S. (1950), 'A system of logic', in E. Nagel (ed.), *John Stuart Mill's Philosophy of Scientific Method*, New York, Hafner, pp. 3–358.

Newton-Smith, W. (1981), *The Rationality of Science*, London, Routledge & Kegan Paul.

Pais, A. (1982), *'Subtle is the Lord . . .': The Science and Life of Albert Einstein*, Oxford, Oxford University Press.

Pastin, M. (1975), 'Modest foundationalism and self-warrant', in N. Rescher (ed.), *Studies in Epistemology*, Oxford, Oxford University Press, pp. 141–9.

Plato (1961), *Collected Dialogues*, E. Hamilton and H. Cairns (eds), New York, Pantheon.

Polanyi, M. (1958), *Personal Knowledge*, New York, Harper & Row.

Polanyi, M. (1967), *The Tacit Dimension*, Garden City, Anchor Books.

Pollock, J. (1979), 'A plethora of epistemological theories', in G. Pappas (ed.), *Justification and Knowledge*, Dordrecht, D. Reidel, pp. 93–113.

Popper, K. (1965), *Conjectures and Refutations*, New York, Harper & Row.

Popper, K. (1968), *Logic of Scientific Discovery*, second English edition, New York, Harper & Row.

Bibliography

Popper, K. (1970), 'Normal science and its dangers', in I. Lakatos and A. Musgrave (eds), *Criticism and the Growth of Knowledge*, Cambridge, Cambridge University Press, pp. 51–8.

Popper, K. (1971), *The Open Society and its Enemies*, fifth edition, Princeton, Princeton University Press.

Popper, K. (1972), *Objective Knowledge*, Oxford, Oxford University Press.

Price, H. (1964), *Perception*, London, Methuen.

Putnam, H. (1969), 'Is logic empirical?' in R. Cohen and M. Wartofsky (eds), *Boston Studies in the Philosophy of Science*, vol. 5, Dordrecht, D. Reidel, pp. 216–41.

Putnam, H. (1978), *Meaning and the Moral Sciences*, London, Routledge & Kegan Paul.

Putnam, H. (1981), *Reason, Truth and History*, Cambridge, Cambridge University Press.

Quine, W. (1982), *Methods of Logic*, fourth edition, Cambridge, Harvard University Press.

Redhead, A. (1982), 'Radio astronomy by very-long-baseline interferometry', *Scientific American*, vol. 246, no. 6, pp. 52–61.

Reichenbach, H. (1938), *Experience and Prediction*, Chicago, University of Chicago Press.

Ross, D. (1963), *Plato's Theory of Ideas*, Oxford, Oxford University Press.

Rudner, R. (1966), *Philosophy of Social Science*, Englewood Cliffs, Prentice-Hall.

Schagrin, M. (1973), 'On being unreasonable', *Philosophy of Science*, vol. 40, pp. 1–9.

Schagrin, M. (1982), 'The failure to be rational', *Philosophy of Science*, vol. 49, pp. 120–4.

Sellars, W. (1948), 'Concepts as involving laws and inconceivable without them', *Philosophy of Science*, vol. 15, pp. 287–315.

Sellars, W. (1953), 'Inference and meaning', *Mind*, vol. 62, pp. 313–38.

Sellars, W. (1963), *Science, Perception and Reality*, New York, Humanities Press.

Sellars, W. (1968), *Science and Metaphysics*, New York, Humanities Press.

Sellars, W. (1974), 'Conceptual change', in *Essays in Philosophy and its History*, Dordrecht, D. Reidel, pp. 172–88.

Sellars, W. (1975), 'The structure of knowledge', in *Action, Knowledge and Reality*, H. Castañeda (ed.), Indianapolis, Bobbs-Merrill, pp. 295–347.

Shapere, D. (1982), 'The concept of observation in science and philosophy', *Philosophy of Science*, vol. 49, pp. 485–525.

Shapere, D. (1984), *Reason and the Search for Knowledge*, Dordrecht, D. Reidel.

Siegel, H. (1985), 'What is the question concerning the rationality of science?', *Philosophy of Science*, vol. 52, pp. 517–37.

Silverman, D. (1975), *Reading Castaneda*, London, Routledge & Kegan Paul.

Simon, H. (1983), *Reason in Human Affairs*, Stanford, Stanford University Press.

Smith, E. and Medin, D. (1981), *Categories and Concepts*, Cambridge, Harvard University Press.

Stove, D. (1982), *Popper and After*, Oxford, Pergamon Press.

Stuewer, R. (1970), 'Non-Einsteinian interpretations of the photoelectric effect', in R. Stuewer (ed.), *Minnesota Studies in the Philosophy of Science*, vol. 5, Minneapolis, University of Minnesota Press, pp. 246–63.

Tennekes, J. (1971), *Anthropology, Relativism and Method*, Assen, Koninklijke Van Gorcum.

van Helden, A. (1974), 'The telescope in the seventeenth century', *Isis*, vol. 65, pp. 38–58.

Vickers, G. (1965), *The Art of Judgement*, New York, Basic Books.

Wartofsky, M. (1980), 'Scientific judgement, creativity and discovery in scientific thought', in T. Nickles (ed.), *Scientific Discovery: Case Studies*, Dordrecht, D. Reidel, pp. 1–20.

Weisskopf, V. (1972), *Physics in the Twentieth Century*, Cambridge, MIT Press.

Whorf, B. (1956), *Language, Thought and Reality*, J. Carroll (ed.), Cambridge, MIT Press.

Wilkes, K. (1984), 'Is consciousness important?' *British Journal for the Philosophy of Science*, vol. 35, pp. 223–43.

Winch, P. (1958), *The Idea of a Social Science*, London, Routledge & Kegan Paul.

Winch, P. (1970), 'Understanding a primitive society', in B. Wilson (ed.), *Rationality*, Worcester, Basil Blackwell, pp. 78–111.

Wittgenstein, L. (1953), *Philosophical Investigations*, G. Anscombe (trans.), New York, Macmillan.

Wolterstorff, N. (1983), 'Can belief in God be rational if it has no foundations?' in A. Plantinga and N. Walterstorff (eds), *Faith and Rationality*, Notre Dame, University of Notre Dame Press, pp. 135–86.

Index

Index